"Ian is a natural prose stylist with a real knack for pacing and the telling detail. . . . [*Society's Child*] a juicily entertaining look at an unusual life in show business."

—*Kirkus Reviews*

"Fans will love the book, of course, but many nonfans, too, should find this painfully candid memoir hard to put down." —*Booklist*, starred review

"Fans will appreciate the candor with which Ian discusses her hardships and her gradual path to happiness." —*Publishers Weekly*

"As Ian writes in this candid autobiography, she has endured . . . betrayals both personal and professional and a lot of unwanted attention from a vindictive tax man. Somehow she survived with good humor mostly intact." —*Mojo* magazine

"Janis Ian was brilliant from the start. Through her songs and poems I have always noticed the grace in her use of language; now I can see her artistic flow in book form. Congratulations, Janis!" —ODETTA

"One of life's greatest pleasures is a book that you simply can't put down—one that transports you from start to finish as it elevates, enlightens, enlarges, and entertains. Janis Ian gives you all of this in *Society's Child*. It's a book that flies on 'glistening wings' straight into your heart, where it will nestle forever."

—KITTY KELLEY, bestselling author of *The Family* and *The Royals*

"I laughed, I ached, I wept, I cheered . . . and ultimately was totally taken by Janis Ian's honest and deeply moving autobiography: an insightful and courageously personal account of her musical, spiritual, and emotional journey!"

—NOEL PAUL STOOKEY, singer-songwriter, of Peter, Paul and Mary

"A splendid retelling of a major life! Janis Ian is a survivor, and her book is an illuminating and inspiring read."

—ANNE McCAFFREY, bestselling author of the Pern series and *The Ship Who Sang*

"Musical genius, lover of life's bounties, survivor of its spectacular bummers, big, big artist in a beautiful tiny package—my friend Janis Ian."

—RONNIE GILBERT of The Weavers, singer, actor, and playwright

"This is a wonderful book. Janis has made something amazing here, as amazing as any of her songs. It's not just her story—it's our story, the story of a generation. She is articulate, and emotional without being self-indulgent, handles tragedy with grace, and tells of amazing involvement with other icons of our time without being in the least pretentious, and her words resonate with our own experiences so that as you read, you will constantly find yourself saying, 'Hey, I remember that!' and 'I was doing *this* then.' It was a kaleidoscopic time, the decades of innocence lost and regained and lost again, and Janis tells it all with the conviction of one who has truly lived it and come out on the other side to hand us our hope again, wrapped in another song."

—MERCEDES LACKEY, author of *The Fairy Godmother,* the Heralds of Valdemar series, and the Obsidian Mountain trilogy

"Janis Ian's songs cut close to the bone. So does her autobiography. Harrowing and inspiring by turns, *Society's Child* is as relentlessly honest as her lyrics, and engrossing from first page to last. A fascinating look at the music business as it was then and as it is now, and at the life of a singer and songwriter whose music helped shape our dreams and define our times, even while she herself was battling racists, rejection, abuse, and the Internal Revenue Service, this book is sure to touch anyone who ever yearned for more."

—GEORGE R. R. MARTIN, author of the bestselling Song of Ice and Fire series

"*Society's Child* is an extraordinary book: brave, wise, and honest—just like the treasured songwriter whose story it is."

—CHARLES DE LINT, author of *Dingo* and *Promises to Keep*

"*Society's Child* proves that Janis Ian's prose is as searing as her song lyrics. To live through all that she has, personally and professionally, and to come through it with her sanity, sense of humor, health, and talent intact is both astonishing and inspiring. For people who think they know Janis Ian, this book not only will surprise them—but may in turn horrify, sadden, yet ultimately enlighten them."

—CHRISTINE LAVIN, singer-songwriter

"*Society's Child* is a truly remarkable story, told by a truly remarkable talent. Janis Ian is a wordsmith who could make anything interesting; with a subject as fascinating as her life, the result is a classic of its kind."

—MIKE RESNICK, award-winning science fiction author

"One of the finest self-written books about the songwriting life in recent years . . . It's nice that Janis Ian conducts the tour in person and allows us to see the undressed side of the stone."

—JIMMY WEBB, songwriter, and author of *Tunesmith: Inside the Art of Songwriting*

"Good autobiographies are rare. It's too tempting to excuse, justify, or conceal one's own mistakes, or absolve them through confession; or worse, to attack other people in the guise of their 'telling the truth.' Janis Ian understands that nobody knows 'the truth' and that all she can tell is how things seemed to her as they were happening, and how they seem to her now. The result is a book that has all the inside knowledge of memoir, yet all the candor, compassion, and toughness of a book written by a wise observer. Add to this Ian's extraordinary talent as a writer, and you have a book of surpassing clarity and truth."

—ORSON SCOTT CARD, award-winning author of *Ender's Game*

"Janis Ian is at once larger-than-life and excruciatingly human. I opened *Society's Child* intending to skim the first page, and looked up thirty minutes later to find myself still standing at my kitchen counter, weeping like a baby. After finishing her book, I feel like I've had a front-row seat to the sound track of my life. The telling of the tale would have been enough, but the insights into her personal ups and downs through it all are the real gift of this book. In the end, she teaches us that stewarding our gifts and living life from the inside out are the true tasks at hand for each of us, messy though this may be. Her extraordinary strength of spirit shines through every page." —KATHY MATTEA, Grammy-winning singer and musician

To Judith
with much
thanks!

Society's Child

MY AUTOBIOGRAPHY

Janis Ian (signature)

Janis Ian

JEREMY P. TARCHER/PENGUIN

a member of Penguin Group (USA) Inc.

New York

JEREMY P. TARCHER/PENGUIN
Published by the Penguin Group
Penguin Group (USA) Inc., 375 Hudson Street, New York, New York 10014, USA ·
Penguin Group (Canada), 90 Eglinton Avenue East, Suite 700, Toronto, Ontario M4P 2Y3, Canada
(a division of Pearson Canada Inc.) · Penguin Books Ltd, 80 Strand, London WC2R 0RL, England ·
Penguin Ireland, 25 St Stephen's Green, Dublin 2, Ireland (a division of Penguin Books Ltd) ·
Penguin Group (Australia), 250 Camberwell Road, Camberwell, Victoria 3124, Australia (a division of
Pearson Australia Group Pty Ltd) · Penguin Books India Pvt Ltd, 11 Community Centre, Panchsheel Park,
New Delhi–110 017, India · Penguin Group (NZ), 67 Apollo Drive, Rosedale, North Shore 0632, New
Zealand (a division of Pearson New Zealand Ltd) · Penguin Books (South Africa) (Pty) Ltd,
24 Sturdee Avenue, Rosebank, Johannesburg 2196, South Africa

Penguin Books Ltd, Registered Offices: 80 Strand, London WC2R 0RL, England

First trade paperback edition 2009
Copyright © 2008 by Janis Ian

FRONTISPIECE PHOTOGRAPH BY PETER CUNNINGHAM
Credits and permissions appear on page 349.

Most Tarcher/Penguin books are available at special quantity discounts for bulk purchase for
sales promotions, premiums, fund-raising, and educational needs. Special books or book excerpts
also can be created to fit specific needs. For details, write Penguin Group (USA) Inc.
Special Markets, 375 Hudson Street, New York, NY 10014.

The Library of Congress catalogued the hardcover edition as follows:

Ian, Janis.
Society's child: my autobiography / Janis Ian.
p.   cm.
Includes index.
ISBN 978-1-58542-675-1
1. Ian, Janis.   2. Singers—United States—Biography.   I. Title.
ML420.I16A3   2008   2008017130
782.42164092—dc22
[B]

ISBN 978-1-58542-749-9 (paperback edition)

Printed in the United States of America
1   3   5   7   9   10   8   6   4   2

Book design by Meighan Cavanaugh

For Stella Adler & Gerry Weiss

Gone, but never forgotten

SPECIAL THANKS TO

My "benign readers" group, who read and commented from the first draft on: D'Lesli Davis, Adrienne Dominguez, Sandra Eikelenboom, Jeff Evans, Mary Faulkner, Mike Resnick, Cathy Sullivan, and especially Ineke Kokernoot and Don Schlitz, whose comments were invaluable.

The fan research group: Kathleen Brogan, Dar Vendegna, Marilyn Manzione, Jim Perota, Karen Redick, and in particular Amy Hoffman and Barb "Roady" Winters, who saved me countless hours by assembling old tour schedules and press.

The Green Hills Public Library, which provided hundreds of research volumes without a whimper.

My first editor, Judy Wieder, who forced me to write prose and whipped me into shape; my second editor, Lydia Hutchinson, who gave me free rein and made me learn to edit myself. Mike Resnick, friend and collaborator, who insisted I begin writing fiction; Mercedes Lackey, who maintained I could do it, then walked me through my first effort. Orson Scott Card, who gave me my first laptop. Kitty Kelley, who was adamant that I not go for the high dollars and write this book too soon—who also unwittingly gave me structure when she said, "Write it like you write your music. Make every chapter a song. The end result will be a symphony."

My business manager, Charles Sussman, and my agents, Tim Drake and Paul Fenn, who helped make it possible for me to stay home a full year to write this book. Jennie Adams, who helped me stay sane through the process. Kat Graham, who kept the house going, and John Leonardini, who kept the website and computers running.

Lula McMillan and Willie Mae Duncan, who cared for my mother like their own until the day of her death.

My partner of two decades, Pat Snyder, who keeps my ego firmly in check, and whose unwavering support makes all the difference.

Last but not least, to the writers who've sustained me, from Rimbaud to Madeleine L'Engle, who opened new worlds to me when I most needed them. And to Anne McCaffrey, whose wit and wisdom remind me daily that life is for the living.

CONTENTS

INTRODUCTION

I was born into the crack that split America.

On one side of the chasm was the America my parents lived in. There, the country was still congratulating itself on winning the war after the War to End All Wars. Men wore suits and ties to work, or laborer's uniforms. Women wore stiletto heels, and kept themselves pure for marriage. Females did the housework, males did the heavy lifting. Blacks knew their place, whites knew theirs, and there wasn't much room between.

On the other side of the crack was the America I grew up in, bounded by anarchy and a passion for truth. In that America, all wars were meaningless, born out of governmental greed and disregard. Vietnam was just the latest in a series of events to help the rich get richer and the poor get poorer. People on my side of the crack wore colorful clothing and water buffalo sandals, made love not war, and believed in the family of man, unbounded by race, religion, or nationality. We lived through an adolescence tinged by the assassinations of those we held dear. We didn't know our place.

To my parents' generation, we had it all. They'd worked hard to give it to us, and they couldn't understand why we were busy throwing it away. What did we want? Didn't we have everything they'd longed for? The economy was booming. We were the strongest nation on earth. Why couldn't my generation just shut up, and accept the good life we'd been given?

To our eyes, those things didn't mean as much as young soldiers dying in mosquito-infested jungles, or blacks being turned away at the voting booths. So despite our parents' love of silence, we never shut up. We marched, wrote polemics, started magazines, took over universities. And in between, we smoked a little pot, made a little love, and changed the world forever.

Like all good things, the halcyon days of the early sixties came to an end. Nixon came to power, and cast an ugly shadow over the fire of John F. Kennedy's memory. The women's movement disintegrated into half a dozen powerless fronts, as did the nascent gay rights movement. The peace movement was back-burnered when we pulled out of Vietnam, and the civil rights movement fragmented with the death of Martin Luther King Jr. Our parents were right: change is the only constant.

I was born into a country that would soon divide. In my parents' America, life was light and easy, and Mitch Miller ruled the airwaves. In my America, we lost all innocence, and pop music was king.

PROLOGUE

Nigger lover! Nigger lover! Nigger lover!

I was standing alone on a stage in Encino, California, halfway through the first verse of my song "Society's Child."

Come to my door, baby
Face is clean and shining black as night
My mama went to answer
You know that you looked so fine
Now, I could understand the tears and the shame
She called you "Boy" instead of your name

The problem had begun with a lone woman screaming out the words *"Nigger lover!"* Then the people sitting around her had joined in, chanting as though they were at a religious service. They were even chanting in time to the song. *"Nigger* lover! *Nigger* lover! *beat* beat *beat*

beat *Nigger* lover! *Nigger* lover! *beat* beat *beat* beat." It was difficult to concentrate on keeping my own time.

The chant degenerated into yelling, twenty or thirty people in the sold-out concert hall. I peered to the left, where the sound came from, and saw some of them beginning to rise. They were shaking their fists in the air as the rest of the audience looked on in stunned silence.

I was having a hit record.

I was singing for people who wanted me dead.

I was fifteen years old.

I felt like crying, but you can't sing and cry at the same time, so I tried to keep going. My fingers were getting clumsy; it felt like I was trying to play the guitar with gloves on. My voice was starting to tremble, and I was losing control of my pitch. More of the crowd began yelling, whether for me or against me, I didn't know. It was hard to hear myself over the noise.

I looked into the house again, walking out of the spotlight to avoid its glare. There, in the center left, dozens of audience members were shaking their fists and screaming at me. One woman was bouncing up and down in a frenzy, shrieking the epithet so loudly that she was bright red in the face. A man, dressed nicely in a suit and tie, was making obscene gestures and shouting something about monkeys. I was trying to block out the crowd's chant and get through the song, but all I could hear was the yelling.

I had no idea what to do. I'd been on a concert stage perhaps a dozen times in my life to date. If this were a club, the bouncer would make short work of the troublemakers, but no one seemed to be doing anything. I could feel tears welling up in my eyes. What was *wrong* with these people? It was just a song, not a combat invitation!

I finally stopped playing and started crying. Not wanting the audience to see me break down, I set my prized guitar on the floor and tried to walk calmly off the stage. As soon as I hit the wings, I went running for the ladies' room. I could hear booing and hissing as I left, along with a few cheers. I wondered which group was doing the booing, and which was applauding. The walls blurred as I bent my head over the sink and began to cry in earnest.

I'd written the song a year before, when we were still living in East Orange, New Jersey. It was a very mixed neighborhood—well, actually, it wasn't that mixed. It was almost all Negro; I was one of seven white girls in my whole school. So I'd seen the problem from both sides. My black friends' parents didn't want them dating whites. My white friends' parents didn't want them dating blacks.

The whole thing seemed pretty stupid to me, so I wrote about it to clear out my system. I never thought of it as a song about an interracial love affair gone bad. I just thought of it as a good song. Now here I was, a year later, with a single that was banned from virtually every radio station in the country, and a career that was turning into a war zone.

People got crazy. A radio station in Atlanta dared to put "Society's Child" in rotation, and someone burned the station down. Strangers walked up to me in restaurants and spit in my food. Sometimes, when I tried to walk onstage from the audience, a person would deliberately put their foot out to trip me. The mail I got spanned the gap between heaven and hell; one letter would thank me for bravely speaking out, the next would have razor blades taped to the envelope so I'd shred my fingers opening it.

The irony of it all was, I wasn't especially brave. At least, I didn't think so. The song was just in keeping with the times, and the times were volatile indeed.

A few minutes after I'd begun to weep, the concert promoter came rushing in. "Why did you leave?!" he cried. "What on earth is wrong? You've got to go back out there!" Now, in retrospect, I can see that he was scared, too. The thought of a thousand people demanding their money back must have been horrifying to him.

I splashed water on my reddened nose, dried my face, then turned to look at him. The tears welled up again when I saw pity in his eyes.

"They were chanting *'Nigger lover!'* at me. I couldn't hear myself. I didn't know what else to do. They were starting to move toward the stage. So I left." It all sounded pretty logical when I said it, now that the threat was in the past.

The promoter wrung his hands. "Well, you've got to go back, Janis. You've *got* to. We have a thousand people who paid good money to attend this show, and you're talking about a few troublemakers bothering you enough to stop a performance? You can't do that. You've got to go back and finish the show!"

I was appalled, and it showed in my face. Just the thought of going back onstage with those people still in the audience was enough to put me in a state of panic.

"I can't go back there. I *can't*. What if they start throwing things? What if somebody takes a shot at me?"

There. I'd finally said it, the secret dread I hadn't admitted to anyone. *What if someone takes a shot at me? What if someone really does try to kill me?* I would never have believed a simple song could provoke such violence, but I believed it now. Oh, yeah, you bet I believed it. And I truly did not want to die. Onstage or off.

I wasn't exaggerating my fear. Based on the hate mail I was getting from the Southern states, my manager and agents had decided not to book me within fifty miles of the Mason-Dixon line. It wasn't just me, either. No one was exempt; the record company and everyone else who worked with me was in trouble over this record. Even Shadow Morton, my producer, was taken aback by the virulence. He'd been producing the Shangri-Las, and the only mail they got was requests for autographed photos and marriage proposals. Now he was getting postcards with his photo in the center of a bull's-eye. Everyone, from the record company secretaries to my manager, was being attacked.

Yet stubbornly, Verve Forecast president Jerry Schoenbaum kept re-releasing it, kept publicizing it, kept demanding that radio play the song. It helped that the reviews were astounding. It helped that the most respected radio tip sheet of the day said, *Magnificently done, but will probably never see the light of day. Too bad.* It helped that *The New York Times* gave me rave reviews. But nothing anyone wrote changed the death threats that came regularly, with my name on the envelope. And no one had any idea of what to do about it; this was all new to my team.

When we cut the single, I didn't have anything resembling a "team." I had myself, Shadow, and the attorney who'd introduced us. Shadow had listened to the dozen or so songs I'd finished, picked one, and a few weeks later I was in the studio for my first recording session. I remember Shadow, myself, and a friend talking on a busy side street during a break. Shadow turned to me and said very seriously, "Janis, if you'll change just one word in the song—just one word—I can guarantee you a number one record. Just change 'black' to anything else. It's your decision."

I thought about it for around two seconds; then our friend looked at me and said, "You whore now, you'll whore forever." Strong words for a fifteen-year-old to hear, but they made sense. To my way of thinking, I had nothing to lose. I was getting to make a record. How cool was that?

And coming from the folk tradition, I couldn't see telling new friends like Dave Van Ronk or Odetta that I'd weaseled out, just to get a hit. After all, in my world a hit record was kind of embarrassing. It meant you'd sold out. Joan Baez didn't have hit records. Peter LaFarge didn't have hit records.

But Bob Dylan did, and he was my hero. Still, he had them on his own terms, and that was what I intended to do as well. The word stayed.

And now, look where it had gotten me. Here I was, standing in a bathroom, blowing my reddened nose and arguing with a promoter over whether my show should be canceled. So much for sticking to your principles.

My hands were still shaking, though the adrenaline rush was dying down. I tried to read his mind. *He probably thinks I'm behaving like a kid, a spoiled kid. Like an amateur. I don't care! Right now, I am an amateur.*

The promoter leaned on the edge of a sink, paused, then said, "It would be terrible if a small segment of the audience ruined it for everyone else. . . . You know, those people who were yelling paid perfectly good money for their tickets, just so they could come here and try to scare you off the stage. Are you going to stand for that?"

I nodded miserably. Yes, I was going to stand for that. Of course I was going to stand for it. Goodman, Schwerner, and Chaney had been found dead in Mississippi, killed just for helping people register to vote. All I'd done was write a song, make a three-minute record, and those same people wanted *me* dead. The stakes were pretty high.

He sighed. "You've got to go back, Janis. You've got to, because if you don't, they win. And you can't let them win. What about the next person they take on like this? You're no coward. I *know* you're not a coward. And I know that *you* know they'll win, if you don't go back out there."

Oh, no. He'd hit on the one thing that would sway me. Hadn't my parents raised me to be a hero? Hadn't I grown up on stories of Judah Maccabee, how he and his brothers and a small band of Jews had fought off mighty Rome for four full years? Hadn't my brother and I played Superman until I half believed I could fly? In my family, in my culture, heroism was expected. Those people who named names before the House Committee on Un-American Activities were traitors, cowards. My grandparents spit after saying their names. I couldn't stand the thought that I might be a coward—I just couldn't stand it.

Then a completely different idea struck. *I don't want to disappoint the real fans out there. And there must be real fans out there, somewhere!*

I thought about all the times I'd heard other performers say, "The show must go on." If there was one cardinal rule in show business, that was it. The only valid excuses were hospitalization or your own death;

otherwise, the show went on. That was tradition. That was the lineage I'd adopted.

Shortly before cutting "Society's Child," when I was still fourteen, I'd run into Ellie Greenwich up at Shadow's office. I was tongue-tied; I loved her songwriting, thought "Da Doo Ron Ron" was brilliant, and couldn't think of a thing to say. Shadow rescued me, telling her I was also a songwriter and performer. With a stern look, she'd turned to me and said, "Kid, this business is about hard work, and don't you ever forget it. It's about getting your period, having cramps that are killing you, then walking onstage to do the show, anyhow—and never letting the crowd know it. If you don't have the guts for that, don't even start."

Yep, that was my lineage now, like it or not. I wiped my eyes with a paper towel, then looked down at the floor, hoping I wouldn't start crying again. The promoter awkwardly patted my shoulder and said, "Well?"

"Well . . ." I lifted my head to meet his eyes, then took a deep breath.

"Well, if I die tonight, you know, if something goes wrong, just tell my folks and my brother I love them." It seemed like the brave thing to say, even though what I really wanted to tell him was, *I'm not a coward, I'm just scared, and I want to go home right now and hide under the bed.*

He walked me to the wings. The houselights had been turned up to half while the crew waited to find out what came next. The lights went out, and a spotlight drifted toward the side of the stage where I stood, taking deep breaths and blanking my mind to everything but the show. I squared my shoulders and walked back to center stage, picked up my guitar, adjusted the microphone, and began singing "Society's Child" again from the top.

At first, there were a few more shouts, but I ignored them and kept going. I closed my eyes to help myself concentrate, tuning out the noise, tuning in to the words and the music. And oddly enough, as I continued to ignore the shouting, the audience members took matters into their own hands. A few rose and walked over to the troublemakers, telling them to shut up. An usher came down the aisle and shone his flashlight in their faces, threatening to eject them bodily if they continued.

Slowly, the claque of people who'd been disrupting things began leaving the theater. As they rose and filed into the aisles, I stopped singing, but I kept playing the guitar chords, tapping my foot to the beat. My eyes were wide open and my head was high as I watched them go. I wanted to let them know I was no longer afraid. When the theater doors closed behind the last of them, I began the final verse.

One of these days I'm gonna stop my listening
Gonna raise my head up high
One of these days I'm gonna
raise up my glistening wings and fly

As I got to the words "I'm gonna raise up my glistening wings and fly," there was a roar from the crowd, and the entire room stood up. Someone began clapping; the rest of the room joined in, and I grinned like a fool as I strummed the final chords. I had a standing ovation, even before I'd finished the song.

My chaperone and I left the theater quietly, me hiding on the floor of the backseat to avoid the picket line and any further disruptions. It had been funny earlier in the day, rolling up to the theater and seeing signs with *Nigger lover go home!* and *No race mixing allowed here!*, but it wasn't so funny now.

I never ate before a show, and I'd spent a lot more energy than usual, so we stopped at a roadside coffee shop about half an hour out of town for a quick bite. This was farm country, and the counter was full of seated men wearing hard-worn jeans and neatly buttoned shirts, the dust of the fields still on their soles. In my bright hippie clothing, dangling earrings, and beads, I attracted a fair amount of attention any time I left a major city. Usually there wasn't big trouble, just a few snide remarks like *Is that a girl or a boy?* or *Who let the animals out of the zoo?* But I'd just been through an awful experience, and I tensed as they turned to look at me.

The waitress grinned as we ordered, trying not to laugh. I must have looked like something she'd seen on television, or in magazines with articles on the "new generation." After she took our orders, the place settled down, but I noticed one older man staring at me out of the corner of his eye. Now, in my fifties, I realize he wasn't so very old at all, but back then he seemed ancient.

Maybe he saw me on TV, and he's just staring because he's never seen a famous person this close before. I tried to tell myself that, but alarm bells were going off in my head.

He kept gawking, and it became irritating. It's hard to relax when someone actually turns around on their counter stool and stares at you without pretense, occasionally whispering something to the person next to them and laughing. I felt like a zoo animal.

By now our food had arrived, but mine tasted like sawdust. It seemed like the entire diner was lining up against me, and I braced myself for the worst. I wondered if he'd come over and spit in my plate, or just take me out back and lynch me, then bury me in a cornfield somewhere.

I just bet he was one of that claque calling me a nigger lover. Bastard. I clenched my jaw. Dinner was ruined. The entire day was ruined. The more I thought about it, picking at my food, the madder I got. Scared as I was, I was also getting really angry.

As I pushed the plate away, he rose and started to walk toward us. *Uh-oh, here it comes.* I could feel my muscles tightening. My chaperone, blissfully unaware, kept her eyes on her cheeseburger and her mouth wrapped around the fries. I felt totally alone.

He came to our table, paused, stuck his hands in his pockets, and said, "Hey."

I looked up with no smile and said, "Hey back at you." He smiled broadly, and suddenly he didn't look so old. Or so mean.

"Just wanted to say, I was at your show tonight. Good job. Thanks."

My confusion must have shown on my face. It took a minute for me to register that he was actually complimenting me, not hawking a gob of saliva onto my food. I could feel myself flushing with embarrassment.

"Uh, thanks for the compliment. . . . It was a rough show." I tried a tentative smile, but my face wasn't working right yet.

"Yeah, it was rough, but you handled it. You showed 'em but good. Nice job, kid." And with that, he turned and walked away.

As we left the diner, my chaperone looked at me curiously and said, "What on earth was that about?" She had no idea; while I was dealing with the crowd, she'd been up in the office, dealing with the money.

I shrugged, then said, "It's nothing. Just that sometimes, you can't judge on first impressions."

ONE

Hair of Spun Gold

When I was but the age of five,
my world had just come alive
Wondrous things to be seen and be done
All that I could think of was fun

It was the best of songs, it was the worst of songs.

But it was *my* song.

I was twelve years old, sitting in the backseat of our station wagon with my brother beside me and my father's guitar in my lap. I'd picked my time carefully; we were headed from our home in New Jersey to my grandparents' apartment in the Bronx, so I had at least forty-five uninterrupted minutes to get my parents' full attention and play them the first song I'd ever written, "Hair of Spun Gold."

Finding a slice of time like that was no easy feat. Dad worked full-time as a high school music teacher, and he also gave private piano lessons—fifteen or twenty a week—in addition to being the director of a summer camp. Mom was head bookkeeper for a local nursing home, and camp treasurer, publicist, graphics artist, and designer, in addition to her civil rights work. We usually spent weekends at the mimeograph machine, stuffing envelopes for various causes, giving slide shows to prospective campers and their parents, or visiting relatives. We ate dinner together every night, but that time was spent catching up on the day's events. After supper, there was homework, and whatever my parents still needed to get done. It was a real coup, trapping them like this. They'd have to listen.

I'd picked up the guitar at Camp Woodland when I was ten, and I'd fallen in love. After the boredom of studying classical piano and practicing relentless scales for eight years, the guitar was a revelation. Unlike a piano, you could carry it anywhere. You could feel the wood vibrating against your skin as you played, forming a direct connection with your voice. Best of all, there didn't seem to be any rules. Piano study was full of rules: hold your hands *this* way, move your fingers *that* way, play the passage *this* way. With classical piano, the dead past lived. With guitar, the present became the future.

I knew my parents were disappointed by my lack of enthusiasm for a career as a classical pianist. At first, all the signs seemed to point toward it. Even to me, that path had a certain logic.

We lived on a chicken farm when I was born; my earliest memories were of candling eggs, and hearing music. I was a curious, articulate kid. My dad used to say, "Janis started talking at seven months, and she never stopped." There's a lot of truth to that. I didn't waste any time being pre-verbal; the minute I could form words, I began using them. Same with walking—I had no patience with crawling, so I'd haul myself up, take as many steps as I could, then fall forward with my butt in the air and yell until someone helped me stand up again.

There was a collie named Boy who appointed himself my guardian. He lay in front of my crib from the time I was born, growling when anyone but my parents approached. There were Mickey and Gilby, who rented the attic apartment of our farmhouse and kept a pet monkey I played with. There were Ronnie and Inga, a mixed-race couple with a son my age, and Mom's best friend, Susie, who'd tried to commit suicide by laying on a train track, but had only succeeded in becoming wheelchair-bound. There was Lonnie, Dad's second-in-command, a huge black man from somewhere down South, who had the sweetest smile I knew. The only time I remember race coming up in our lives was when I asked Lonnie if I could also have chocolate skin when I grew up, because I thought it was so pretty.

I had a tribe of family living in nearby Lakewood, and my favorite cousin, Donna, just six months older than me, would often spend the weekend. I'd tell her bedtime stories that continued long after she'd fallen asleep; my father would listen at the door, vastly entertained as I tried to remember the tales he'd told me.

It was an ideal life for a child with a lot going on in her head. We were a mile from the next farm, five miles from the feed store. People were in and out of the house all the time, but I had long hours alone to think. Fortunately for me, Mom had memorized Dr. Benjamin Spock's *Baby and Child Care* well before I was born. Everything I asked was patiently answered. Anything I wanted to try, we tried, whether it was keeping caterpillars in a glass jar to see if they'd become butterflies, or visiting Mr. Appleby's farm next door and milking a cow by myself. My bedroom had a huge oilcloth on one wall, where I could finger-paint and color in chalk to my heart's content. When I woke with the sun, I could sit on the green linoleum floor and play checkers with Peter, my guardian angel, who wasn't real but was real to me.

Worried about the isolation of farm life, my parents tried to make sure I was exposed to as much "culture" as possible. A friend of theirs was in the cast of *Oklahoma!* so we drove into New York one morning and watched a rehearsal. For weeks after, I marched around the barnyard directing the poultry, singing "Poor Judd is Dead" to the ones who'd already keeled over.

Dad took me to see a couple of Chaplin films soon after, and I spent the next few days in silence, miming everything and driving my mother crazy. It stopped when she mistook my signs for "I'm hungry," and plunked me down in the middle of the chickens with a feed basket in my arms. I spent the next few minutes frantically throwing meal at them while the hens tried to peck holes in my feet, then finally opened my mouth and screamed to be rescued. That was the end of my career as Marcel Marceau.

We were rich in culture, but there was never money to spare. I can't remember a time when I didn't know that. We weren't poor, but we sure as heck weren't rich. My grandfather was a bagger in a fancy New York fruit and vegetable store; we depended on the two free bags of food he could give us every other week. My grandmother was a wonderful seamstress, and we depended on the clothes she made for me. Still, I didn't feel like I lacked anything. I cut up newspapers and made my own picture books, creating paste from flour and water. I had an entire drum set from pots and pans and wooden spoons. Most of the time, I created my own entertainment, with the help of the grown-ups around me.

I knew enough not to ask for anything, no matter how much a bar of chocolate or a pretty pair of shoes tempted me when we went shopping. My parents loved me; that was obvious from the hugs and praise I received all day long. To ask for *things* when I knew we couldn't afford extras seemed like ingratitude of the worst sort. Still, it had to happen sooner or later. . . .

With the help of my grandparents, my folks had splurged on a television set shortly after my birth. It was one of the first in our neighborhood. I think everyone was a little worried that my mom, who loved going out and giving parties, would go nuts if she was alone in the house all day with only an infant for company.

I was allowed to watch *Romper Room* and *Howdy Doody* in the mornings, and I must have seen the ad for a Tiny Tears doll on one of them. I was entranced. She had curly hair, just like me. Her eyes opened and closed. You could even bottle-feed her, and she cried real tears. I didn't ordinarily have much use for dolls, but with her porcelain face and sweet smile, I thought she was the most beautiful thing in the world. I wanted her so badly that I actually asked my mother, and was gently told there wasn't enough in the till for such a luxury. I didn't mention it again, but I kept wishing and hoping.

The morning of my third birthday, I woke to find a bassinet by the side of my bed. When I sat up and looked in it, there was a Tiny Tears doll! My Bubby and Zaddy (grandmother and grandfather) had bought her for me. I was so happy, I think I cried. It was the beginning of hope. My blind optimism began the morning I woke to that doll. To this day, my glass is always half full, and I believe things turn out for the best in the end.

Make no mistake, reader—the lack of money wasn't due to a lack of hard work. My parents both came from a long line of hard workers, people who toughed it out because the only other choices were death or surrender. My mother's father, my Zaddy, was fifteen when he traded passports with an older cousin so he could come to America. Otherwise, the Czar's army would have taken him into service, holding my Zaddy for twenty-five years before allowing him to return home.

Jews weren't allowed to travel without special papers; Zaddy was arrested on his way to America, for leaving his province. Put to work running machinery in the jail, his hand was caught in a thresher and never set. The family myth was that a prison guard's beautiful wife had fallen in love with him, and set him free in the dead of night.

My Bubby, my mother's mom, had seen half her family slaughtered by the Cossacks after her uncle hid her in a hayloft. She drove herself home in a wagon, and was stopped and questioned. Jews weren't allowed to travel without permission; Bubby was saved from rape and arrest only because she spoke fluent Ukrainian, and could pretend to be Christian. She was just fourteen.

My father's father, Yashe, had died when Dad was nine. In our eyes, Yashe had died a hero. Diagnosed with Hodgkin's disease, knowing he would be dead in a year or two, leaving my Bubby Fink with three small children and no money to raise them, he decided to take matters into his own hands. One day, in the hospital, he asked the nurse to get him a cup of tea. He never asked for anything, so the nurse thought it was odd. Besides, she wasn't supposed to leave his side. He insisted. All he wanted was a glass of tea, something to take the chill off his bones.

While she was getting the tea, he walked to the balcony and threw himself off, dying when he hit the ground. Because of his illness, it couldn't be ruled a suicide; it was entirely possible he'd walked out there, become dizzy, and missed his footing.

My Bubby Fink received the entire insurance policy payout, enabling her to open a little rooming house. She took in boarders and did all the work herself: cleaning, cooking, collecting. She kept her family together with an iron fist, insisting they all get an education, reading poetry aloud to them after the day's work was done.

Like the rest of our family, my dad was a hard worker. He'd wanted to be a concert pianist, but he'd started far too late for that, though he still played for his own enjoyment. Meanwhile, he ran the farm. He gave piano lessons. In addition, he spent long hours on the road selling eggs to regular customers as far afield as Long Island. He had a chicken vaccination business as well; the crew was integrated, a rarity in those days.

He was also going to college, courtesy of the GI Bill. He'd served his time in the army, gotten an honorable discharge, and was now entitled to an education at the government's expense. In other words, he was really, really busy. But he always made time for music, and he always made time for me.

One evening when I was about two and a half, as I sat in the living room listening to my father play Debussy's "Clair de Lune" on our battered upright, I had a sudden epiphany. The music coming from the piano was flowing through my father's fingers. *He* was making that noise!

What a revelation . . . it was as though a part of me that had always floated around in the stratosphere suddenly fell to earth with a thud, then sat up, hungry for more. I rushed over to the piano and tugged at his arm. "Daddy, I want to do that. Teach me to do that!" I begged.

My father was amused. I was the apple of his eye, his *shayne punim* ("pretty face"), his curly-haired wonder. He loved making Egyptian one-eyed sandwiches for me, folding a piece of bread in half, biting out the center, then dropping it into a sizzling frying pan and cracking an egg into the hole as I looked on in awe. The brightest spot in my week was when he'd take me for breakfast at the diner where Mom worked part-time, and I'd get to sit at the counter with the other farmers like a grown-up. He called me his *macheshayfe*, his little witch, and everything I did delighted him. Now here I was, demanding piano lessons. It must have seemed very cute.

He tried to break it to me gently. "Jan, before you can learn the piano, you have to know the alphabet. You have to be able to tell time. You have to be able to count to ten." With that, he picked me up and carried me off to bed, where he told me a story about a little hunchback who fell in love with a princess.

The next morning, I went to Mom and explained what I needed to learn. I can still see her taking the bedroom alarm clock and showing me what the big hand and the little hand did. We conquered time, then moved on to the alphabet. I had a head start on that, because my grandparents wrote to me every week, and I'd been trying to read the letters myself for a while. We made short work of the alphabet, then she drilled me in numbers. The numbers made sense because of the clock.

That evening, I presented my new skills to my father, and piano lessons began.

I can only wonder, now, what my parents must have thought. I was their first child; they had no basis for comparison. All the families we knew were bright, all the homes we knew were filled with books. No one seemed to think I was anything out of the ordinary, so I didn't, either.

My father was a master teacher, something I only understood much later. When I started piano lessons with him, he was the only teacher I'd ever known, and after about a year, he began driving me crazy. He had terrible eye-hand coordination, and he played the same wrong note in "Clair de Lune" every time, no matter how often I pointed it out. Then I began getting into arguments with him over interpretations and fingering.

You can imagine how it made him feel, being critiqued by a three-and-a-half-year-old. For my father, music was a joy. For me, it was sacred. I distinctly remember our final argument, which ended with his yelling to my mom, "I don't have to take this shit from a kid!" I remember it, because I'd never heard him curse before.

There followed a succession of truly awful (but inexpensive) piano teachers. It was a real economic struggle for my parents. I knew I ought to be grateful, but I hated practicing. The constant repetition, the strictness of it, seemed stupid to me. Life was already strict enough. We had to be careful about what we said, who we befriended. Even in nursery school, I knew I had to be careful, because there was always someone watching.

THE FBI HAD DEVELOPED an interest in my family shortly before I was born. One morning, Dad attended a meeting of local chicken farmers to discuss the price of eggs. Two agents picked him up as he walked home, and questioned him about possible Communist ties. A few years later, after we'd lost the farm and moved into a rented house in Lakewood, they tried to interview him again. When Dad refused to speak with them, the FBI placed us on the "watch list."

Those were the HUAC years, when a Communist lived under every bed. We were under surveillance my entire childhood, carefully stalked and photographed by men in dark suits and shiny shoes. It was scary, because my family's fortune hung in the balance. When Dad graduated from Rutgers University, he became a teacher, a public employee.

Teachers were eligible for tenure after two years at the same school, and tenure meant lifetime job security. With tenure, we could buy a house. With tenure, we could settle down. So I was forbidden to do anything that might jeopardize his chances, whether it was taking a copy of the *National Guardian* (a leftist paper) to school, or telling friends about the guitar chords I'd learned from Robbie and Mike Meeropol, the children of Ethel and Julius Rosenberg.

Sadly, the precautions were useless. At the end of Dad's second year at a school, the FBI would meet with the principal and ask whether my father consorted with known Communists, and that was the end of tenure. We moved every second summer so Dad could start over again in a new school system. It was jarring, always leaving places and people. It meant I couldn't really form deep friendships with anyone; my closest friend became my brother, Eric, because he was always there. Besides, I was responsible for him.

It was a marvel when he came home. Mom had done everything right (courtesy, again, of Dr. Spock). Months before the birth, I'd been given a life-size doll. I practiced taking care of it with my mother's help, putting it to sleep in the bassinet next to my Tiny Tears doll. All our relatives were there when Mom came home from the hospital. They sat me on the couch, then put pillows all around me. When Mom walked in, the first thing she did was carefully place my brother on my lap so I could hold him myself. I was three and a half, and overjoyed to be so trusted. From that moment on, he was the light of my life.

Eric was bright, curious, and so lively that I soon despaired. When Mom went back to work full-time, I was told he was my responsibility while she was gone. I took that responsibility seriously, and happily, because I adored him, but it made life more complicated than ever. Eric had truly boundless energy, and once he became mobile, he was a handful.

We would lose him in department stores. He ran right through plate-glass doors. He moved so fast that nothing around him was safe, including his own body. His brain was as busy as mine, but somehow it short-circuited when it came to thinking about consequences. Coming back from school one winter's day, he took a walk up to his knees in the creek and came home with frozen feet. I had to look up frostbite in the first-aid book to get the boots off. Another time, he decided to see what would happen if he threw some of my science kit chemicals into a test tube and lit it. He blew off his eyelashes and eyebrows, sending me yet again to the Red Cross handbook to figure out what to do.

Despite all that, he was my best friend and confidant. Moving every two years as we did, thrust into strange school systems where most of the kids had known each other since kindergarten, left me feeling like an outcast. We migrated from Farmingdale to Lakewood, then to a succession of garden apartments in New Brunswick, and finally to East Orange during my tenth summer. By that time, I'd attended five different schools.

My family, and music, were the only constants in my life. Eric was a comfort, and a source of stability, but even Eric couldn't understand the restless urgency I felt. I had a lot of energy, coupled with a fair amount of drive. I'd gotten into Rutgers Prep on a full scholarship when I was nine, and catching up to the other fourth graders took a good three or four hours of homework each evening. At the same time, there was a veterinary book I wanted, but I was too young for a regular job. Girls weren't allowed newspaper routes, so I bribed a boy down the street to get one, then fulfilled it for him and kicked back a portion of the money. Between school, the paper route, and playing with the neighborhood kids, I was pretty busy, but something in me kept saying it wasn't enough.

I had nowhere to put it, this restlessness that consumed me. Sometimes I wanted to crawl out of my skin and send my soul out to skitter along the sewer lines like a fish, sloughing off daily life and mindlessly racing against nothing as fast as I could. My impatience was all-embracing; it included everyone and everything around me, as well as myself. My appetite was voracious, but I couldn't find anything to fill my belly. Playing the piano satisfied a bit of it, reading sometimes took the edge off, but nothing really fed that hunger—until I discovered the guitar.

Now here I sat, propping the instrument up on my lap, singing a song I'd written myself for parents who'd thought all those hours of listening and practicing in my room were just for fun. And not to brag, but for a first effort, it was a pretty good song. A little long, perhaps; it takes years to learn to condense. A little trite, but I knew that. I'd used phrases like "lips of ruby red" and "eyes as deep as the deepest sea" deliberately, to make it sound more like an old folk song. I was very proud of the guitar part; most of it was up around the twelfth fret, where even angels feared to tread.

We stopped at a light. I finished singing, and there was silence. *All right*, I thought, *maybe it's not a great song, but it's a start.*

I waited. Finally, Mom turned around in her seat and faced me.

"Jan, that's a beautiful song. Where did you learn it?" she asked.

"I wrote it," I replied.

With that, Dad turned around, too, and they both stared at me like I was a two-headed calf.

It's moments like that you remember in your life as an artist. Never the endings; always the beginnings.

THE WHOLE IDEA of becoming a singer had started out, innocuously enough, with Odetta's appearance on *The Harry Belafonte Show* when I was nine. At that time, it was impossible to find black people on television unless it was a documentary about Africa. I still remember the first Doublemint gum commercial with black twins in it; at school the next day, no one talked about anything else. For a black man to have a prime-time TV show was astonishing, a real sign of the changing times.

I was taking a shower when I heard the most incredible voice coming from the living room. Throwing a towel around me, I raced out of the bathroom, yelling "Who is that? Who is that?!" *That's Odetta,* my mom replied. I stared at the television screen. Even in black and white, she was absolutely beautiful. Dressed simply, with large hoop earrings framing her face, her hair in the first Afro I'd seen, she sang a song I'd always heard done as a quiet lament.

Well, there was nothing quiet about this! She had power in her voice, and she used it unmercifully. Each time she strummed the guitar, it was as if John Henry's hammer collided with the strings. I felt like I'd been smacked across the face with a two-by-four. She was bigger than life, and I wanted to meet her more than anything in the world.

A few months later, I saw in the newspaper that Odetta would be performing at nearby Rutgers. I begged for tickets. I pleaded with my parents. I scrimped and saved so I could buy my own. The night of the concert found me and Mom sitting in the cheapest seats available, last balcony, last row. Performers call that the nosebleed section. I didn't care; I was enthralled. In that ninety minutes, my life was changed. I knew what I was going to do when I grew up. When I wasn't busy with my veterinary practice, I was going to sing, and play guitar, and perform all over the place.

After the show, we stood outside the dressing room for what seemed like hours, hoping to meet the great woman. Sadly, it was a school night, and we had to leave before she came out to greet the fans. Still, it was a momentous evening in what turned out to be a momentous year for me.

Over those short twelve months, lots of things happened. School-work challenged me, for the first time. I realized I was attracted to women. I read *Scottsboro Boys,* and understood why my folks worked so hard for civil rights. And I discovered God.

My parents were atheists, as were many Jewish immigrants and their children. Somehow, in throwing away the need to keep kosher and study *Torah,* they had also become "free thinkers." But like most Jewish atheists, they were also fervently Jewish. We celebrated all the holidays:

Purim, Passover, Chanukah. We were never allowed to have a Christmas tree in the house. We might have been atheists, but we believed in Judaism. In later years, when we'd argue about it, my mom would always close the discussions by saying, "Janis, God doesn't care if I'm an atheist!"

I was raised to think for myself, and I did. Our bookshelves were open; Dad's theory was, "What she doesn't understand will go over her head; what she does understand won't hurt her." So I read *The Diary of Anne Frank,* Freud, *Fahrenheit 451,* books about the Holocaust . . . pretty much whatever I could get my hands on. And because I was aware that there were so many worlds out there, I remained open to change.

That summer, we went for a picnic with our friends the Cazdens. On the way, the car radio warned of two escaped convicts in the area. When we reached the picnic site, my parents cautioned me to stay within earshot. I wandered off, following the creek, and eventually hit a clearing with a big sturdy tree on the banks. I leaned back against it, watching the water flow. I could smell the sweet bouquet of moss on the rocks, and I filled my nostrils with the scent of running water. It was completely silent but for the noise of the creek—silent in the world, and silent in my heart.

Suddenly, in one huge gestalt, I realized that each drop of water in the creek would never be in that exact place again. At the same time, each drop of water would eventually return to the stream, because the water was part of something much bigger than itself, constantly regenerating through rain, snow, mist.

I let my mind float with the idea. The creek seemed to slow until it stopped moving. There was complete stillness, within and without. Everything was totally in its place, and so was I. Everything was *right.* It was as though a curtain had lifted, and my mind woke up. *I* woke up. And in that moment, I knew God was there, around me and inside me.

I ran my hands down the tree trunk, feeling its age and majesty, and I understood that the water and the trunk were both made of the same stuff. I didn't know to call it "molecules" back then, but I knew instinctively that the trunk would someday disintegrate and turn into earth and water, and that same water would run through other trees and cause them to live and take shape.

I call this a revelation, in the old-fashioned, miraculous sense of the word. I don't know how to explain it better than to say that in an instant, everything made sense. There was a shaking of the world around me that turned everything upside down and right back up again, leaving it all brand-new and slightly different. Like a familiar city street just after a hard rain. I knew, without a doubt, that God existed. I couldn't explain it; I just *knew*.

I was stunned by joy; my mother was horrified. Her reaction was a funny corollary to the typical believer's reaction when her child says, "I don't believe in God anymore!" Mom worried that she'd done something wrong, something that made me need "the crutch of religion."

I went back and sat at the campfire, eating my hot dog and staring into the shadows. At about the time I ran out of sauerkraut, one of the shadows moved, and two men approached the fire. Our parents grabbed us, sure these were the convict escapees, until I noticed that one of them was dressed like a medieval minstrel. I didn't think most prisoners wore tights and shirts with poofy sleeves; this guy was either a lunatic, or a man on a mission.

He held a lute out with one hand, put the other up palm forward, and said, "Good evening. My name is Serafyn; I'm a minstrel, traveling through this country and trading songs for food." He and his friend were walking across the United States. We made him welcome, and spent the rest of the evening swapping songs with him. It was a magical night all around, and I snuggled happily against Eric on the ride home, my heart happy and full of music and faith.

A week or so later, we discovered Dad had again been denied tenure. My folks told us he'd managed to find another teaching job in West Orange, New Jersey; at summer's end, we'd be moving to adjacent East

Orange, which had more affordable housing than Dad's new district. It was a huge wrench for me; I'd done so well at Rutgers that they'd guaranteed my scholarship through high school, hinting at further help for college and graduate school. I couldn't stand the thought of leaving a place that had finally challenged me to do my intellectual best, and I pleaded with my parents to let me go to boarding school there instead. But my father, whose own father had died young, insisted the family stay together. And my mother, already concerned that I was almost "too smart" and would miss out on a "normal" childhood because of it, agreed.

Partly to ease the transition from New Brunswick to East Orange, my folks sent me to Camp Woodland that summer. We couldn't afford it, but Dad took on the job of music counselor, which entitled him to my tuition and a cabin of his own. Mom visited weekends, Eric in tow. I studiously avoided them; the embarrassment of having my parents at camp with me was excruciating. Outside of that, it was a fantastic summer.

Woodland was an unusual camp. Started in the mid-1940s by Norman Studer, a folklorist and educator, it was a haunt for red diaper babies like myself, kids whose parents were left-leaning or even outright Socialists or Communists. It was unusual in that it was also a "work camp"; we built bunkhouses, helped in the kitchen, and learned all sorts of things you'd never run across in the city.

Though Woodland was leftist, it bore little resemblance to others of its ilk. Norman was a true folklorist, who firmly believed that the stories and songs of the people in the surrounding mountains should be collected and cherished. I remember traipsing up a mountain with my dad one day, carrying a battery-run tape recorder. After a few hours' climb, we reached a small house—actually, little more than a shack. No electricity, no running water. Inside was a man who knew some songs and played a bit of fiddle; Norman wanted him captured on tape. When my father asked the man why the fiddle had only three strings instead of four, he grinned and said it had always been that way. He just played around it.

Folks from the towns and mountaintops would come to camp and call square dances on the weekends, playing dulcimers and fiddles and staying to show us how they worked. The townspeople would be invited to join us for dances, or sit in the audience when we put on plays like *Sojourner Truth*. In return, we learned farming songs from farmers, logging songs from lumberjacks, and local history from one and all. Norman made Camp Woodland a real part of the community. He extended his "collecting" beyond songs, to the skills of the people living nearby, inviting them to camp so we could learn from each other.

We made paper from bark, collecting it carefully in the woods, pounding it to a pulp, then smoothing it out so we could take the quill pens we'd sharpened, dip them in ink we'd created from berries, and write letters home. We made our own candles from ashes and lye, taught by a local farmer's wife who'd been supplying the region for decades. Instead of celebrating the Fourth of July, we had Hiroshima Day, complete with memorial services and discussions about nuclear disarmament. I learned phrases like "strontium 90" and discovered that all those bomb drills at school, hiding under the desk with my butt in the air, were not going to save my ass when the big one fell.

Anyone who attended school in America during the sixties still flinches when an air raid siren goes off. Bomb drills were held in every classroom; the siren would start, and we'd scramble to the floor while the teachers pretended we could survive a nuclear attack. But after that summer, I knew safety was a myth. Even if we survived the initial blast, the windstorm, and the firestorm, we'd be cut down by radiation sickness. The government knew it. I knew it. My family and friends knew it. The only ones who didn't know it were the rest of America, busy building fallout shelters that only guaranteed they'd die alone.

But enough depressing cold war memories! More than anything else at camp, we had music. It seemed like every counselor and CIT (counselor-in-training) played *something*—usually guitar, but also banjo, harmonica, autoharp. During free time, someone would start a song, and within minutes there'd be a crowd of singers and players. We had incredible musicians among the staff, people like Eric Weissberg of "Dueling Banjos" fame, and John Cohen. And of course, Pete Seeger, who would come up and stay for days, singing and teaching.

I began learning to play the guitar. A couple of counselors showed me some chords, and I stole my father's copy of *The Leadbelly Songbook*, picking out songs so I'd be able to contribute something to the Sunday meeting services. I fell in love with the strings, the body, the sound, and was soon imitating Odetta around the campfires.

That summer, Joan Baez was queen. She'd made her first appearance at the Newport Folk Festival two years earlier, in 1959, and had swept through the folk community like a storm. To my bunkmates, Joan was the epitome of cool. Some wanted to look like her, some wanted to be like her, and some (including me) just wanted to *be* her.

Our camp uniform was jeans, a work shirt, and water buffalo sandals—most of the time we looked like complete slobs. But on Joan, those jeans and sandals were transformed into a political statement. She stood for everything we believed in. She sang for civil rights causes. She marched with Dr. Martin Luther King Jr. She refused to appear on the *Hootenanny* TV program after it blacklisted Pete Seeger. Best of all, she was easy to copy.

At least, she was easy to copy for everyone but me. My hair was curly and short; every other female at camp had long, straight hair, parted down the middle like Joan's. They were tall and willowy; I was short and stocky. They played "Silver Dagger," or sang interminable verses of "Barbara Allen"; I was still singing "John Henry." So when I got home that fall and started fifth grade, I also embarked on a series of maneuvers to make myself more "folk-like."

It wasn't easy. The hair thing was useless; I tried putting it up in huge rollers overnight, and that straightened it, but at the first hint of humidity it sprang back around my head in twists. Tall and willowy was just not going to happen; one look at my family tree of short Russian peasants knocked that idea out of my head. As to clothes, there was no way I'd be allowed to wear jeans and a work shirt to school.

But I could do the music part. I practiced to my Baez records, slowing them down and figuring out the fingering. I memorized every folk album in my parents' collection, and hungered for more.

Records were expensive. I got just enough allowance to cover school lunches; if I wanted more clothing than the one new outfit I got each fall, I had to earn the money myself. I might get one record for my birthday or Chanukah, but that wasn't nearly enough, so I embarked on a fund-raising drive. I cut out sodas, saving a nickel a day. I took baby-sitting jobs in our apartment building for a quarter per hour, safe in the knowledge that my parents were nearby. I got a job washing counter-tops at the local soda shop for twenty-five cents an hour, and occasion-ally a generous soul would leave me a nickel tip. I cleaned out people's basements and taught guitar. Every cent I earned went toward albums, and later, as I began writing, toward paper and pens.

It's a funny thing about writers and their tools. When you're young, those tools assume a mystical importance. Even when you're older, there are writing adjuncts that seem to bring you luck. I feel sorry for con-temporary writers brought up on word processors. They'll never know what it's like to stroke the black keys of an old Remington, and cherish the memories they hold. Even now, I like to write on thin-lined legal pads, with a Pilot Precise V Extra Fine pen. One year, my partner, Pat, gave me a ream of the pads I like, and a dozen boxes of those pens in assorted colors. She said she felt funny giving me pads and pens for my birthday rather than jewelry or clothing, but I was ecstatic.

I think the reason for that mysticism is twofold. First, somewhere in the back of our minds, every writer is worried about running out of pa-per and pens. What if they stop manufacturing the kind I like? What if there's a war, and it's all requisitioned? These are vast worries, particularly to a child songwriter growing up during the Cuban missile crisis.

Second, we have no idea where our creativity comes from, or why it's so elusive. Why did I write a great verse Tuesday, and find myself unable to come up with anything even vaguely decent on Wednesday? Why are some shows incandescent, while others leave me feeling like I'm nothing more than a good craftsman?

As I grew older, I realized that a lot of things affect my creativity. Fatigue, illness, emotional life. I accept that some moments are more creative than others, and try to let it go. But at its heart, the process of creativity is just as mysterious to me as it is to the listener or reader, and that's frightening.

Stella Adler, my teacher and friend, used to say, "Trust your talent. The talent knows better than you do." I try to live by those words, because I know they're true. But like every artist, a small space in my heart worries that I'll never write another good song, that the talent will just up and leave me one day. Hence the thin-lined pads and Pilot pens.

But I digress. . . .

TWO

God & the FBI

They could fingerprint my heart
I knew it from the start
Ain't no place for a face to hide
from god & the fbi

We were living in East Orange when I started writing songs. Back then, it was noted for its fine school system and its award-winning public library. The town was almost all black, as were the schools.

There were only three white kids in my fifth-grade class, and they were already good friends. They were blond and redheaded, blue- and green-eyed. I had black hair, brown eyes, and a suspect family. The white kids avoided me like the plague.

Fortunately, the black kids were more welcoming, especially when they found out I could play any song by ear. *Bang!* I was suddenly popular at parties, where I could provide the bass part to James Brown's "I'll Go Crazy," or chords to the Drifters' "There Goes My Baby." Everyone at school listened to the soul stations coming out of Newark, so I became steeped in Lou Rawls and the Coasters, and later the Motown groups. This was an entirely new world to me, but strangely enough, it dovetailed with the music I'd been listening to at home. Big Bill Broonzy wasn't that far away from Ray Charles. Reverend Gary Davis ran right beside Marvin Gaye. The main difference, so far as I could see, was that these newer soul singers didn't play instruments.

Like folk music, the music I was now hearing spoke to what I was feeling. Songs like "Get a Job" dealt with the real world we inhabited, where good jobs were hard to come by, and everybody wanted one.

I was branching out, omnivorously listening to anything I could get my hands on. My parents' LP collection stretched from Bessie Smith to the Weavers, from Beethoven to the Missa Luba. Now, with my new-found friends from camp and school, and my earnings from babysitting and cleaning counters, I was bringing us into the sixties. I listened to everything but white pop music, which my friends and I looked on with disdain. To our minds, the pop music of the late fifties and early sixties was just stupid.

I'd seen *American Bandstand* years before; the show was everything I loathed. The singers looked manufactured, stamped out with cookie cutters by evil music-haters who just saw dollar signs instead of ways to change the world. The songs, too, sounded manufactured, with the same chord progressions and awful guitar parts. Fabian, Frankie Avalon—what was with these guys? Not to mention their hair . . .

Smokey Robinson was my hero; it was impossible to compare "Tracks of My Tears" to "Teen Angel" and not switch sides. I couldn't understand how anyone could enjoy such vapidity, and my friends agreed.

White pop music was something Republicans listened to, not people like us.

I guess it was inevitable that I'd start writing songs. I'd always written as a way of getting out whatever was inside me. It was rare that I found someone I could really talk to; there was so much going on in my head at any one time that even I could barely keep up. My parents were busy, Eric was younger, and I was always in a new school system. So I turned to music.

Before I could start writing songs, though, I had to learn my lineage. Not just what I'd grown up on, but the trail from Ma Rainey to Bessie Smith to Billie Holiday to Nina Simone. I followed the Childe Ballads to Hedy West and Hank Williams, coming full circle with the Weavers and Pete. I begged records from older friends, from families we knew, from anyone who owned a turntable. I ran across women like Victoria Spivey and Sister Rosetta Tharpe, both great players and bandleaders. Like Odetta, they became my role models. And I dove into contemporary folk music with a passion.

There was a "folk show" broadcast out of Newark once a week. It didn't begin until ten o'clock, past my bedtime. My Zaddy had given me a transistor radio, still an astonishing thing in 1962, and I'd hide under the blanket with my bedroom door shut tight, a towel shoved under it to muffle the noise. With the radio pressed against my ear, I would lay there and listen, discovering Phil Ochs, Eric Andersen, Judy Henske. I worshipped them, and each time I managed to save $1.99, I'd buy one of their albums. (In mono, because mono was slightly cheaper, and I reasoned that the notes would be the same either way.)

I'd bring the record home and play it again and again, learning the guitar parts, lyrics, and phrasing. I spent all my after-school time like that, copying their words onto yellow legal pads, wearing my fingers out on the strings.

There weren't enough hours in the day for me to do everything I needed to do. My priorities were guitar and the library. As far as I was concerned, school was a complete waste of time. When I'd entered kindergarten in Lakewood, the teacher proudly told us we were going to learn to read. I raised my hand and explained that since I could already read and write, I saw no need to practice those skills anymore, and wanted to be excused. Instead of trying to find out my reading level, the teacher told the class I was a liar, and made me stand in the corner.

That absolutely stunned me. Up until then, I'd never known a grown-up to be unfair. Yet there I was, standing with my face against the wall, burning in shame, for telling a simple truth! I arrived home that afternoon and informed Mom that I hated school and was never going back. My mother was outraged, and the next morning she had a long talk with the principal. After that, the teacher let me read quietly while the rest of the class struggled with their ABCs, but my feelings about school never changed.

Unfortunately for me, I didn't have any really good teachers until junior high. In my eyes, school remained a prison I had to put up with while I did my time and waited for parole. When I did the math, it was horrendous. School wasted six or seven hours of my day, five days a week, thirty-five weeks a year. I was losing 175 days a year to this idiocy, 1,225 hours that could be spent making music, or reading a new book. I resented every second of it.

I spent the school year waiting for camp. Woodland had closed, and Camp Webatuck had opened. Dad was now director, Mom was financial officer, and our roving music counselors included Pete, Richie Havens, and Bernice Reagon of the SNCC Freedom Singers. Because of my folks' positions, we got to go up early and meet them first. Counselors and CITs arrived a week early for training, so we got a head start on meeting them as well.

We also got to open the bunks for the summer, clearing away the red pepper we'd scattered over the mattresses to keep rodents out, and sorting through the kitchen supplies and foods the government gave nonprofit organizations like ours. There was a lot of work, but there was also plenty of time for singing and swimming. My goal in life at that point was to become a lifeguard; I couldn't think of anything nobler than spending my summers saving lives. I knew lifeguards didn't make much money, so I intended to become a veterinarian, too, and then make music on the side.

It was a seminal summer. I got my first kiss, from a CIT named Yadi Montalalou. He was darkly handsome, and he let me hang around him the first week. Seeing the case of hero worship I'd developed, he came over to me as I sat on a Ping-Pong table and kissed me sweetly on the lips. Then he asked me to do his laundry. As I dragged the bag, bursting at the seams with filthy clothing, up the hill to the laundry room, my dad caught sight of me. When I told him what I was doing, and why, Yadi was quickly moved to another section of the camp. I can't say I was sorry to see him go; it hadn't been much of a kiss.

As camp progressed, I found my first boyfriend. Tall, thin, serious, we'd have long, intense talks about the problems of the world, as you can only do when you're starting adolescence and able to take everything, including yourself, seriously. We tongue-kissed a couple of times, which was weird and sticky. We'd subtly hold hands in the rec hall as we watched *Alexander Nevsky* or *Battleship Potemkin,* films the camp managed to get free from grateful parents and leftist organizations. We went to the folk dances Friday nights, learning Greek and Israeli circle dances and watching Mike Peters, later to become a hugely successful choreographer, leap higher than anyone else. We sat arm in arm around the bonfire on weekends and listened as my father told us the story of Leiningen and the ants, or scared us silly with *The Green Hand.*

Camp felt safe. For the first time, I felt completely accepted by everyone around me. I hated returning to school, although it was a bit more bearable. For one thing, I was now one of the "old kids." I had a few friends. For another, I'd gotten to know Anna Baker, our local librarian.

Anna saved my emotional life. The first time we spoke, she asked what I wanted to read, because I looked so intense. I shrugged and told her I didn't know; I'd just started with the left shelves and intended to read right through to the opposite side. I confessed it was a little frustrating, because I was only allowed to take home three books on my child's card, and often all three turned out to be boring.

Anna changed everything. She immediately pulled a copy of Madeleine L'Engle's *A Wrinkle in Time* off the shelf, along with *Half Magic*, by Edgar Eager, and Jean Craighead George's *My Side of the Mountain*. Then she told me if I wanted to take more than three home, she'd check them out on her own card. I had a friend who understood! We couldn't afford to buy a lot of books, and as fast as I read, it really would have been a waste of money. The library and Anna were my salvation, and we corresponded until her death many years later.

By the start of sixth grade, I'd exhausted the juvenile and young adult sections. And I really had more pressing things on my mind than whether Willie would win the baseball game and become a hometown hero. My IQ had been tested in kindergarten, and again when I applied for a scholarship to prep school. I knew it was high, because someone from Rutgers had called my mom and said, "Do you know what you have here? Do you have *any idea* what you have here?!" My mom was rudely awakened to the possibility that I wasn't just different. I was really, *really* different.

She laughed, and told him, "I don't want to know. She's just a normal child." So that was how I was raised, and that was how I thought of myself. A little smarter than some, maybe, but certainly no Einstein.

It wasn't until sixth grade that I became aware of just how much importance my teachers placed on those numbers. My closest friend was a very tall girl named Pat McCormick; we spent our time together singing bad harmonies and being silly, cracking up over nothing and playing hopscotch on the sidewalk. The other kids called us "Mutt and Jeff," but I didn't care. It was great for a solemn child like me to have a friend who liked running and jumping rope, and didn't expect anything more of me than some fun now and then.

One day our homeroom teacher, an elderly white woman, took me aside and said I should choose someone else to be "best pals" with. I bristled, thinking it was because Pat was black. *No,* she said, *it's because of your IQ. You're just too smart to be friends with someone like that. You're out of her league.*

Yikes! I guess she meant to reassure me by showing me my scores, but it scared the pants off me instead. According to the numbers, I was a genius. I didn't feel like a genius. Geniuses were crazy, or they went crazy at an early age. Everybody knew that. Geniuses were kids who started college at eight, and died young—everybody knew that, too. You couldn't have a happy life if you were a genius; you were all head and no heart. Was that going to be my fate? Had I just been faking it until now?

I went home and asked my mom if I was a genius. She laughed, sat me down, and said, "Honey, a genius is someone who makes something absolutely new, something that was never there before. A Beethoven, or a Picasso. You're a little young to be worrying about that." I was relieved, but not relieved enough. It worried me all month, as I struggled to look as "normal" as possible around the other kids. So I finally went to Anna for help.

Rather than scoffing at my concerns, she took me upstairs to the adult section, where we checked out the voluminous *Terman's Genetic Studies of Genius.* Most of it went over my head, but I walked away reassured on several fronts. Being smart didn't mean you would go crazy or die young. Smart people seemed better adjusted, and lived a bit longer. Best of all, they had hearts, too.

Phew.

That concern aside, I could explore the other big thing that was bothering me—girls. I'd known I was attracted to women since fourth grade. I'd been reading something by Freud that my parents had on their bookshelves, and it set me to thinking about my homeroom teacher. Sitting on a knoll, watching her during recess, I thought, *What I'm feeling isn't some little girl thing. It's real.* My next thought was, *Better not tell Mom. She'll think it's just a phase.* The idea of my feelings being discounted in that manner wasn't pleasant.

Now that I'd hit adolescence, sex became an issue. My classmates were dating, making out, talking about boyfriends, and dreaming of marriage. I was dreaming of saving Joan Baez from drowning, of her eternal gratitude as she kissed me chastely on the lips and adopted me into her life. I was a late starter; my sexual fantasies ended at the neck. But they were always about women.

I was desperately in love with my guidance counselor. In my fantasy, she pulled me out of class to confess undying devotion. In my daydreams, she said she would leave her husband for me, then kissed me on the forehead. Eventually we went to her car, where Other Things Happened. I didn't know what Other Things were, but I was busily leafing through James Baldwin's *Another Country* to locate the sex scenes and find out.

I also worried about our FBI surveillance team. We'd seen them at camp the summer before, watching us through binoculars as we played baseball. I reasoned that when the guidance counselor and I eloped, she probably wouldn't appreciate being tailed by men with tape recorders pretending to be shooting a documentary. How could we ever run away to Poughkeepsie (at the time the sum length of my geographical boundaries) if we had to bring all these people along?

I turned to the library again, and found "homosexuality" cross-referenced under "deviant behavior." I picked up *City of Night* and read about male homosexuals; everyone seemed miserably unhappy. I checked out Radclyffe Hall's *The Well of Loneliness*. Throughout the book, Hall spoke about wanting to be a boy, wanting to be a man, wanting to be male. I felt nothing of the kind. I *liked* being a girl. I just also liked other girls.

Still, it was good to know I wasn't the only one out there, even if I was probably the only one in New Jersey.

Once I entered junior high, a couple of older kids noticed me reading Allen Ginsberg and befriended me. I fell in with an interesting group of nerds, people who wrote poetry and talked about assassination conspiracies, which was a whole lot more exciting than my classmates' discussions of poodle skirts versus wraparounds.

My new school friends passed around rumors like lightning—Oswald was a tool of the CIA, the Mafia killed Kennedy, Marilyn Monroe was Bobby's lover, and had to be eliminated because she knew too much. They made fun of the FBI, who they said were anti-female and anti-intellectual. J. Edgar Hoover ate lunch every single day with Clyde Tolson, and liked to dress up as a woman—that's why there were no homosexual agents allowed, because "it takes one to know one," and their cover would be blown.

This was a new concept for me, that one of the most powerful figures in the nation had to lead a secret life. I became fascinated by famous homosexuals, staring at their photographs and wondering what we had in common. Could we be spotted by physical type?

I was hyperconscious of my body and the way I moved. One of my teachers had told me I walked "too heavy," so I started trying to be light on my feet. The result was ridiculous, a sort of Dumbo meets Pavlova. I gave it up and moved on.

I put a picture of J. Edgar Hoover next to one of Gertrude Stein, added Radclyffe Hall to the mix, and immediately decided I could not be gay. If these three typified my kind, forget it! Better to marry than to burn. I would become straight. I would get married. I would join the FBI. I'd surveil myself, and take some control over my life.

God knows, it felt like we had little enough control in general. To my immense relief, we'd managed to stay in East Orange for more than two years. Dad had to change school systems when the West Orange high school refused him tenure, but he found a job in neighboring Jersey City, so Eric and I could stay in the same school system.

I couldn't understand why my father never got tenure. Everyone said he was a great educator. Each time it was denied, parents' organizations signed petitions and students picketed on his behalf, but he still couldn't keep a job for more than a couple of years.

Losing tenure didn't just mean we had to move again. It meant we couldn't buy the house he dreamed about, or have the garden my mother yearned for. I wouldn't get my own guitar, and my grandparents would still have to send bags of groceries home with us on the weekends when we visited. In the race to be upwardly mobile, we were falling sadly behind. It was depressing. I wondered if maybe there was something wrong with us.

My life was pretty compartmentalized. I lived in two worlds: the world of camp and the world of school. On weekends, I'd take the bus to Greenwich Village, meet up with other kids from Webatuck, and stand around the fountain singing. We'd talk about politics, Vietnam, voter registration drives. A couple of the CITs, Teddy Gold and Nicky Wechsler, had gone down South to register black voters; they were our heroes.

It was tremendously exciting to be a kid in the Village back then. Things that were only whispered about behind closed doors were visible on the street. Interracial couples walked freely, holding hands. No one stared. Gay couples kissed by the fountain, sat in earnest discussion over thick Italian coffee while holding hands across the table, and no one arrested them. Transvestites paraded outside the clubs, talking makeup and shoe size. Poets stood on corners reciting nihilistic verse that never rhymed. The bookstores carried strange titles by authors like Leroi Jones. I even found a book where the type was different for every word!

We roamed the streets in packs, completely ignored by the adults around us. Hippiedom was just beginning, and in our jeans and work shirts, we felt adult and "with it." It was exhilarating, confusing, momentous.

Then I'd go home and back to school, where people worried over whether tongue-kissing could get you pregnant, and interracial dating was frowned upon by both colors. Where I had to watch my step in case one of my girlfriends figured out why I never looked at anyone when we changed for gym. Where people laughed at my idea of becoming a singer.

I stayed hidden in both worlds, keeping secrets, swinging between the two poles. One part of me was fiercely brave, role-modeled on Batman comic books and Jewish champions. That part would join SDS to protest the war in Vietnam. That part was almost brave enough to ask my best friend if she wanted to practice kissing sometime.

The other part worried about looking "dykey," got straight As, and wondered if the government might just be right. They didn't want gay people in the schools; maybe we *were* all child molesters. They kept a close watch on my family; maybe we *were* a threat to the government.

I lived in dread of discovery—by nameless agents who'd somehow discover my fantasies and lock me away until I could be "cured." By my parents, who'd realize I would rather stay home playing guitar than go to a political meeting. By my friends from camp and school, who'd notice I was neither fish nor fowl. It was crazy-making.

Oh, wait. There was one more secret, one more hidden world. Gosh, I almost forgot.

I was being molested by our dentist.

It feels so strange to write that. "Molested." What a word. Every time I think about it, and the body memories return, all I can think is "Yuck." But that's not much of a description, is it?

When we moved to East Orange, we needed a new dentist. Both my parents had bad teeth, and I seemed to have inherited the worst of it. My parents found a nice married fellow who had built on an addition to his house and put an office there. It was homey, laid-back. There was just a small waiting area, usually empty, and his treatment room.

I vividly remember the first time we went, because somehow Eric got ten steps ahead of Dad and me. By the time we entered the room, every single machine was going berserk. The chair was lunging up and down, the drills were spinning, water was spewing out of the little faucet. Eric looked so innocent that all we could do was laugh.

The dentist took X-rays. Eric was fine, just one cavity. I, however, was in a world of trouble. It would take several months to get me straightened out. Lots of cavities. Lots of work. We were fellow leftists, he'd cut his rates, no need to worry about immediate payment. Reader, remember, this was the age before credit cards. My folks didn't have enough money for all that dental work, so his kind offer came as a relief.

No one thought to wonder why our previous dentist hadn't seen all these cavities the year before. Everyone, including me, just figured I'd drawn the genetic short straw.

My dad came into the treatment room with me as the dentist explained that he'd be using hypnosis instead of shots. It sounded so easy, it made me smile. He said, "One part of you will be here, in the chair, while I'm drilling—but that part will feel no pain. I'll send the other part far away, to a place I call the Waiting Room. That part will feel the pain. You'll never really have to deal with it."

Sounded great. I never wondered if the part that felt the pain, which was still a part of *me*, might think of it as torture.

He held a small spiral in front of my face, telling me to look deeply into it and relax. Then he pressed a button and the black part began spinning. I concentrated on the red center and tried to relax. He began counting in a monotone, and I felt myself slipping away. Dad was there the whole time; it felt safe enough. And, heck, part of me did indeed go away! When the dentist began drilling, the part of me in the chair didn't feel anything but a mild buzzing sensation. It was terrific.

Dad or Mom came with me the next two or three times; after that, they'd just drop me off on Saturday mornings and pick me up an hour later. No big deal.

Now, understand: I'd started puberty pretty early, in fourth grade. I had to get a brassiere that year; I remember that it annoyed me, because it got in the way when I played baseball. Every time I lifted my arms, it was there, cutting into my skin. An impediment. Suddenly, there were these breasts to deal with, two of them, one on each side. There was no escaping them, because they grew and grew. By the time I was in fifth grade, I was a B cup. By sixth or seventh, I was a C.

So when I met the dentist, there was already a fair amount of female visible on me.

One morning, after he put me under, he told me we were going to play something he called "the tickle game." He'd tickle me somewhere, and if it felt good, I should smile. The part of me in the chair thought that sounded okay, kind of like something I'd do with Eric. So he tickled my arm, and I giggled. Then he tickled my neck, and I giggled again. Then he tickled my thigh, and I stopped giggling.

"Does that feel good?" he asked.

I couldn't respond. I was confused, and a little frightened.

He did it again. "Doesn't that feel good? Tell me it feels good."

Well, he'd given me a direct order. I told him it felt good, and his fingers moved further up my body.

From then on, every time I went, he'd play the tickle game. And as his hands moved higher, and my body began to respond, he became more excited. Finally, after the third or fourth time, he touched me, then went to the little bathroom connected to the treatment room. I stayed in the chair; no one had told me I could get up, or put me back together. Part of me was missing, so I sat and waited. There was silence, then the toilet flushed, the sink turned on, and eventually he came out, wiping his hands.

It took me months to figure out what he was doing in there. Yuck. But I couldn't tell anyone. I really couldn't. First, because every time he put me under, he'd remind me that if I told, my parents would be ashamed of me. I'd be sent away because I'd been bad. I wouldn't be allowed to see my brother again.

Second, because *I* was ashamed. I couldn't imagine anything more humiliating than my parents finding out. Here was this body that I'd thought I owned, but there was a stranger pawing at it now, making it feel things it had never felt before. It felt good sometimes. It felt grown-up. And I kind of liked having a secret with a grown-up.

The only problem was, the part of me he sent away each time didn't like it at all. That part was screaming in outrage, running up the walls of the Waiting Room trying to claw its way out. That part wanted to kick him, hurt him, do anything to make him stop. But that part wasn't going anywhere, and the dentist never had to face it.

Only I did.

As the years progressed (and, yes, it went on for years), he added insult to injury. After one particularly "friendly" session, I protested. I told my parents I wanted a new dentist. I wouldn't go back there. I just couldn't. I was on the verge of tears, and they called him to discuss it.

He met with them before my next appointment and told them I'd become scared of the drill. It was something most children went through at one point or another, not to be concerned, the best thing to do was ride it out. Wait a few weeks, give me some time off, then resume treatment.

So we kept the same dentist.

The next session, Dad stayed with me until I was under and the drilling began, then left to give a piano lesson. And that bastard proceeded to tell me that I was a "dirty, filthy girl" who should be punished for telling. He said no one would ever love me if I kept "acting up like this." He looked at me sadly and said, "I really don't know why you're making such a fuss. You like it. I know you like it."

A tear rolled down my cheek. And he licked it off.

Really. He licked my cheek. Like a cow. How disgusting is *that*?

Then he did something that still makes my stomach turn over. He held the big drill over my molar, and told me I was now going to see what happened to disobedient girls. The part of me in the Waiting Room was going to feel everything, just like always, but this time *I'd* feel it, too. Then he plowed into that molar like there was no tomorrow.

It hurt. Jesus Christ, it hurt. It hurt so much that I thought I was going to throw up. And in my little head, I swore to myself that I'd never, ever, do anything to make him angry again.

Impossible. Just impossible. At ten, at eleven, grown-ups hold all the cards. They have all the power. I'd been taught grown-ups were to be trusted, were to be obeyed. You went to a grown-up if someone hurt you. You went to a grown-up if you were in trouble.

This was incomprehensible. I had no framework for it. But there was no way out, so I buried the whole thing and just didn't think about it unless I was there. And so it continued, until we moved to New York four years later.

That's another reason camp felt so safe. There was no dentist there.

To this day, I can't believe he didn't know what he was doing to me. My partner is a criminal defense attorney; she works with molesters, with pedophiles. She says they have no empathy; they only get upset when they're caught, and then their concern is only for themselves. How can that be?

How could it have meant so little to him, when forty years later I can still smell his sweat, still see the hair on his hands, still see his big pores hovering over my face? I can still hear him as he breathes harder and harder, until he finally goes off to the toilet to relieve himself. Forty years later, I can still feel my thighs clenching and unclenching, seeking some rude release that never came. While he masturbated and emerged, businesslike, to finish off the dental work.

Once in a while, I actually managed to say, "Stop it." I can hear my voice now, whispering, tiny, shaking. Saying it under my breath, like my voice belonged to someone else. He liked that, hearing me ask him to stop. Those were the times he'd remind me that he didn't have to stop, that no one would believe me if I told, that I was dirty.

Maybe he wanted me to beg. He warned me to be cooperative, or else. "There are worse things than this, you know." Like he was saving me from a worse fate. Like he was good.

I can still feel him pushing me back in the chair, feel him spreading my legs apart.

Yuck.

My mom worried over me. She'd look at me with concern and say, "What's the matter, pussycat? You look so sad." I didn't know. I couldn't put a name to it. There were so few people to talk to, and no one to discuss my fears with. There was just too much going on. I didn't realize that Carl Jung had described this oceanic feeling decades before; I just knew that I was separated from the rest of the world by a thin glass sheet I could never get past.

Except for music. Music filled my world. It filled my soul. It saturated my heart, and made it feel so full that there were moments when I thought I would burst from the sheer joy of it.

THREE

Silly Habits

Why bother waiting
When you can have it all today?

etween all these worlds, the only safe retreat was music, so there I stayed. I was over thirteen now, and according to my Jewish heritage, responsible for my own actions. I began testing my wings, taking the bus to visit my friend Merka at her Philadelphia dorm on weekends. We'd met at camp when I was just ten and she was sixteen; she was riding bareback on a white stallion, saw me watching goggle-eyed, and offered me a ride. I felt like a combination of the Lone Ranger and Sitting Bull. It was heaven.

With the passing years, we'd become friends. Merka treated me like a peer. She took me seriously, and I adored her for it. It was Merka I wrote to when my head felt like it was exploding, and it was Merka who told me things would get better as I got older. She was as close to a big sister as I've had, and the thrill of being treated like an equal was something I could cling to during the tedium of social studies or grammar. She and her friends Bif and Graham would pick me up at the bus station, playing harmonica and singing. Then we'd go to a coffee shop, where there'd be more music and lively discussions about art, politics, and people.

There was also Janey, my bunkmate from the previous summer. Janey was a lifesaver; like me, she played guitar and sang, and saw nothing weird in my determination to become a singer-songwriter. Most of the campers looked on popular music with disdain, but Janey worshipped the Rolling Stones and introduced me to pop music. We'd spend hours holed up in her bedroom, listening to Bessie Smith and the Beatles, harmonizing with each other before slipping out to get an egg cream at Irv's corner store. We thought nothing of taking the train into Manhattan, pulling out our guitars, and amusing the other passengers with high-spirited takes on "Satisfaction" or "Love Me Do."

Janey got away with murder. She did things that had never even occurred to me. She didn't bother showing up for school half the time. She begged and cajoled her parents for book money, then spent it on jeans and records. Her folks cracked us up. They were avid golfers, but the golf club wouldn't let them in if everyone in the party wasn't present. So on weekends, Janey's mother would rouse us before dawn, yelling for us to haul ourselves out of bed and accompany her to the golf course, where we'd stand in for the golf partners until they arrived.

I think in large part it was my friendship with Janey that saved me during the early, violent years of "Society's Child." From the outside, she looked uncomplicated; the class clown. Once I got to know her, she was as deep as I was—she just hid it better. But she gave me a childhood. It was impossible to be serious around her. She behaved like a kid, so I could behave like a kid, and we laughed and wept and swore eternal friendship as only newborn adolescents can. I began to feel at home in a few more places, and safe enough to step out a bit.

My father subscribed to *Broadside,* which billed itself as a "topical song magazine." The scruffy mimeographed pages arrived in our mailbox monthly, showcasing the best of young songwriters. Unlike the larger circulation *Sing Out!*, which featured traditional folk songs, *Broadside* published people who were still alive and kicking. Bob Dylan got his start there. Buffy Sainte-Marie, Phil Ochs, and Tom Paxton contributed. The editors, Sis Cunningham and Gordon Friesen, were a couple of leftist Okies bent on rousing the masses and making a better world; it showed in the songs they chose. Their Upper West Side living room was a haven for songwriters too intense, too political, or just too weird to make it on Tin Pan Alley.

They also ran a series of "hoots" (hootenannies) at New York's Village Gate, normally a premiere jazz club. The owner, Art D'Lugoff, donated his space to *Broadside* once a month, and the hoots were fast becoming a place where record companies and agents could discover new talent. The great folk boom (or "great folk scare," as Dave Van Ronk called it) was in full flourish. Joan Baez was on the cover of *Time*, Peter, Paul & Mary had a No. 1 album, and the huge bloc of baby boomers were just coming of age.

It was a heady time to be young. The civil rights movement was everywhere. President Kennedy was dead, President Johnson was pulling on his beagles' ears, and the Vietnam War was a lightning rod for dissidents all over the world.

I'd been reading *Broadside* for about a year when it occurred to me that, with five or six pieces under my belt, I was now a songwriter, too. So that August 1964, I modeled a lead sheet on the ones I'd seen in the magazine, neatly printing the melody and lyrics to "Hair of Spun Gold" with the chords above. I put my name and telephone number in the upper right, and sent it in. Then I promptly forgot about it.

I entered eighth grade and proceeded to dream my way through class, jotting down songs in the back of my loose-leaf notebooks and writing bad poetry for the school paper. Sometime in early September, Sis Cunningham called our house and got my father on the phone. Did a songwriter named Janis live there?

Yes, but she was out; could he take a message?

Broadside wanted to publish her song in the October issue, and wondered if she would be interested in playing a hoot?

My dad sputtered, saying, "But . . . she's only thirteen!"

"Oh," said Sis, "in that event, would you mind driving her?"

My stunned father barely managed to say yes.

So we made our way to Greenwich Village one Sunday morning, and I shyly presented myself in the dressing room, where Sis and her family made me welcome. No one knew whether I could actually sing on key, but I'd had a song published, so here I was. Before the show, I sat quietly in a corner, trying not to stare as my heroes walked in and greeted one another. Everybody seemed to know everybody else. Occasionally, someone shot me a curious glance, but no one spoke to me. I probably didn't look like I wanted to be social. I was busy tuning and retuning my low strings, nervously telling myself this was no different from singing for the local student nurses in their dorm room back home.

A dozen chairs were arranged in a row on the small stage. At show-time, all the performers filed out, holding their guitars, and took a seat. I was sandwiched between Tom Paxton and Len Chandler, thrilled to be there and determined to do a good job. When my name was finally called, I walked to the center microphone and sang the first song I'd ever written, finishing to a rousing standing ovation. The singers behind me pushed me back to the mic for an encore, and I sang the second song I'd written, "Here's To . . . ," to yet another standing ovation, then walked back to my chair in a daze.

After the show, Len picked me up and hugged me so hard I thought my ribs would crack, while Eric Andersen and Lou Gossett Jr. pumped my hand and congratulated me. I went out into the audience and was surprised to see my folks speaking with Judy Collins and the president of her record company, Jac Holzman. My folks looked bewildered as Jac told them Elektra Records would like to bring me into the studio and record a few sides for an upcoming album of singer-songwriters that would include Pat Sky, Bruce Murdoch, and Richard Fariña.

They seemed pretty involved, so I walked over to a group of guitarists who were studying with the Reverend Gary Davis, and wrote down his phone number.

That night, I overheard my parents talking about Holzman's offer. Elektra was highly respected, but it scared my folks. I was too young, too innocent to be exposed to that kind of world. The only other performer to compare me to was Stevie Wonder, and he had the Motown machinery behind him. What about school? What about college?

Finally, Mom turned to my father and said, "You know, Vic, she's going to do this whether we want it or not. If we say no, she'll find some other way to get into New York and start recording. If we say yes, at least we'll be able to watch over her." So on February 12, 1965, two months before my fourteenth birthday, I signed a contract with Elektra to record four sides.

We did the session just after my birthday on April 7. I don't remember much about it except that Jac seemed weird. All the "folkies" I'd met were warm, friendly people, while Jac felt disconnected and cold. He saw everything in the abstract, one step removed. It unnerved me, and I don't think I performed very well. That May, I received my first check, and promptly bought a hardcover copy of *A Wrinkle in Time* that I have to this day.

Back home, I was trying to join a band, playing the lead part to "Satisfaction" for my auditions. One thirteen-year-old bass player looked on in surprise, then said to the boy who'd brought me, "Wow, she really *can* play!" I never got a job, though, because I was a girl, and they thought it would be embarrassing to have me in the group. It was all right with me; I was interested in other things.

I'd seen Reverend Davis around Washington Square, preaching the gospel with his guitar in hand, and I soon began taking lessons from him. I paid for them out of babysitting money and my pitiful allowance, skipping lunches to make up the shortfall. It was painful trying to make my small hands play the patterns his giant fingers had invented. Gary played a huge Gibson J-200, and his fingers flew around the strings. Mine just clattered, landing with a thud. It was a losing proposition, and my lessons quickly became social occasions instead. His wife, Miss Annie, took a liking to me, feeding me Southern comfort foods—corn bread with stewed chicken, fried okra, black-eyed peas. I'd take the bus home in the evening, stuffed full of music and food.

Gary loved telling jokes. He'd crack himself up for hours. Soon I found myself acting as occasional "lead boy," placing his hand on my shoulder and guiding him through the maze of New York streets while other students trailed behind. Gary might have been blind, but he didn't miss a trick. He never messed with me because of my age, but he had roving hands nonetheless. One of us would say, "Reverend, there's a beauty at two o'clock!" He'd swerve to the right, put both his hands straight in front of him, and collide with her breasts, crying, "I can't see! I can't see! Help a poor blind man, please!"

In retrospect, it probably wasn't funny for the women he encountered, but it made us howl with laughter.

I went off to camp in June and spent the summer singing with Janey and writing songs. She was impressed that I had a recording contract, but the following September, Jac called me in to tell me they'd decided to use David Blue for the project instead of me. Jac said he thought I could be a great singer, but I should forget about a career as a songwriter—I'd never be great.

That same afternoon, I went to see Harold Leventhal, who managed Judy Collins, Arlo Guthrie, and Pete Seeger. Harold told me I could be a great songwriter, but should forget about a career as a singer—I'd never be great.

On the bus going home, I thought about what Jac and Harold had said. It was confusing. How could these two men, so respected in the folk world, come to such opposite conclusions about me? I knew I wasn't great yet, but I was good. Sis and Gordon said so. Buffy Sainte-Marie said so. I wasn't deluding myself, so why didn't these two men see it?

The conclusion was obvious—no one on the business end knew what they were talking about. I gave a mental shrug and set the conversations aside. I knew I was going to be a good songwriter, and I knew I was going to be a good singer. So they were wrong. I could live with that.

My parents were relieved; they had enough on their plates without worrying over my budding career. The FBI kept ensuring Dad wouldn't get tenure. He'd had to go to New York to get a new teaching position the year before, and commuting to and from Manhattan was wearing him out. If we moved there, he'd be able to take the train to work. Camp Webatuck had an office in a grimy downtown building. If we moved it into our apartment, our living space could be subsidized.

I didn't know any of this was going on. I was concentrating on writing, singing wherever anyone would allow, and trying to maintain my grade average. Writing had become a necessity, like breathing. I didn't find it strange that I was writing songs at my age. My friend Janey wrote plays. My friend Jim Washington wrote poetry. I wrote songs.

Sitting on a bus one day, I saw a couple holding hands. They were just a little older than me; he was black, she was white. The occupants of the bus moved away from them, but they seemed oblivious as they smiled and whispered to each other. I started wondering what the outcome of their relationship would be, and began writing "Society's Child." It took a while to complete, because I wasn't sure how I wanted it to end. I was excited when I came up with the refrain:

> *I can't see you any more, baby*
> *Can't see you any more*

and when I finally resolved it to my satisfaction at the end:

> *No, I don't want to see you any more, baby*

That solved the hardest part, because I didn't want the breakup of their relationship to be just society's fault. I wanted the girl to take some responsibility for it, too. I saw that last "baby" as an ironic comment on her cowardice.

Frances Stern, my school guidance counselor, helped me enormously. She told the administration I needed heavy counseling, then let me sit outside her office and write instead of attending classes. I wrote most of "Society's Child" like that, holed up in an uncomfortable chair trying to ignore the bell that signaled the start of the next period.

I was proud of the song, but no prouder than of any other song I'd written to date. All twelve of them. I'd started dozens, but was rapidly reaching the point where I knew whether a song had any promise, or whether I should just move on.

At Thanksgiving dinner, my folks announced we'd be moving to New York over Christmas vacation. I was horrified; they'd never yanked us out in the middle of a school term. Couldn't I stay with a friend for the rest of the year, and finish up ninth grade in East Orange? I swore to get straight As. I promised to be good, to no avail. Yet again, there was no way I'd be allowed to stay.

I was devastated. Things finally felt stable, and here I was, moving again. The prospect of living in New York didn't make up for the loss of familiar faces. So I grudgingly packed, and said good-bye to my friends.

Our first night in Manhattan, I wandered from our apartment on Eighty-fourth Street and West End Avenue up to Broadway, one block east. I'd only been to Manhattan on Sundays, and then only during daylight hours. I was always under strict instructions to be home before dark, so I'd never seen the city at night.

Sitting on a wooden crate in front of the local A&P, I stared at all the movement around me. It was nine o'clock, and people were still rushing through the streets! In East Orange, only Howard Johnson's stayed open late; it was big news when they decided to keep the doors open past eight on Fridays. By ten o'clock everyone was home in bed, and the streets were silent and dark.

What a different world I'd entered. I could feel the rumble of the subway as it raced through the tunnels under my feet. The trains ran all night; they never stopped. New York never stopped. Everyone I watched had busy looks on their faces, like they had appointments to keep. At this time of night! Women in high heels and fur coats dashed across the street, rushing to beat the lights. At the Eighty-sixth Street subway stop, junkies crammed the benches, huddling together for warmth, competing for space with the elderly people who met there every evening to discuss the day's events.

Most astonishing of all, the bookstore up the street was open until midnight—who'd ever heard of such a thing? I strolled in and was amazed at all the books I'd never read. I stood there leafing through them for a while, then walked home whistling. Maybe this move wasn't such a bad thing, after all.

It had been so long since we'd changed school systems that my parents had forgotten to register me. When they realized their mistake, the only school that had room for another student was Commerce Vocational, so off I went. It was January 1965, and New York was in the throes of a fight between mayor John Lindsay and pretty much everyone else. There was a transit strike; no buses or trains were running. Radio stations were asking drivers to put signs on the dashboards if they were willing to give students a ride. I hopped into a car with a bunch of other kids and made my way to what I hoped would be a good school.

The shock was enormous. In East Orange, classes were small, under twenty-five students per classroom. The kids were middle-class, bent on getting into good colleges. There was tremendous academic focus; books were new, teachers were patient, and much as I detested going, I did learn something every day.

Commerce was a vocational school, set up to teach children with no interest in academia how to make a living. It was also mostly Hispanic, a completely unfamiliar culture to me at the time. There were forty and fifty kids to a class. They were building Lincoln Center next door, tearing down the adjacent building, and the classrooms shook from the wrecking balls all day long.

My first morning, I saw I'd been assigned two home economics classes, one in cooking and one in sewing. I went to my overworked guidance counselor (here called a "placement assistant," or someone who'd help you find a job) and asked whether I couldn't take shop instead. He smiled and told me I'd need the home ec one day, so I could be a better wife and mother. I couldn't believe it.

Some of the girls in my class were pregnant, which also shook me. In my old school, we had just progressed from tongue-kissing to petting, meaning everyone kept their shirt on and tried to imagine what was on the other side of the cotton. Here, they were already making babies.

It was a completely alien world, but there was nothing I could do about it. Or almost nothing. I heard about a different high school, Music & Art, that was geared toward people like me. I called and got an application for the next term, then began practicing Beethoven's *Moonlight Sonata* because the second movement was flashy and might give me an edge.

At the same time, I was still hanging out with Reverend Davis, who started taking me around to his shows and letting me sing a song here and there. *Broadside* published "Society's Child," then titled "Baby, I've Been Thinking," in issue #67 that February. I was now a regular, getting to perform at the Village Gate hoots every other month. I spent a lot of time in Sis and Gordon's living room, trading songs and learning my craft. Weekends were spent with Merka or Janey, or hanging around the Village looking at instruments I couldn't afford.

We lived next door to Sri Swami Satchitananda, a devout Yoga teacher from India. He held classes in his apartment, and would often send his students to help us stuff envelopes and send out flyers. I loved being around him; looking into his eyes was like falling into a clear, deep lake. In a time when people my age were becoming fascinated by Indian culture and spirituality, imitating it and sometimes using it to outright con people, his honesty and dedication inspired my respect.

Satchitananda visited us often, and so did the FBI. Our phones were tapped, though I doubt they ever heard anything more interesting than Eric talking to his friends about a new game, or me trying to figure out my math homework. Still, my camp friends and I made a game of it, buying police whistles and blowing them into the telephone at earsplitting volumes whenever we heard the click of a tape recorder turning on.

My father grew increasingly tired of the surveillance; one of Swamiji's students told us the feds were asking questions again, and the landlord warned us that they were also making inquiries about *me*. I'd actually been placed on the "Reserve Index-B," with a page of my very own. Their investigation of me went on right into December. When my father found out, he was furious. That was it, all bets were off.

On the pretext that our summer camp was advertising itself as "multicultural and multiracial," and thereby warranted an investigation, two hawk-faced men carrying laminated ID cards came to our door one evening. They demanded the names of any counselors who might be heading south to be Freedom Riders.

My father asked if they had a warrant. No, they said, but they were sure that as a good American he'd want to cooperate. After all, my grandparents were naturalized citizens. Perhaps they'd lied on the forms. The citizenship could always be revoked.

My father, furious, told them to leave. The lead G-man argued, saying they just wanted information. Dad grabbed the door handle to close it, and one of them thrust his arm inside to hold it open. My father slammed the door shut on the agent's wrist, and with a howl of pain, they left.

My pacifist mother objected to the violence, but Dad said he hadn't attacked anyone, he'd just made sure the door was securely closed. It wasn't his fault there was an arm in the way. Watching from the kitchen, I was proud of him, though grateful none of the neighbors were home to see.

I got my first real paying gig, at a New Jersey coffeehouse, opening for a band whose claim to fame was that they'd be opening for Sam the Sham & the Pharoahs at Shea Stadium soon. I excitedly wrote to Sis and Gordon, *I have 4 days' worth of a job—2 weekends—$37.50 a night, which is a decent start. Now I can buy a guitar case!* I was desperate for a soft case, one like all the professionals carried. Mine was cardboard, and it embarrassed me. With my first earnings (about twenty-five dollars after bus fare, for six shows over a March weekend), I bought the case. With my next, I bought a pair of green suede boots, a set of dangling hoop earrings, and a hardback book. I was rich!

I went to a Be-In at Central Park March 30, playing background for a group called the Pennywhistlers, and wrote to Merka, *I attended a march with the Pennywhistlers. I went disguised as a banjo.* I played with words like that all the time, relishing the way new things would pop out of my pen unexpectedly.

April ushered in the spring, and it was glorious—the streets came alive with people of all colors and shapes. Overnight, it seemed, everyone was young, brightly dressed, and socially conscious. "Dancing in the Streets" was what we all felt; the air was heady with change, and our power was reflected in the music. You knew who your friends were by the way they dressed, and the length of their hair. Not since the French Revolution had youth held such power, and we were just beginning to flex our muscles.

Reverend Gary was playing the Gaslight Café, a folk club famous for introducing Bob Dylan to the world, and Miss Annie brought me along to the sound check. She went up to the owner, Clarence Hood, and told him Gary wanted me to be his opening act. Mr. Hood declined, citing everything from my age to the fact that people were paying to see Gary, not some unknown kid.

Miss Annie walked over to Gary and whispered in his ear. He whispered back, then started making his way to the door. Miss Annie went back to Mr. Hood and explained that Gary really wasn't feeling very well, they'd probably have to cancel that night's show.

I got the gig.

I was delirious with joy. Even though I was unadvertised, unpaid, and essentially unwelcome, *I was playing New York!* And at the Gaslight, no less!

It was a real trip. The Gaslight was tiny, holding around a hundred people. There was a tenement above, so some nights the audience had to snap their fingers instead of clapping, or the residents would throw garbage down the airshaft. No air-conditioning to relieve the sweat of summer months. The toilet was almost in the center of the room, and when someone flushed, it would get picked up by the microphone and resound through the tiny speakers. To get to the "dressing room" (a couch on the far side of the kitchen), you had to step over an open chest of ice that was sunk into the floor. But there was music in the walls.

Mr. Hood had been a wealthy Democratic committeeman in Mississippi who got in trouble over civil rights. He came north and bought the Gaslight in 1961, put his son Sam in charge of it, and spent the rest of his time playing poker. He was never called "Clarence," always "Mr. Hood," and despite his reluctance to hire me, he gave an amazing number of performers their first big break. Robert Shelton, music critic for *The New York Times*, hung out at the Gaslight, and his review of Dylan's show had cracked open a lot of doors for Bob. It was a huge deal for me, playing there.

Between sets, I could go next door to the Kettle of Fish and try not to stare at Dylan and Phil Ochs, getting drunk and picking fights with each other. There were tons of clubs, and now that I was an actual performer, I was usually allowed in free. We had a bit of time while they turned the house between shows (two a night, three on weekends), so I began watching other performers and meeting my future colleagues. There was a wonderful mix of genres at the time, and pretty soon I was hanging out with the Young Rascals and Jimi Hendrix, watching Frank Zappa and the Mothers of Invention, the Lovin' Spoonful, and the Blues Project, precursor of the group Blood, Sweat & Tears.

One night, after my set, a fellow came running backstage and yelled, "Kid, I'm gonna make you a star!" It was such an incredibly hackneyed line that I laughed and responded, "Yeah, you and what army?" But he was serious. His name was Jacob Solman, and he wanted to meet with me the next afternoon. I shrugged, told him it would have to be after school, and arranged to meet him at the office of an attorney he knew.

The attorney, Johanan Vigoda, turned out to be one of the most powerful lawyers in the music industry, though a little strange around the edges. When we met, he shook my hand in silence, then sat down and said, "Play, kid!" I pulled out my guitar and sang a couple of songs. Without another word, he motioned to the guitar case. I put my instrument away, then he grabbed my arm and rushed me out of the building and into a taxi. A few minutes later, we entered an impersonal building on West Sixty-first Street. We took the slow elevator up a few flights to an office that had "Phantom Productions" on the entry door, and walked through into a small, crowded reception area.

Johanan barked, "Tell him I'm here!" at the receptionist. Not pausing for her to buzz anyone, still holding my arm in an iron grip, he ushered me into a tiny office where a man wearing a cowboy hat held a newspaper in front of his face. His feet were propped up on the desk, and I remember thinking that his boots looked pretty expensive.

There were gold records all over the walls with names like the Shangri-Las on them. Shadow Morton had produced a ton of hits. I wasn't impressed. This guy didn't even have the courtesy to put down the paper, let alone say hello.

Johanan sat down in the only other chair and said, "George"

(Shadow's birth name). The paper didn't move, though a thin trail of cigarette smoke began making its way over the top.

"George," he said again. "George. You have to hear this girl."

The paper still didn't move. A heavy Brooklyn accent muttered, "I'm quitting the music business."

Johanan rolled his eyes, then gestured for me to unpack the guitar. I strapped it on, tuned, and waited. A page of the newspaper turned. All was silent.

Johanan mouthed "Sing" to me, and I began a song. As I sang, my annoyance level rose. Bad enough this stuck-up guy had his feet on the desk. Bad enough that he was ignoring us. But now, he was insulting my music!

I finished the song, packed up my guitar, and pulled a lighter out of my pocket. Not looking at Johanan, I walked up to the desk, and carefully lit a corner of the paper. Then I walked to the elevator, a stunned Vigoda behind me.

Just as the door opened, a gorgeous man in a cowboy hat and boots came running up to me, shouting, "Wait! Wait! I'm sorry, kid, I'm sorry. Really, wait!"

"Why should I?" I asked. "You're incredibly rude."

I entered the elevator and pushed the button. The door began to close. Shadow stuck a boot in the gap, jamming the door and asking me to please, please come back and sing for him.

"Why should I?" I asked again.

Shadow grinned, one of the cutest things I'd ever seen. He looked like a puppy trying to get away with something. "Because I'm an idiot, and you should always let idiots have a second chance."

We went back to his office, and I sang him all twelve songs I'd written. When I'd finished, he asked about one in particular.

"That's called 'Baby, I've Been Thinking.'"

Shadow rolled his eyes. "That last verse, where you say *Baby, I'm only society's child.* . . . 'Society's Child.' That's a *song title.* Baby Whatever? That's not a title. We change the name."

He rose, looked at Johanan, and said, "Okay. We go in the studio first week of May. Atlantic will pay for it."

Turning back to me, he asked if I needed anything for the session. "Like what?" I wondered aloud.

He snapped his fingers with impatience and said, "Like rental instruments."

Oh. Wow. Figuring I'd never get the chance to play a real harpsichord, I asked for one. Shadow was amused; why on earth did I need a harpsichord? I thought quickly, and said, "For the introduction." I could always make something up over the next couple of weeks, given the incentive of a new instrument under my fingers.

Okay, anything else? I asked for a twelve-string guitar, because my dad was going to need his Martin during the day. Besides, I might never get to play one otherwise.

We shook hands on it and that was that. I wrote down the date and place, then went home to my parents, who grounded me for two days because I hadn't telephoned to say I'd be late. I tried to explain that I couldn't possibly have stopped everything just to call, but no one was listening. So for the next two afternoons, I was grounded, and for a week I spent my after-school hours doing the ironing.

One afternoon, while I was slaving over one of Dad's collars, Jacob came by with a songwriter named Bruce Murdoch. I continued ironing while Bruce sang me some of his songs, but Jacob really wanted me to concentrate on the music, so he took over the ironing. My mom came in and was furious. This was *my* punishment for *my* bad behavior, and not only were they making it pleasurable, but Jacob was taking my punishment for me! He was banned from the house for the rest of the week, and I now had to do the ironing *and* the washing up.

What a way to start a career.

FOUR

Society's Child

When we're older, things may change
But for now, this is the way they must remain
I say—I can't see you any more, baby

We recorded "Society's Child" shortly after my fifteenth birthday. When I entered the run-down Midtown hotel that housed Mira Sound Studio, I saw a bloated policeman sitting in the lobby behind a table that held a sign saying "WARNING. THESE PREMISES HAVE BEEN RAIDED." It was a little disconcerting.

Shadow had assembled the A-list players for our session, although I didn't know it at the time. The two most important for me were Artie Butler, who'd double on harpsichord and organ, and George Duvivier, the great upright bass player. I went over to Artie and pulled out a scrap of paper with the harpsichord introduction I'd written the week before; he looked at it, then said, "What about lead sheets?"

I'd never been to a recording session before. I didn't know what a lead sheet was. Where I came from, you sang the song, everyone learned it by heart, then you played. It took as long as it took. Completely oblivious to the clock ticking away by the dollar, I started to play him the song. Artie Kaplan, the bandleader, came over and shook his head.

"Kid. *Kid.* Stop a second. You don't have a chart for this song?"

I shook my head. What the heck was a chart?

The two Arties laughed, and Butler pulled out a sheet of music paper. As I played the song, I called out the chords, and they taught me how to write a chart. Once the chart was done, each musician made his own copy. Now they could play the song without having to memorize it.

I looked up at the control room to see whether Shadow had any instructions for us. No response. I was kind of proud that he trusted me to lead the band. I didn't realize he was busy getting through his first Bacardi bottle of the day. He'd drink one bottle of Bacardi Light, then follow it with a bottle of Bacardi Dark. By the time a three-hour session ended, both bottles would be empty.

Brooks Arthur, the engineer, gave me a thumbs-up sign, and I started singing. The band struggled to play along the way they'd play on a standard pop session, but because the tempo changed with each chorus, things immediately fell apart. We played it over and over again for almost three hours, until my fingers were numb from the effort of pressing down on the twelve-string's neck. It just kept getting worse.

The band members took their designated union break. Shadow came in and asked me what was wrong. I replied that it didn't sound like it should, but I didn't know what to do about it, and my stomach was starting to hurt. I was in agony, but I didn't speak the language of studio musicians yet, and I couldn't fix what was wrong.

Seeing me about to cry, Duvivier walked over and put a hand on my shoulder. He was the only one in the room who'd listened to the lyrics, and he knew exactly what the record needed. It needed their full attention. So when the players came back, Duvivier looked up and said, "Gentlemen. Let's listen to the song." With Shadow standing beside me, the musicians gathered around, and I sang it from top to bottom. They nodded to one another; this was not an ordinary song. This should not be an ordinary record.

They conferred, sorted out the arrangement, and we cut it in one take. My stomach stopped hurting, and I grinned as I sang, because Artie Butler had to run back and forth between the organ and the harpsichord at the start and end of each chorus. It was comical watching him try to silently leap over cables and into a chair. After the last note finished ringing, he added an explosive organ comment, and we were done.

I didn't realize it, but we were in overtime. That was a serious financial problem, and normally the producer would have stopped after three hours to avoid it. Shadow had no intention of doing that; he believed in the song enough to spend whatever time and money it took. Although, now that I think of it, it wasn't his money but Atlantic's. We spent almost $6,000 on "Society's Child"; the rest of my entire first album cost a total of just $7,000.

The next day, Shadow sat down with Brooks and tried to mix the record. It shouldn't have been hard; there were only eight tracks, and he thought he could easily mix it himself. But like everything about "Society's Child," it was difficult. After three days, he finally let Brooks take a shot. Brooks got it mixed in one take. I guess when things are right, they're right.

I was on cloud nine. I'd made a record. It would be coming out on Atlantic, a real record company. I was going to miss the first few weeks of camp and work the Gaslight twice, then fly to Chicago to play the W.E.B. DuBois conference, my first out-of-town gig. My parents arranged for one of the counselors, Liz McMillan, to chaperone me. Everything was great.

But with this record, nothing came easy. Atlantic turned it down. Jerry Wexler, vice president of the company, handed the master tapes back to Shadow, saying, "Good luck finding a home for this. We'll eat the costs, but we can't put it out; it's too controversial." They never did get their money back.

Two years later, at the Grammy Awards, Wexler surprised me by apologizing, saying that if any company should have released it, Atlantic should have. He said it in front of everyone present, and I thought, "What a stand-up thing to do."

However, there were no apologies then. Shadow and his partners pitched the record without success. They were convinced it was a hit, and so was everyone who heard it, but no one would dare to release it. He approached twenty-two labels in all, and every single one said, "Love the record! Can I keep the acetate? Sorry, can't put it out."

Then, suddenly, jazz giant Verve Records formed Verve Forecast, hiring Jerry Schoenbaum to run the company, with instructions to go out and find the best young talent in New York. Schoenbaum, bless his heart, made my record a cause célèbre, releasing it three times over the next eight months.

The first release was that August. Given the climate of the time, we would never have had a hit but for two important things. First, FM radio was just beginning to take hold, uniting young listeners across America. There was a revolution taking place in radio, with stations playing long album cuts instead of only singles, sometimes even playing three or four in a row by the same artist. Stations across the country jumped on the format, and for the first time, we baby boomers were all listening to the same thing. We now had, not just a common spoken language, but a common musical language. And since the music soon became infused with the politics of social change, we had that in common, too.

Second, New York station WOR-FM changed its playlist to free-form rock that July, letting the disc jockeys choose their own material. That meant the program director or music director, who traditionally decided which new records would be played and how often, no longer held all the power of choice. The head of WOR's all-star lineup was

Murray the K, who'd been known as "the Fifth Beatle." Murray made it his personal mission to break my record, playing it every hour on the hour. So did Scott Muni and Rosko, two of the other DJs. Pretty soon, you could hear "Society's Child" throughout New York's five boroughs, in the supermarkets, in the parks, blaring out of transistor radios on the street. Several other stations went the same way, up and down the East Coast, and the record slowly climbed the local charts.

I had a hit, though only in scattered pockets. Most radio stations were afraid to play it, and with good reason. Radio stations depend on listeners for their advertising revenue, and the volume of hate mail and angry calls my record generated was astounding. The program directors made excuses—it was too long, it was too depressing, it changed tempos, you couldn't dance to it. But the real reason was fear, and we knew it.

How on earth do you combat that? I spent long afternoons at Shadow's office, calling stations to thank them for playing my record, calling others to ask them to get on the bandwagon. I started doing record hops to pay back the disc jockeys who were helping us. They'd send a limousine to pick me up, along with someone from Shadow's office. We'd drive to New Jersey, or the Poconos, and meet up with the DJ. There'd be a small stage backed by huge signs advertising the station, with an unplugged microphone and a crowd of teenagers. I'd lip-synch the song, then go home.

I never thought of it as payola; I thought of it as gratitude.

I was suddenly famous in New York, Philadelphia, and Flint, Michigan, for some unfathomable reason. Where they would play it, the record was a hit. July 29 saw me opening at the Gaslight for a full week, with Gary Davis headlining. By mid-August I was actually carrying my own show. Between sets, I'd hit the streets, which were becoming more and more crowded as tourists bused in to see the freaks. It got so bad at one point that a group of us began greeting the tourists as they disembarked, calling out, "Ladies and gentlemen, on your right you see a typical suburban American worker! Note the shiny shoes, the neatly pressed jacket, and the stunned look on his face. Yes, fellow freaks, be grateful that you will never have to have one in your home! They're all right to look at, but you wouldn't want one to marry your daughter." We laughed ourselves silly over how annoyed they'd get, because we were surrounded by people "like us," and the boring middle-class people stepping off the bus were just bewildered outsiders for once.

After my shows were over, I'd gravitate to the Dugout and drink soda, while Dave Van Ronk argued politics with all and sundry. My mother was at the Gaslight with me most nights, and she and Dave would usually end the evening singing "The Internationale" while I tried to hide behind the jukebox. Dave and his wife befriended me, having me over for dinner and trying to teach me a bit about business.

Odetta came to a few of my shows, sitting next to my mother and reassuring her. Mom worried about me all the time—was it too soon? Was I growing up too fast? What about voice lessons, didn't I need more? Odetta would sit with her and pat her hand, saying, "Pearl. She'll be all right. She'll be all right."

On August 19 I signed a second contract with Shadow's production company, this time in front of the Surrogate's Court for the Protection of Widows and Orphans. There was something called the Coogan Law in effect then, because when Jackie Coogan had reached his majority, he'd discovered that his parents had spent all the money he'd earned as a child. The Coogan Law said that no contract signed by a minor, even with parental signatures, was valid unless overseen by the court. All monies earned would be held in trust until I reached twenty-one, watched over by the court and my mom.

I could, however, apply for an allowance, and with the help of a yearly case of the judge's favorite whiskey delivered to his chambers, I got permission to purchase an upright piano and some other equipment. Otherwise, most of my earnings stayed in the bank, which would matter a lot three years later when I found myself back-taxed at a

90 percent rate, with none of the monies having been sheltered or invested.

Mom went back to camp, and I stayed in the city alone for a couple of weeks to do press, our neighbors alerted to keep an eye on me. On September 1, I woke to a frantic knocking on the door. Lisa, Shadow's secretary, rushed into the apartment, saying, "Pack a bag and come with me!" I asked what it was about and she put her finger to her lips, shook her head, mouthed "Later," then helped me pack. She hustled me out of the building through the service entrance, and into a waiting cab. We arrived at her basement apartment and she said, "You'll sleep on the couch, right here. It's only for a few days. DON'T GO OUT."

Then she showed me that morning's newspaper. The headline screamed "Young Reds Bud in Upstate Valley." The article went on to say that a "Commie Camp" had been discovered in Wingdale, New York. It identified the camp as Webatuck, then said, "The camp is run by VICTOR and PEARL FINK, who live at 500 West End Avenue." Shadow was protecting me from the photographers and reporters camping outside our building.

A little while later, spurred by that article, a lunatic fringe group called the Minutemen planted homemade bombs all over camp, mostly in the area reserved for five- to eight-year-olds. The irony was that the FBI had to come and dismantle them.

Later that September, I started life at the High School of Music & Art. I had really high hopes, but they were soon dashed. It had never occurred to me that teachers would find my budding career a threat, but they did, and school became a nightmare. My parents had brokered a deal so I could take days off to perform; the school said so long as I pulled an A average on all the tests, it wouldn't matter. Imagine our surprise when my first report card arrived, and I'd failed every subject due to absences.

The kids were all right; they just wanted autographs, or to come to recording sessions. But the teachers made my life hell. It became normal for me to enter a classroom and hear a teacher say, "Oh, Janis. Or should I say, *Miss Ian*? How kind of you to grace us with your presence. I'm sure you're *much* too busy being a *star* to attend class." One told the class I was absent because I was a heroin addict. The voice teacher said, "You think, because you're famous, you don't need lessons?"

The final straw was a report I turned in for Miss Hermann, my English teacher. Titled "The Present Me," we were supposed to describe our lives as we were living them, so she could get to know us. I wrote about music and playing in the clubs. She failed me, the first F I'd ever received, writing, "Leave the jazz for your hobby" in the margins. It was a monumental insult. I wrote in my journal: *Fame doesn't change you—it changes the people around you.*

We began work on my first album that October, and Verve released "Society's Child" for the second time, with full promotion and publicity. MGM, the parent company, sent me on a tour of radio stations and record hops, hoping to convince a few more stations to be courageous enough to play the record. *The New York Times* ran an article about censorship in the music industry, saying:

> *"'Society's Child' marks a new boldness in popular music, while also proclaiming the radiant new talent, Janis Ian."*

My parents were thrilled; clubs and *Broadside* were one thing, but this was the *Times*.

My life separated again, into the world of school, and the world of the entertainment business. I made new friends. One of the closest was a drag queen named Harlow. She was absolutely the most beautiful woman I'd ever seen, and my publicist, Kenny Schaeffer, who'd introduced us, didn't bother telling me much about her.

Harlow was a platinum blond, with legs that looked great in a miniskirt, something I couldn't say for myself. We spent long hours together, talking about everything from parents to politics, drawn by a mutual sense of ourselves as outcasts. I wasn't in love with her, but I was immensely flattered that an older woman (she was at least twenty then, to my fifteen) would be interested in me. I envied her style, the ease with which she wore her clothes, the fabulous way they clung to her body. I envied her long fingernails, which I as a guitarist could not afford. Most of all, I envied her directness. She seemed to know herself in a way that left no room for self-doubt, while I was consumed by it.

Harlow told me she was taking part in a beauty contest, and a film might be made of it. I was thrilled for her, even though she seemed to grow increasingly distant. I put it down to nerves, until one day at lunch she blurted out, "Janis, there's something I've got to tell you." I waited, hoping for some good gossip.

She leaned forward. "I'm not what you think I am, Janis. . . . I'm not female."

Okay, that made a certain amount of sense to me. It was the sixties; everyone was redefining themselves. In the global, eternal, metaphysical sense, I wasn't female, either. I was Part of the Human Race. I was Beyond Race. Beyond Religion. And quite willing to be Beyond Gender. I told her as much.

"No, really," she insisted. "I'm not a girl."

I shrugged and waited for the punch line. Harlow grimaced, then said, "Janis, I'm a transvestite." My jaw dropped as I involuntarily stared at those perfect legs.

Absurd. It couldn't be true. Transvestites were people with a five o'clock shadow. They wore badly fitting dresses, and choke collars to hide their Adam's apples. Not possible.

I shook my head and laughed, saying, "Yeah. And I'm the queen of England, right?" We argued until she lost patience and led me off to the ladies' room, where she hiked her miniskirt even higher, and proved beyond a doubt that she was telling the truth. I was completely blown away.

I was blown away a lot that year. I was getting heaps of fan mail, much of it from strippers, hookers, and other folks living on the margins. The strippers would enclose autographed pictures of themselves in various poses. I don't know why, really, except that they identified with the songs I wrote, which were mostly about the disenfranchised and dispossessed. At a time when people didn't speak about "ugly things" like prostitution, I was singing about it.

I was also beginning to get a fair amount of hate mail, which was scary. People threatened to burn down the venues I worked in, to run me over in the street, to shoot me while I was on stage. It was so frightening that I ignored it.

I hired a manager, Jean Harcourt Powell, a lovely British woman who stood as my friend and protector for the next fifteen years. I hired attorneys, signing a retainer agreement. I had a record company, a publicist, an accountant, and a publisher. Even better, I had all the work I wanted, and was soon making the munificent sum of five hundred dollars a week at places like the Main Point in Bryn Mawr, Pennsylvania. Life was good.

I hung out in the Village as much as possible, learning my craft by watching other performers play through the flu, hecklers, and uncaring, drunken tourists. There were a million clubs, and I was now welcome in all of them. The Bitter End, Gerde's Folk City, Café Wha?, the Night Owl . . . it was never-ending. On any given night, I could club-hop and meet up with Odetta, Van Ronk, Tim Buckley, the Rascals, Eric Burdon, Tim Hardin, and dozens more, sometimes all in the same room.

We recorded my first album, *Janis Ian,* in just under a week. I'd written all the songs, and I was very proud of it. The day I got a test acetate, I brought it home to play for my parents. Mom wasn't there, but Dad sat and listened with me. Toward the end, there was a song called "New Christ Cardiac Hero," comparing the youth of today with Jesus Christ, and finding both wanting. My father looked at me and said, "Jan, between the single and this song, you're going to have big trouble." I shrugged it off. How could things possibly be worse than death threats and school?

Christmas vacation came and went; I struggled to keep my grades up, and fought to maintain my writing output. Going to school was terrifying. The principal had asked me to do a show in the auditorium, and I'd refused. He told me I needed to pull up my grades, saying, "If you can write all those songs, you can be a straight-A student." What he forgot was that I *was* being a straight-A student; it was the absences that pulled down my averages.

For the first time in my life, I talked back, saying, "Look, if you want my grades up, tell the kids to stop asking for autographs. Tell the teachers to stop asking how my records are selling. And while you're at it, ask them to stop making it their personal mission to destroy my life here."

My next report card showed zeros in courtesy, effort, responsibility, and self-control. Not to mention 40s and 50s in everything else. The chorus teacher put me in the back and told me to just mouth the words; if I wasn't willing to sing solos in assembly, I had no business singing in the chorus. It got to the point where the two friends I'd made waited for me outside the doors each morning, then physically pushed me inside.

I begged my parents to let me quit. I'd soon be sixteen, and could legally leave with their permission. It infuriated my father, who said no child of his was going to quit high school. So I endured.

That next January, Shadow and I got our big break. TV producer David Oppenheim had been given a copy of "Society's Child" by Bob Shelton. After hearing about our problems at radio, David had played it for Leonard Bernstein. Bernstein was determined to see pop music recognized as a valid form; to that end, he was about to film a one-hour special called *Inside Pop: The Rock Revolution*. It would feature Jim McGuinn of the Byrds, Brian Wilson of the Beach Boys, and now, me.

I spent an entire day with Bernstein, talking and taping my portion. At the end, he called me something like "a marvelous creature," and I went home happy that his wife had helped me with my Spanish home-work. I didn't think much about the effect the show might have, na-tionally broadcast at prime time Sunday night, in an era when there were only seven TV channels available to watch. My parents and grand-parents were happy because it was Leonard Bernstein, but I was getting used to having a fuss made over me. I'd been on several magazine cov-ers, was mentioned in the *Times* at least once a month, and had even had a feature in the *Los Angeles Times*. So it really didn't faze me. I was more concerned with the effect my new album would have on things.

The record came out in February, and sure enough, Dad was right. The single had gotten big airplay in Boston; I'd even headlined at a club there for a week. I remember it because when Jean and I drove up in a cab, there was a huge line that stretched all the way around the block and halfway down the next street. I wondered aloud what was going on, that people were so excited about, and Jean laughed and said, "That line's for you, Janis!"

So when the album came out, it was natural that a major Boston pe-riodical review it. What wasn't natural was their devoting an entire page to it. The author quoted extensively from "New Christ Cardiac Hero," and was promptly fired for it. My publicist had a field day, arranging for a lady from United Press International to interview me for a feature.

We met at Sardi's, a theater hangout. Jean told me I could order the London broil, even though it cost a fortune, because the news service would be picking up the tab. When my plate came, there were three small, thin strips of steak, two small carrots, and two baby potatoes. I was horrified, saying to the reporter, "My mom could feed us for a week on what this lunch is costing, and this is all they give you?!" Later, she told Jean I "wasn't nearly as nice as Shirley Temple." In the article, she wrote that I wasn't nearly as nice as Patty Duke. In fact, she said I was a very rude girl.

I honored her decades later by naming my publishing and record companies after that comment.

The Bernstein show aired, and suddenly all the radio stations were apologizing. KRLA Los Angeles even took out a full-page ad in *Billboard* saying they were sorry. *Time* and *Newsweek* wanted my opinion on everything from Vietnam to the generation gap. My album started climbing the national charts, as did the single. Soon both were in the Top Ten. Verve took out ads saying:

Janis Ian: The Youngest Pop Legend Alive

It was confusing; was there also a dead youngest pop legend around somewhere?

I became really famous. In some major cities, the single had already been on the charts for eight staggering months. We watched its progress toward Middle America with interest; an East Coast station would go on it, then, as it started to fall, a station west of that one would go on it, and the same process would occur. It charted across the country for months and months.

As I got more famous, things started getting weird. Globally weird. My father's brother and his wife read a free-form article I'd written for *Seventeen* magazine and informed my parents that I was "hooked on LSD." My paternal grandmother wanted me to record an album of Yiddish folk songs. My mother's parents wanted to know why I didn't come for Friday dinner every week. The record company held meetings to discuss my clothes, my hair, my persona.

The pressure was enormous. We were supposed to start cutting my second album just as the first began climbing the charts. Shadow and the record label wanted to know where the songs were. Somehow, in the preceding three months, I was supposed to come up with ten brilliant new songs, at least two of them hits. I was also expected to continue promoting the first record, which meant interviews, hops, concerts, and whatever else anyone could find. At my parents' insistence, the next album was postponed until summer, when I'd be off from school.

I signed with William Morris, a huge booking agency, and started getting offers to write film scores. My agents, David Geffen and Hal Ray, were busy going through them. We had a meeting one day where they presented me with a script for something called *The Graduate,* and advised me to pass. One of them said, *"It's going to be directed by Mike Nichols, who is good, but as a director of a major motion picture he's pretty much untried. It stars some short, big-nosed unknown kid with a funny name and bad hair. The story line is silly—Up with People–type graduates from college, has an affair with his mother's close friend and neighbor, falls in love with the neighbor's daughter, then runs away with her after breaking into the church where her wedding's being held. Oh, and he locks everyone else inside the church with a big cross, while he and the chick make their escape by bus. Ridiculous."*

We passed, Paul Simon did the score, and the rest is history.

I rented a studio apartment next door to my parents' so I could have a place to work. At home, Dad needed the piano most of the time; there was no way to write songs in my bedroom while he was pounding away two doors down. It was a relief to be away from everyone, to sleep late and work on my own schedule. It was also my escape when things got too hard, and they were definitely getting hard. Outside of the jealousy at school, there was jealousy in the folk world. People were turning on me.

I'd changed my name legally, from the family name of Fink to my brother's middle name of Ian. My parents weren't happy, but I reasoned with them that Fink wasn't really our family name. Dad's father, Yashe, had been given the name when he landed at Ellis Island. It wasn't like we'd come over on the *Mayflower* with it.

I also had no desire to involve my family in my career, particularly after the violent reactions my songs were getting. I'd begun using "Ian" long before going into the studio, and it was natural that I formally change it so I could use it on my passport. Songwriter Julius Lester took umbrage, though, as well as being angry over the national success of "Society's Child." *Broadside* published an open letter from him, saying:

"Now she's on TV with all sorts of lights and camera angles and I just know she's not protesting anymore. She's making it and it's sad. Like there goes another one chasing that American dream of fame and money. . . ."

When I confessed how hurt I was to Janey, she said, "Sheesh. We're only fifteen. We've got years of this shit ahead of us."

A lot of people in the folk community turned their backs once I had a hit record. The Newport Folk Festival was the ultimate for a folk performer; you weren't really anyone until you'd played their main stage. I'd grown up listening to the Vanguard series *Live at Newport,* and for a while my sole goal in life was to play there. In a three-to-four vote, they refused to book me, reasoning that I was "too young," and that older players who might die soon needed the break first. I accepted that until I found out Arlo Guthrie, just a few years older than me, was headlining one night. Then I was devastated.

What I remember most about that period was my confusion. What was so wrong with having a hit, especially one like this? Here I was, breaking ground at radio, a lightning rod for hate groups all over the country, and all the folkies could think about was how unfair life was, to let some kid "make it" before she'd even paid her dues. From my vantage point, I was on the front lines, playing to boos and catcalls, bravely standing up in front of audiences who sometimes threw things and screamed epithets while I tried to continue singing. When I'd walk down the street, strangers would tell me how much the song meant to them, how it had changed their lives, and that was great. But strangers would also walk up and spit in my face, telling me how much they hated the song, and me along with it. I expected the folk community to support me, but only Van Ronk and Odetta and a handful of others did. The envy was incredible.

My parents were weird, too. As alien as I'd always felt, my family now seemed like they were living on another planet, more and more disconnected from my daily life. I still ate dinner at home, when I wasn't performing somewhere, but there was a lot of silence at our table now. Mom had suddenly begun writing poetry, and would stare dreamily into the distance as she picked at her food. Dad was a bundle of nervous energy, unable to sit still, and flying into a rage at the drop of a hat. My kid brother was scared; we'd never had to deal with yelling or violence in our home, and here Dad was, about to beat the dog because she'd gotten into the garbage. I grabbed his arm and stopped him, yelling, "Dad! Dad! You always told us it was *our* fault if the dog did something wrong! Whatever's going on, don't take it out on her!"

No one would tell me what was happening, and to be honest, I don't think I wanted to know. I just wanted to write songs, and tour. Eric took the brunt of it, because I was home as little as possible. Sometimes I'd get back from doing a show at midnight or later, and Dad would be sitting on a kitchen chair, watching old movies on our little black-and-white TV set. We'd sit together for a while, and things would seem all right again. But they weren't.

My album got nominated for a Grammy, and *Life* magazine decided to profile me. I had permission to spend most of the summer working, and hired Merka as my tour manager. We went to California, where the Byrds opened for me and I played to sold-out houses. I did the Berkeley Folk Festival with Big Brother and the Holding Company, and Janis Joplin became a good friend. She was seven or eight years older than me, but it didn't matter. We both had bad skin. We both felt overweight. We were both outsiders. The only difference is that she'd slept with more people than I had. We went to a party at Peter Tork's house one night, where everyone was wearing bright silk Indian clothing and crashing on a floor filled with pillows and hashish pipes. There were dozens of naked people lolling around; I shrugged it off, trying to look cool.

Joplin took me to another party and introduced me to Olive Watson, granddaughter of IBM's founder. Olive in turn made us matching suede pants, and at the next party, I watched as a heroin dealer went around the room, giving free shots to all and sundry. When Janis's turn came, she looked up at me and rasped, "Kid, time for you to go home." As I turned at the door to tell her good-bye, the shot was just sliding through her brown suede pants and into her thigh.

You could hear my record at the grocery while you shopped, or playing in the background of a clothing store. It was amazing, wonderful, scary. I felt landless and homeless, on the road, with Merka and my guitar the only constants. Between the press and the shows, I was tired all the time, and would often fall asleep sitting in Merka's lap between appointments. I was being a pretend adult most of the time, and it seemed like Merka was the only person who realized I was also just a clueless sixteen-year-old. With Merka, I could giggle, play on swings, confess my confusion.

Taking a nap with her arms around me made me feel safe, like it was all right to be young and confused. She behaved like a big sister, and I could hide in her arms without worrying she'd think I was acting like a baby.

Unfortunately, not everyone saw it that way. My business advisors landed on me with both feet after I taped the *Smothers Brothers Comedy Hour.* According to them, a very well-known television star had spied me asleep in Merka's lap during a break, and had proceeded to tell several industry people that I was obviously a lesbian and shouldn't be allowed on national television.

I was appalled. Here I hadn't even slept with a *boy* yet, let alone a girl, and an industry veteran I'd long admired was trying to get me blackballed!

For my first appearance on *The Tonight Show,* Jean booked us into the Hollywood Roosevelt Hotel, a bastion of respectability. When she tried to make a long-distance call, the hotel demanded a five-hundred-dollar cash deposit, on the grounds that I was a hippie and entertainers never paid their bills. Jean was offended; I was amused. MasterCard and Visa didn't exist yet; you paid for things with a check, or with cash. American Express cards were notoriously hard to get, but I'd had one for a year, so we tried that. It wasn't good enough—the hotel thought it was fake. My age and clothing conspired against us. It's laughable now, when you can wear anything you like, but back then my high boots, paisley shirts, and tights really set me apart.

It's hard, in this day and age, to realize how divisive things were in 1967. The country was already polarized by Vietnam and the civil rights movement; people like me split it still further. The world was divided into "us" and "them." "They" wore suits and crew cuts, high heels and bouffants. They got married young, had the requisite number of children, and drank martinis every night. "We" wore long hair, flowered ties, and sandals. We slept with our lovers instead of marrying them, used birth control, and smoked pot.

They saw us as a danger. We saw them as a drag.

It was *Easy Rider* out there once you left L.A. or New York. We'd routinely get pulled over in small towns, hauled out of the rental car, and inspected for drug use by sheriffs who hoped to parade us before their friends, snickering behind their hands at the freaks wearing love beads and headbands.

I felt like an outlaw much of the time, estranged from my family because I was never home, no longer welcomed by the folk community, and out of sync with the mainstream pop people. I fell in with a group of outsiders who were also unacceptable to the mainstream, people like Hendrix and Joplin. They didn't care how old I was, or what my opinions were about "the generation gap." They just cared about making music.

I loved Jimi. To him, I was always "that girl who wrote that song, man, you know." A lot has been written about his life and his death, but nothing's been said about his grace. And he was beautifully graceful, both as a musician and as a man. I used to love watching his hands— long and slender, the perfect players' fingers. I envied him that. We'd spend entire nights at the Café Au Go Go, jamming. The club had a Hammond B3 I played incompetently, but I could set up a pattern and Jimi would fall into a reverie, playing his ass off for the winos who'd help us close the bar at 3 A.M.

Things were a lot looser than they are now. Club owners would stay open so artists could sit around and jam—not because it would attract paying customers (even in New York, there weren't a whole lot of tourists out after midnight), but so we could play together. The informal late-night jam sessions helped hone your talent, and completely disparate musicians would congregate together, forming friendships and trading licks. It was a gloriously free feeling, playing for the sheer joy of it. No audience, no manager, no record company—just people making music.

I went to visit Jimi while he was recording in L.A. After the session, alone with me in the studio, he pulled out a small bag of cocaine and took a few snorts. I'd been bugging him to let me try it for weeks, and he finally gave in. I took a snort, then sneezed, blowing several hundred dollars' worth all over the console. Jimi started laughing, and I joined in. Then I realized something was radically wrong; my heart was pumping like a jackhammer, and all the color drained out of my face. It felt like I was about to spin into oblivion as I slumped against a wall and slid to the floor.

Jimi grabbed me, saying, "Girl, your face is so white, I can see right through it." He was frantic, trying to figure out what was wrong with me and fix it. Neither of us wanted to call the paramedics, who'd leak the story to the press and get us in trouble. I muttered that I'd be fine, and he got me some cold water to sip on. After a few more minutes, my heart settled down, but I was definitely done with coke.

Years later, I discovered I was allergic to vasoconstrictors, and anything with speed in it. Lucky for me, because cocaine could easily have become my drug of choice. I'd have loved the extra energy, the sense of power, and I'd have ended up like so many of my friends, strung out or even dead.

I played the Troubadour that July, a prestige gig at the time. After my second show, Merka and I went next door to Dan Tana's for some Italian food. We were soon joined by Doug Weston, owner of the Troub, and a few other performers. As we toyed with our pasta, chatting amiably, a woman came over and sat down next to me. By then I was used to strangers making themselves welcome, so I nodded and ignored her. The next thing I knew, she was whispering in my ear, telling me all the things she'd like to do to my body. I looked around the table; Merka had gone to the bathroom, and everyone else was studiously ignoring us. I pulled my head away a little, and she laughed, then put her tongue in my ear!

Things continued to get more surreal as I became more famous. A national magazine asked what lotions I used on my face; I answered "Duck saliva," and they printed it as a serious statement. MGM took a million-dollar insurance policy out on my life, sending me for a physical with a doctor whose sink was full of bloody instruments. My manager and agents joked that at sixteen, I was now at the peak of my career, and if I would just die, they'd all make a fortune selling me as a martyr. Somehow, I didn't find the thought as funny as they did.

On a typical day, I'd be up at five or six in the morning to tape television and radio appearances. Then we'd fly to the next town, where I'd visit several radio stations, have lunch with a program director and local record company rep, go to sound check, do a few more interviews, do my show, then go back to a cold room-service dinner the hotel restaurant had left in my room before closing. I tried to escape the pressure by writing songs, but I never had time to finish anything, and that began to wear on me. I loved my work, loved the performing and writing, but the rest of it was coldly unsatisfying.

It was a vicious cycle. No one would put out my records if I didn't perform and do press. I couldn't make records without writing songs, and I couldn't buy time to write songs without the money I earned from performing. I felt like a cornered mouse. I started having nightmares, waking sweat-drenched and shouting in the hotel rooms I shared with Merka.

Life magazine followed me around through all of it, wanting photos of me "acting like a normal teenager" to intersperse with pictures of me onstage and in TV studios. It was truly strange, being before a lens so much. At first, I was really self-conscious, but after a while it just seemed normal.

That's the problem with being famous: things that are not normal start feeling normal, and eventually you just accept them as part of daily life. Having my meals interrupted by autograph-seekers seemed normal. Wearing hats so fans couldn't snip off a lock of my hair for a souvenir seemed normal.

Being followed by the government, too, seemed normal. All the performers I knew were being followed; you could never tell how many people at a party or backstage were actually informers. We used to joke that organizations like the National Student Association could never have existed without CIA funding.

We joked, but we didn't really understand just how serious it was until 1976, when a Senate Intelligence Committee started investigating the CIA's involvement in domestic affairs. The CIA had started something called "Operation CHAOS" in 1967, to wage a clandestine war against the youth and civil rights movements. Who knew? I was staggered to read a description from the CHAOS files of their goals in targeting war protestors, civil rights activists, and other public figures:

Show them as scurrilous and depraved. Call attention to their habits and living conditions, explore every possible embarrassment. Send in women and sex, break up marriages. Have members arrested on marijuana charges. Investigate personal conflicts or animosities between them. Send articles to the newspapers showing their depravity. Use narcotics and free sex to entrap. Use misinformation to confuse and disrupt. Get records of their bank accounts. Obtain specimens of handwriting. Provoke target groups into rivalries that may result in death.

Scary stuff.

For us, it was impossible to separate protesting against the war from the civil rights movement, using drugs, and living on music. The rest of the country had managed to ignore most of it, until San Francisco's "Summer of Love" got national attention from the press, and large portions of America that still yearned for the simplicity and rigidity of the fifties had their minds blown. People were afraid their children would be infected, would drop out of the mainstream and into the counterculture, advocating free love and free sex and turning into drug-ridden lunatics dancing on the streets of Haight-Ashbury. A backlash was beginning.

Just before summer vacation ended, we recorded my second album, *A Song for All the Seasons of Your Mind*. We'd taken ten days this time, but Shadow and I were both disappointed with the result. Most people have years to prepare for their recording debut and its follow-up. I'd had months, and it showed. I felt like what I heard in my head wasn't making it onto the vinyl. I was hungry for a different kind of music, something with more jazz and less pop. Naturally, the record company wasn't thrilled with that idea. Besides, they wanted the album released that fall, eight months after the first one, to make their year-end financials. It was odd being a commodity, but a No. 1 record had ensured I'd be working on the company time frame, not my own.

There were perks to being well-known, though. I had access. People like Johnny Mercer stopped by my dressing room to talk. Henry Mancini wanted to meet with me. And my record company was willing to listen to my ideas.

My first album cover had been a painting by Joseph Solman, and I wanted to continue that by having my second cover a painting by Salvador Dalí. Jean arranged to meet him in the bar of a nearby hotel. We sat down in front of the fountain area and waited. And waited.

About forty-five minutes later, Dalí swept in, wearing his cloak and twirling his famous mustache. Jean explained what we wanted. He looked down his nose at us and said, "Dalí paint picture. You pay Dalí ten thousand dollars. Dalí keep picture." Then he swept out.

That was the end of that.

One night I was sitting on the aisle at the Café Au Go Go when the stage manager came over and whispered, "Frank Zappa's here. He wants to sit next to you." The news thrilled me; Zappa was one of my heroes. A couple of times, friends had snuck me in to watch him rehearsing the Mothers of Invention. I was fascinated by the hand signals he used; a lifted second finger might mean "Repeat the chorus," a lifted third "Take the second ending." It was classical in its precision.

I moved one seat in, and Zappa sat down on the aisle. He folded one leg over the other, folded his hands in his lap, and stared intently at the stage. Then Cream came on for their first New York show. It was like being blown out of your chair and through a window; I'd never heard playing like that, and I kept waiting for Frank to show some sign of life, or make a comment between songs. But Zappa just sat there, folded and silent, for the entire show. While the rest of the audience were standing and cheering, he stared straight ahead at the stage.

After the band exited, and most of the audience had left, he finally moved. He stood up, stepped into the aisle, looked down at me, and said, "You're doing a great job entertaining the troops, kid. Keep it up."

Life sure was getting bizarre.

Amidst all this strangeness, my folks and school persisted in acting like my life was nothing unusual. I was still expected to pull good grades, learn arias for voice class, and silently submit when the vocal teacher critiqued me by saying, "You think just because you're a big star, you know how to sing?" In between learning arias, I was playing Carnegie Hall with Pete Seeger and Tim Buckley.

That October, I toured as the opening act for Donovan. He was carrying a string quartet that came onstage for one song, which seemed pretty wasteful and self-indulgent. He had a manager named Ashley Kozak who was very concerned with "image." One day, we were all ready to board our flight, when Ashley discovered there was no first class because the plane was so small. He canceled all the tickets and made us wait for a larger plane, just so he and Donovan could sit up front, disconnected from the rest of us.

In the folk community, everyone was pretty friendly. Backstage, waiting for the show to begin, you'd sit around swapping songs and guitar licks, or telling "war stories" about life on the road. Donovan was my first real exposure to British pop music hierarchy. He barely spoke to any of us, including his own players. He ate separately, with his manager. He arrived separately in his limousine. Naturally enough, he became an object of mystery, and a lot of our time was spent speculating on whether he wore anything under his long tunic onstage.

Once the tour was done, Jean tried to collect my fee, but Ashley was abruptly unavailable. I was due ten grand, a fortune, but she couldn't get it out of him. We were sitting around her office one afternoon, trying to figure out what to do, when Shadow's business partner, Larry Martire, walked in.

"Why the long faces?" he asked. Jean explained the situation. Larry looked thoughtful, then said, "Huh. Where's this guy staying?" Jean gave him the name of the hotel and Larry grinned, saying, "I'll be back."

An hour later he walked into the office holding a paper bag. Dumping its contents on the desk, he laughed and said, "No problem. The guy was just being inconsiderate. I taught him a lesson in manners." We stared at the money on the desk and laughed along with him.

I fell in with a group of people closer to my own age who were hanging out in the Village and living on the Upper West Side. There was Bobby Mikels, who hypnotized me so I could remember the vocabulary for my Spanish year-end exams. Olive Watson, still making suede clothing, was one of them, too. We'd hang out until all hours, talking about holographs and holograms and wishing we belonged to the Rand Institute, where someone would pay us just to sit around and think. It was an incredibly diverse group of teenagers when I think about it now.

My closest friend was Carol Hunter, an astonishingly versatile musician who soon joined Jimi and me in our late-night jams. Carol could switch from electric guitar to acoustic twelve-string to percussion or keyboards without effort. She was an incredible bass player, prompting one musician to say, "When you hear bass being played like a guitar, doing all the things a bass shouldn't be able to do, that'll be Carol." She would drag me to readings where I'd fall asleep in the back of the room while pale poets dressed in black recited bad verse. We started talking about doing an album together, just the two of us playing all the instruments. It was a novel idea at the time, before synthesizers and electronic keyboards made it so easy.

I'd done well over fifty live shows that year, plus all the interviews and television. Between work and school, I was exhausted. It was difficult to take the subway to Music & Art each day; strangers thought nothing of grabbing my arm to discuss my records, refusing to let me get off until I'd satisfied their curiosity. I started taking taxis to school, when I bothered going. Somehow, staying up past midnight at the clubs didn't gel with getting up at six to attend school. I didn't mention the absences to my folks.

I was booked to play at Lincoln Center that December 8, the first pop artist to play there. It was exciting and frightening. I was going to use a band for the first time, the New York Rock & Roll Ensemble, led by Michael Kamen. I wanted to wear jeans and a work shirt for the concert, but Verve and Jean were united against it, so we compromised;

I'd wear tights, boots, and a bright red Indian Nehru-collared shirt I'd found while shopping with Joplin one day. I sent a limousine for Sis and Gordon, invited my grandparents and cousins, and worried about whether the twelve-string prototype Ovation Guitars had given me would hold up.

Avery Fisher Hall was packed, and every music critic in New York was there. Nervously pacing backstage, I tried to find some time alone to settle myself down. I hadn't reckoned on my father's side of the family. My grandmother somehow got herself, my aunts, uncles, and cousins backstage before the show. When one of the ushers tried to direct her away from my dressing room, she said in her thick Yiddish accent, "Get out of my way, or I'll give you such a *zetz*, your whole family will walk crooked!" I expect he looked down at this elderly woman, all four feet nine inches of her, and decided he'd met his match.

It was an odd show. I had fun playing with the band, but it was a cold stage. Usually, while you're performing, you can feel something coming back to you from the audience. When it's going well, there's almost a physical connection. It's reassuring, and necessary, because it dictates your timing—how long you take between songs, when you get a drink of water, even which song you do next.

There was nothing of the sort that night. I didn't know that they'd have to tear the inside of the hall apart two or three times in the future to make the room warmer and fix the acoustics. I only knew that nothing was coming back at me.

I got a standing ovation, and took two encores, but I wasn't happy. I'd slowly begun to realize that I didn't know what I was doing—not as a performer, and not as a songwriter. I had to write twenty songs to get to one I liked. There was something wrong with that. I sang my heart out each night, but I was pleased with only a couple of performances a year. Something was wrong with that, too. Going onstage used to make me feel full, and free. Now I walked into the wings feeling empty, and shackled.

As I walked offstage, I said to Jean, "I think I need to quit, I really do." She laughed and said, "Oh, you all say that when you're tired," but I remember thinking, *I'm not "you all"—I'm me, and I have to get off this merry-go-round.* Still, the reviews were great, everyone was congratulatory, and I went to bed thinking of Chanukah, just around the corner.

The next morning, still feeling good, I went into the kitchen for breakfast with my family. I sat down at the yellow Formica table and opened my mouth to say something, but Eric kicked me.

I looked at him, and he nodded toward my parents. Something was terribly wrong. Mom had been crying; her eyes were all swollen and her nose was running.

I looked over at my father. There was a thunderous look on his face. He stared straight ahead, not meeting anyone's eyes.

"Tell them, Pearl," he said.

Mom shook her head. No.

Dad waited, then said it again. "Tell them. Now."

My mother said, "I can't, Vic. I can't," and shook her head again. Neither of them would look at us.

Silence passed. Mom began weeping full tilt. Eric and I looked at each other, embarrassed. I'd only seen my mother cry once before, on the farm, when she'd finally saved enough money for a new couch cover, and I'd finger-painted all over it. What was going on?

Eric's eyes were filling with tears. I patted his hand to reassure him, and waited.

My father finally looked at my mom. His eyes were cold. I shivered to think of those eyes on me. "Pearl, *tell them!*" he shouted.

Mom jumped up and yelled, "You tell them, Vic! I just can't do it!" With that, she rushed from the table, slamming the door behind her.

Dad rose like he was going to go after her, then sighed and sat back down. He looked at Eric, then at me.

"We're getting a divorce. We wanted to wait until after the concert to tell you."

We were stunned. Everyone we knew thought my parents were the perfect couple. They made each other laugh. They loved being together. My own teenage *angst* notwithstanding, I'd thought we were a happy family. They'd seemed fine when I saw them over the summer. They'd seemed fine at the concert, just half a day earlier. They'd seemed fine. Really.

I knew I'd been away a lot, but I couldn't believe I'd have missed something as serious as my parents splitting up. I couldn't wrap my head around it, so I stupidly said, "Are you sure?" My father nodded.

Eric began crying in earnest. I walked him back to his bedroom and wrapped my arms around his small body. He kept saying, "I'll get good grades, Jan, I really will!" I told him it wasn't his fault, but I wasn't sure he believed me. I finally gave him one of my books, which were normally off-limits, and left him reading.

The bedroom door was closed; I could hear sobbing coming from the other side. I walked back to the kitchen, slowly and carefully. Maybe, if I didn't make any noise, I could go back in time. Maybe I'd walk in and everybody would be smiling, Dad flipping an omelet while Mom set the table. Maybe my heart would stop thumping so hard then.

Dad was still at the table, head in hands. He looked up as I walked in, shaking his head. I sat down and waited for my hands to stop trembling.

"Does this have anything to do with me performing, Dad? With me being away so much?" I asked.

"No," he said, "nothing to do with that. Your mom's been having an affair. I told her she had to choose between the affair and her family. She couldn't make the choice."

Oh. Wow. That was bizarre. Men had affairs. Women didn't. Men slept around on their wives—everybody said so. Women didn't do that.

Mothers didn't do that. My mother didn't do that. How could she do that?

Women who slept around were whores. I couldn't stop thinking of it like that.

Then he said, "Of course, the fact that we're always worried over money didn't help the marriage. And it's hard, seeing you make so much every night."

My heart sank like a stone. I hadn't given the money much thought. Most of it went into the bank accounts my mom and the Surrogate's Court had set up. I had an allowance, which sat in a coffee can on the table in my little studio apartment. My friends were welcome to take what they wanted. I had a place to live, a place to work, and a couple of guitars. I didn't really need much else.

It hadn't occurred to me that my folks might have a problem with it. Mom had even turned down the small percentage she was entitled to for managing the money, telling me all my earnings were mine. They didn't need it, she'd said.

But even with Dad holding down two full-time jobs, and giving private lessons, he grossed only $8,275 a year. Mom barely grossed $5,720. They dreamed of a combined income that would reach $15,000. By the end of 1967, I was making that almost every month. It was frightening to discover how much it bothered them, and I wondered what else I'd done to help cause the split.

I went off to school the following Monday, still in shock, to find my homeroom teacher reading a *New York Times* review of my second album to the class. A bunch of kids got up and came over to me, congratulating me on the Philharmonic concert and the review, which opened with "Nobody is safe from Janis Ian anymore." My classmates seemed proud of me, not envious, and that realization cut through the commotion my arrival had engendered, making me feel a little better.

It took a few minutes to get everyone calmed down and seated again. When I finally opened my textbook, I realized I hadn't done my homework for the weekend. I'd totally forgotten about it. The teacher posed a question, I gave the wrong answer, and she said impatiently, "If you're so smart and making so much money, why don't you ever get the right answer, Janis?" The class went silent; everyone was uncomfortable. One of my friends tried to explain that I'd been working, but the teacher told her that was irrelevant.

Afterward, she came up to me and suggested my presence was too disruptive, and it was time to leave school. Throughout the day, as I moved from class to class, the teacher in charge would make the same suggestion. After the fifth teacher, I was called into the dean's office, and told my having such a visible career was wreaking havoc in the school. I was uncooperative, refusing to give a concert for assembly. I was ungrateful, and it would show on my permanent record. If I ever wanted to go to college, the minus-one on my personality card would count against me, he could guarantee it. My final report card would say it all, noting, "Cannot take directions—rebels against authority."

It was definitely time to leave.

FIVE

Haven't I Got Eyes

Haven't I got ears to hear
Haven't I got breath to breathe
Haven't I got eyes to see
what's happening to me

I t was January in New York, slushy streets and sidewalks, bums cadging cigarettes and shivering in the crosstown wind. My family was gone. School was gone. My folk friends were gone. It was The Year of Leaving.

Janis Ian was falling off the charts, but *Seasons* was rising. Still, no one toured in bad weather if they could avoid it, so I hung out at the clubs. My mother was staying at a cheap boarding house called the Lucerne, about three blocks away from my studio apartment, but we weren't speaking. I blamed her for the divorce. It seemed to me that everything would be okay if she'd only go back to my dad. She wouldn't speak about the affair, wouldn't offer any explanation for what had gone wrong, so I was free to make up whatever scenarios I liked. I visited her out of a sense of obligation, but it was depressing and confusing, so I avoided it as much as possible.

And, of course, the woman always got the blame.

A few years later, I discovered her affair hadn't come out of nowhere. Dad had been playing around on her since I was a little girl; each time he promised to stop, and each time he returned to the same woman. I can't imagine how that must have hurt my mother, and I still cringe to think of the years I spent being so angry with her.

One afternoon, I was told to go see my parents' attorney. Jean came with me, her warm presence a safety net around the chaos I felt. I'd never have admitted it, but I found the whole ordeal terrifying, and I wanted someone to lean on.

When we arrived, the lawyer told me that since Eric was only thirteen, the court would decide who he'd live with. I, however, was expected to choose a guardian.

I sat there, dumbfounded. The attorney faced me across his desk, my folks flanking him on either side. No one would meet my eyes. How could I choose between these two people? How could I take sides in front of them?

I couldn't seem to get any words out. I wanted to say: *I'm sixteen years old. I have my own place, earn my own living. You people have screwed everything up—let me take custody of* myself *until you get things sorted out!* Instead I sat there, mute.

One of my parents said that given my age, they'd abide by my decision, but I had to make a choice. *How?* Angry as I was with my mother, she was still my mother, and the part of me in the most pain loved her deeply. Angry as I was with my father, he was my dad, the man who'd given me music. It was impossible, so I looked down at the floor and started to cry.

Jean walked over, grabbed my hand, and hauled me to my feet. Then she turned to them all and said, "I don't know what the American divorce laws are, but I do know one thing. What you are doing to this child is absolutely disgusting." With that, she pushed me out the door and took me back to her apartment, where I could hide out and cry in peace.

I worked really hard at being adult after that. I moved out of my parents' old place and into my little studio, lock, stock, and barrel. I got involved in choosing which dates I'd accept, and which I'd turn down. I stopped laughing; I was full in the throes of teenage angst as it was, and saw nothing to laugh about anymore.

I tried to learn about business, money, investments. I thought about buying a brownstone, and asked Sam Weintraub, my accountant, whether I could afford $7,000 for one on the Upper West Side. "Whaddya need that headache for?" he asked. "New York's topped out. You won't make your money back. You've got two hit albums on the charts. Enjoy your success!"

Everyone kept telling me that: "Enjoy your success." It was great, wasn't it? People worked decades to get to this point. So why, with all this great success, did I still feel like I couldn't do anything right? I couldn't seem to meet my own expectations, but I couldn't confess my feelings to anyone—they thought I had it all.

And I did, in a way. I'd gotten everything I wanted. I was emancipated, living on my own, out of school. My friends were envious. I was officially a star, with two Top Ten albums to my credit, but I still had no follow-up single to "Society's Child." MGM was concerned; my lack of care about whether I ever had another hit song didn't make sense to the company. But between the divorce, the touring, and just plain trying to grow up, I had my hands full.

And I was in love, which complicated things immeasurably. With a boy, no less.

Merka had come to visit the previous October, bringing a friend of hers from Wesleyan College. When I answered the door of my parents' apartment, Peter Cunningham smiled down at me. He wore jeans, and a work shirt with a yellow flowered tie, and he was clutching a small pumpkin. He handed the pumpkin to me as if it were a rose, then said, "Happy Halloween." I looked into the bluest eyes I'd ever seen. He was absolutely beautiful. We began seeing each other occasionally, and by January, I was in love.

For months, things had been falling apart around me. School ended in disaster. My parents were divorcing. People were sending me death threats. I was getting stomach cramps on the road; my doctor ran some tests and asked whether it was possible someone was poisoning my backstage meals. I didn't know how to speak about what was going on inside me, so I didn't try. I just kept turning my emotions off, and getting through the days. Everybody wanted something from me, all the time, and I had nothing left to give.

Peter was an oasis of stability. He was in college, like a normal person. A baseball enthusiast who'd grab dirt from the field when the Red Sox won, he was an athlete, too. He broke all the high-jump records with a stunning six feet four inches a day after he'd stayed up all night with me. He was cocaptain of the track team, and a pole vaulter to boot. He had a tall, rangy body, and eyes that reminded me of every summer's day I'd known. He was kind, and considerate. Best of all, he didn't seem to care that I was "Janis Ian." I got a dozen marriage proposals a month from strangers in love with my work. Peter was in love with *me*.

I called my father, now my legal guardian, and asked him to okay a prescription for birth control pills. I had no intention of getting pregnant, and wanted to make sure everything was covered before the question of "going all the way" came up. My father wasn't thrilled; we were barely speaking, and he had no idea what was going on in my life. When he objected, I told him I would get them one way or another, but life would be a lot easier if he'd just call the doctor.

Dad and Eric were still in our old apartment, and I wasn't real happy being next door to them, so I rented a room for two months at the cheap Lexington Avenue hotel Carol was living in for fifty-five dollars a week. There were a ton of addicts and prostitutes on the premises, renting rooms by the half hour, but it was relatively clean, and they didn't mind noise. We were starting to put my third album together, playing constantly as we worked out the arrangements. I'd tried to record it with Shadow earlier that year, but he was living up to his name. He'd disappeared.

I'd arrive at the studio to find the musicians and engineers playing cards, while they waited for the producer to show. I wasn't allowed to start without Shadow. The band had to be paid full rate every day they were booked, even though not a note was played. After a few weeks of watching them play cards, and my budget go down the drain, I postponed the project.

With the money that had been wasted, I had only enough left in my budget to hire one extra musician, so Carol and I didn't have any choice. We'd have to play everything but the drums ourselves. We hired a drummer and began recording. I lied to MGM, giving them the impression Carol was much older, with a lot of credits under her belt. I didn't feel like I was in any shape to make an album, but the bottom-line people at MGM wanted it for their third-quarter returns. Besides, what else did I have to do with my life? Everything I touched turned to dust.

There were bright spots. I went to the *Tribute to Woody Guthrie* at Carnegie Hall, and saw Dylan make his first appearance after his motorcycle accident. I remember it because Phil Ochs was there, too, very upset at not being invited to sing. It was a great lineup—Pete, Judy Collins, Arlo, Tom Paxton, Richie Havens, Odetta—but there's only so much room at any one show. Still, I could see how it galled Phil, and he walked out early. I felt a little funny sitting in the audience, too, but I was used to being on the outside. Phil wasn't.

I also finally got invited to Newport, via a personal letter of apology from Pete. It didn't quite make up for the hurt of the previous two years, but it helped to know he thought I should have been invited sooner.

On February 17, Carol and I went to the Anderson Theater to see Big Brother play their first New York show. Janis was thrilled; the place was packed, and people were passing bottles of Southern Comfort up to the stage for her to drink. Backstage after the show, she was glowing.

Joplin was as gracious as ever. She gave me a big hug, then put her hand out to shake Carol's, introducing herself by saying, "Hi. I'm the other Janis." I loved her for that.

We worked on the album in fits and starts, cadging time whenever we could. It slowly began to take shape, though the initial engineering was so poor that we had to bring Phil Ramone in to remix the entire thing.

A series of bizarre things happened that April. I went to the studio one day, and discovered the master tapes had been seized. Why, I don't know to this day, but someone had taken them away.

I freaked. Never mind divorce, school, my state of mind—this was my music! I went to Jean, wringing my hands and crying. I'd never dreamed anything could hurt so much. She finally got them back, a long while later, but the album was never the same to me.

On April 4, I went down to the Village to see B.B. King. He wasn't an icon yet; he was still playing some dive clubs. Jimi had introduced me to his music, and we made it a point to go see him together whenever possible. I loved that B.B. had named his guitar "Lucille." When he played it, he treated it like I imagined he'd treat a woman—gently, but with a lot of strength behind it.

B.B. was opening at the Generation Club for Big Brother & the Holding Company, so it was old home week before the show. Jimi finished his own gig early, and came to watch B.B.'s set with me. He was pretty pleased, because he'd bought the club just a little while earlier, intending to turn it into a studio. The two of us stood at the back of the room, slouched against a wall. The place was only half full, but somehow B.B.'s music always sounded better if you stood up.

At some point during the show, a man walked onstage and handed B.B. a note. B.B. read it, looked down at the floor for a while, then announced that Martin Luther King Jr. was now officially declared dead.

We stood in silence against the wall, watching as B.B. clutched Lucille in his arms. Time stopped. We'd been through Kennedy's assassination a scant five years before. That had been shocking enough. But Dr. King? Who would want to assassinate the most famous pacifist on earth?

B.B. began to play, rocking Lucille back and forth as he clutched her to his chest, and the guitar moaned as tears streamed down his face. Tears streamed down all our faces. With Kennedy, we had lost a president. With King, we'd lost a future.

I stayed at the club with Jimi until early morning, then made my way to Midtown for a meeting. It was funny, the way the world continued about its daily business in the face of such tragedy. People seemed a little more solemn than usual, but the good weather had finally arrived, and every so often I'd catch someone smiling or nodding as they scurried along.

Around ten that morning, business finished, I decided to walk home. I strolled casually up Sixth Avenue, checking out the store windows, taking my time. It was surprising how unfazed Manhattan was. In New York, no matter how bad things get, a few hours of great weather and everyone's happy again. Even "the suits" looked relaxed as they hustled to their day jobs. High heels made clicking sounds against the pavement, beating out a staccato rhythm that jangled in my ears. We were miles away from the riots beginning to fester all over the country.

There were a couple of bongo players on the corner of Fifty-second Street, so I stopped to put a dollar in the hat. A block later, I stepped under a hotel awning and collided heavily with a large, florid man who knocked me to the ground. I remember thinking as he approached that he was dressed too warmly for the weather; his tie was unknotted, and his face was red from the heat. I expected him to move out of the way, but he made a beeline for me and we crashed.

I thudded to the sidewalk and lay there for a minute, dazed, as he hurried off. When I opened my eyes, I could see pedestrians carefully stepping around me. I'd landed so hard that I couldn't catch my breath.

The mass of humanity just rolled right by, no one pausing to give me a second glance. *They probably think I'm stoned,* I thought.

I pulled myself up to a sitting position just as a thin man in a lightweight suit stopped and put out his hand. He helped me over to a corner of the hotel entryway, and I sat down again, propped against a wall. He reassured me, saying something like, "You're fine, kid. You just had the wind knocked out of you. Nothing broken." I thanked him for the help, and he handed me an open bottle of Coke, saying, "Here, take this. I just opened it, haven't even had a sip. It'll raise your blood sugar, get you back to normal in no time." And with that, he walked away.

I sat for a few more minutes, nursing my bruised butt against the hard pavement and sipping on the Coke. It was way too sweet, so after a while I rose and threw most of it away. I started back uptown, still feeling a little wobbly, but grateful I hadn't broken anything.

A block or two later, I started feeling even shakier. For some reason, I wasn't seeing well. The air was shimmering; I could see dust motes floating down from the sky above. Then the streetlights came on, one after the other, like dominoes, which didn't make any sense because it was still daytime. But I could see them glowing, could feel the heat from them hitting the top of my head.

I stopped and leaned against a wall, staring at the road. The asphalt looked like it was starting to bubble. I raised my eyes to look across the street. I could just make out the revolving door of an office building. The windows above it were glaring at me, gaping and malevolent.

I'd been dosed. If I'd drunk the entire bottle, I might never have come back.

I looked down at the ground again, trying to get oriented. There were cracks in the sidewalk, and they were starting to catch fire. Little flames danced around me, sucking at my pants legs, but I felt no heat from them. A car began sinking into the road as molten lava bubbled and burst all around it. A nearby fire hydrant exploded into flames.

Buildings were melting all around me. People's faces were liquefying, running like open sores into the street. It was horrendous.

I pressed back against the wall, trying to fall through it and escape to some other place. It was hard to think. It was hard to not think. I wondered why I couldn't hear people screaming as they and their cars got sucked into the abyss.

My shoulders pressed against the bricks. My eyelids were propped open.

The whole world was drenched in blood. It was pouring from my eyes. It was pouring from my ears. It was gushing from my pores, until I couldn't see for the metallic red surrounding me. It went on forever.

Then, abruptly, the scene shifted. The fires went out, and the blood seeped into the gutters. The cars became cartoon figures, running up the avenue on little centipede legs. They busily exchanged information with the feelers coming out of their headlights. They chittered in loud, high voices, while the voices of people around me slowed down, deepened, sped up, like a tape recorder run amok.

I heard someone laughing, and realized it was me. I looked down at my arms and saw that my hands were on fire. I watched in astonishment as the flesh melted away and only charred bones remained.

Through it all, I kept thinking, *I have to get to Carol's. I have to get to Carol's. She'll know what to do.* So I started walking, in a direction I hoped was uptown. I stopped at every corner, not sure whether the light was actually red or green, and didn't step off the curb until the people around me began moving. A few times, I sat down on a bench or sill and closed my eyes, but that made it even worse.

At one point, a policeman stopped me and asked if I was all right. I looked at him uncertainly, unable to tell whether he was real or not. Then I turned and kept walking. With each step I took, time slowed and expanded, until I felt like I was wading in water over my head. I had no idea how I continued to breathe; it was a miracle.

By the time I arrived at Carol's apartment, I was completely incoherent. It should have taken an hour or two to walk there, but I arrived after dark. I couldn't tell her what was going on; I just stood at the door, eyes unfocused, until she took me by the hand and pulled me into the kitchen. She made me a cup of egg drop soup, and I sat on a mattress and sipped at it, telling myself it was just eggs swimming around in the cup, not wriggling worms. I finally went to sleep, and fell into a nightmare that found me alternately dozing and screaming, yelling things that made no sense, and trying to break out of my body. To where, I don't know.

Peter came down from Wesleyan, and someone must have called my dad, because I remember him trying to get into the room. Peter barred the door with his body, yelling, "This is all *your* fault!" Everyone thought I'd finally cracked under the stress of my career, the divorce, the tapes being taken.

After three or four days, I calmed down enough to speak a little, and Carol told me Dad insisted I be taken to a psychiatrist he'd found. She'd wanted to take me to a therapist she knew in Philadelphia, but my father said I was a minor, and no matter what anyone wanted, he was still my legal guardian. If she took me out of state before I was cleared by the psychiatrist, there'd be hell to pay.

She made the appointment.

I was still hallucinating on and off, so Carol took my arm as we walked into his office, making sure I sat on the chair and not the empty air. I remember thinking to myself that this was all nonsense. I disliked him on sight; he was an ugly little man seated behind an absurdly big desk, diplomas hanging everywhere on the wall behind. I stared at his bald head while Carol described what had happened as best she could, and I wondered whether he had a wife who loved him. Unlikely, I decided. He was much too awful-looking.

When Carol finished, he put down his pen and asked me what I saw. Still staring, I said, "A turnip. You look like a turnip." Which was pretty accurate, but also weird enough to convince him to put me on something called Stelazine. I didn't realize it then, but Stelazine was the drug of choice for bringing someone down from a bad acid trip. I took it, and *voilà*! Just like that, in a few hours, I was my old self again.

Except I wasn't. Not just emotionally, but physically. The doctor had forgotten to tell us that the drug's effects were cumulative, and would quickly cause something called tardive dyskinesia. I took the Stelazine for about a week while I remained with Carol, who made sure I took the pills as prescribed throughout the day. By the time we left town for Philly, the drug was having its secondary effects. My tongue was thick. I was drooling. I couldn't keep my head from lolling around. I must have looked like a complete idiot when we walked into the shrink's office. He took one look, pulled out some serum, and gave me a shot. Five minutes later, all the symptoms went away.

He asked what had happened, but I couldn't really tell him. Between the Stelazine and my psyche's desperate efforts to protect me, the entire scenario had become sketchy. I knew I'd been dosed, but I also knew that in my business, plenty of gossips would prefer to think I'd just lost my mind. "Too much too soon," and all that. No one would hire me if I seemed unstable. So I kept silent, and told everyone I was fine, just fine.

The doctor told me he'd like to do a follow-up, so I arranged to return and take a battery of psychological tests from his partner. My father was horrified. People like us didn't seek psychological help. People like us got through, whatever the cost. We toughed it out. Hadn't he just done that with my mom? What was wrong with me, that I needed to talk to a stranger about my problems?

Once they found out I was over my mysterious illness, the world descended again. The record company needed an album cover to make their release date. The agency needed decisions about touring to publicize the album. Jean needed to make sure I was ready to go back to work. Dad suddenly decided to get involved in my life, and he thought if I was crazy enough to seek professional care, I should probably be institutionalized for a while. He began making noises about doing just that.

Carol, sticking to my side like a shadow, took one look at the lunacy going on around me and thought, *These people are crazy. I've got to get her out of here.* So she booked two flights to Bermuda, and made a reservation at a shabby cottage with two tiny bedrooms behind someone's main house.

The night before departure, Carol and I went back to the Generation Club. Jimi had started construction, and cables and studio equipment were everywhere. There were enough instruments to open a shop, including a nice Hammond B-3. I made myself at home in front of it, while Carol grabbed a bass guitar. We sat around what would become Electric Ladyland and jammed for hours. At the end, Jimi invited Carol back to his place, and in one of the biggest sacrifices of her life, she said no, we had a plane to catch.

Bermuda was fantastic. No telephones, just ocean and sand and time to relax. We rode mopeds, ate seafood, rested, and read. I started feeling guilty toward the end; I'd let a lot of people down, and I wanted to make it up to them. So I returned to New York determined to "get my act together" and work my butt off.

I finished up six songs for the score to a short film by Paul Leaf called *Sunday Father,* starring Dustin Hoffman, then got busy remixing the new album, *The Secret Life of J. Eddy Fink,* for its release in July. I had a full tour schedule over the summer and fall to promote it, and was also slated to produce an album for my friend Andy Robinson in November. Right after that, I was committed to scoring a movie called *Four Rode Out,* which would necessitate going to Spain for a few weeks. My time was spoken for, right up until Christmas. That was good. It left me no time to feel.

Because feeling was bad. Feeling just bought trouble. I could see that every single day of my life.

At some point, muddled with fatigue after a bunch of shows, I came home to New York and wanted to make a connection with my family. I dropped my suitcase in the studio apartment and went next door, expecting to find Dad and Eric. I knocked, hoping I could join them for dinner. No answer. I went back to my studio for a key, and tried to open the door. It didn't work.

I went downstairs to the superintendent and told him the lock was broken. My key didn't work. He looked at me quizzically, then said, "They moved. Your dad and brother, they moved to a smaller apartment downstairs. Didn't he tell you?"

Tell me? Why should my father bother telling me he'd moved? Why should he still consider me part of the family? It would never occur to him that I might need him, might want to put my head on his shoulder, feel his arms around me, and weep with exhaustion.

It made me feel bad, but I told myself he was just busy. He probably thought Eric had told me. No use crying over spilled milk. I repacked my suitcase and left a few days later for more touring.

July 27 found me walking into the dining room of the performer's hotel at Newport. I went down to breakfast feeling a little apprehensive, because most of the other performers were strangers to me. Still, even though I'd been shunned by some folkies in New York, I reasoned it would be different now. "Society's Child" had come and gone. I was recording my third album; I was a bona fide member of the community. Surely no one still held my age or success against me?

Thinking hard, I barely noticed where I was going. The buzz of conversation was loud; the place was packed with performers and crew. Grabbing a tray, I stood at the breakfast bar with my back to the room and filled it with food. The room grew silent, and I could feel eyes on my back. I slowly turned around, searching for a friendly face. There were none. One by one, every performer I could see turned away from me, deliberately avoiding my eyes.

I went beet-red with shame. Here I was, at the pinnacle of my dreams, and I was being treated like a pariah. In front of everyone. I squared my shoulders, decided to take the tray up to my room, and began walking toward the door.

Suddenly someone grabbed me from behind. I whirled around,

ready for a fight, and saw Joan Baez. Her face was wreathed in a huge smile. She slung an arm over my shoulder and walked me to her own table, saying, "Oh, Janis! I really want you to meet my mother, Big Joan. We adore you!"

No one dared to mess with me after that.

I went home the day after my main stage performance to play the Village Theater with Jake Holmes. The next morning, I woke feeling lost. A few weeks earlier, I'd begun having pretty bad flashbacks. I could never tell when they'd hit, onstage, in the hotel room, at dinner. They were short, but vivid, and after a while I just treated them like a free movie someone was running in my head. Still, it was disorienting, and I was having nightmares again. It was better on the road, where I constantly had things to occupy me, but once I got home it was rough.

Dad and Eric were at camp, and I was abruptly consumed with an urge to see them and my old friends. I wanted the reassurance of familiar faces, people who'd known me before I had a career. People who'd take care of me. I hailed a taxi and asked the cabbie to take me upstate to Wingdale, New York. "That's gonna cost you two hundred bucks," he said. Fine. I had the money. He made me show it to him before he'd start driving.

I got to camp and went looking for my family. Someone told me Dad was in town, having dinner with a bunch of people. I got a ride to the restaurant and walked in, grinning, expecting to be greeted like a returning hero. Dad hadn't seen me in months. I was sure he'd be thrilled.

Instead, he turned gray as I approached the table. Then he looked embarrassed. Finally, he rose to greet me, saying, "Jan! Jan . . . what on earth are you doing here?!" I stopped in my tracks, afraid to reach for him. Who was this stranger?

I didn't know what everyone else knew, that he was having an affair with someone just a couple of years older than me, and she was sitting beside him. I found out a day or two later, when one of my old counselors decided to fill me in. I left as soon as possible after that, and went back on the road.

Like I said, feelings just bought trouble.

While I was busy touring, Peter was finalizing the details on our first apartment. Mort Schuman, who along with Doc Pomus had written songs like "This Magic Moment" and "Save the Last Dance for Me," was moving to France to write *Jacques Brel Is Alive and Well and Living in Paris*. He wanted to sublet his apartment. It was perfect, a venerable old building on the corner of Seventy-second Street and Riverside Drive. The price was right. Best of all, it was fully furnished, with a baby grand and room for a pool table in the living room. When I got back to New York, we moved in.

I had a standing invitation to do *The Joey Bishop Show*, so Jean and I flew to Los Angeles to publicize the upcoming album. The other guest was Gypsy Rose Lee, and I got my first taste of what being completely upstaged felt like. Gypsy was an ex-stripper, flamboyantly energetic, and always center stage. She was first up, charming her way through the interview and making the audience guffaw with laughter. I came on next, sang my song, then walked over to the dais where they sat. Gypsy immediately stood up to hug me, managing to get my back turned to the cameras, while her face looked over my shoulder at the TV audience. As we sat down, she mentioned her grandchildren and how much I reminded her of them. I politely said, "Oh, you have grandchildren?" She pulled out a scrapbook and spent the rest of my segment showing us their photographs, talking about her life with them.

I didn't understand I'd been upstaged until after the show, when Jean said, "Well. That was interesting. . . ." and explained it to me. She was annoyed at my naiveté, and somewhat contemptuous. Coming from the British theatrical tradition, she expected me to pay attention to things like how I walked and stood, to make sure I was visible in group photographs, and to claim my stage time as my own. She saw it as a competition, the way Gypsy did. I had a hard time feeling that viscerally. To me, it was about music. People liked mine, or they didn't. Everything else was secondary, including me.

It drove Jean crazy that I wouldn't wear makeup unless I was performing. "Marlene Dietrich spends more time putting on makeup to greet her fans after the show than she spends putting it on for the show!" she'd fume. I'd shrug and mumble that, much as I admired her, Dietrich was nine hundred years old, and probably enjoyed putting on a mask.

Back home, Peter's friend Steve Rudy was staying with us. A brilliant Russian scholar, he eventually went to Harvard, until they ran out of courses and sent him to MIT. When they, too, ran out of courses, they sent him to Russia to study. Now he was back home, with amazing wooden icons tipped with gold that he'd smuggled out of the country, trading pairs of Levi's for them.

We were having a great time. We'd all started smoking pot, and we'd sit around stoned out of our minds while Steve recited Russian poetry and read Dostoyevsky aloud to us. We had a little parrot, and once we spent four or five hours chanting "God's in the tree trunks" at him, trying to raise his consciousness.

Perhaps it sounds like we were doing a lot of drugs. We were, make no mistake. But drugs were different then. You could smoke an entire joint and just be high enough to get happy. There was no PCP to lace them with yet. And we confined ourselves to marijuana and hash, although once in a while something else snuck past.

Out in California, Peter and I had met Stanley Owsley, a chemist who was the first to produce LSD in massive amounts. Neither of us had any interest in acid—in fact, it scared me to death. So we declined, politely, and Owsley said, "Wait! I've got something even cooler!" and slipped a few pills into our hands. "This is THC, short for tetrahydrocannabinol, the main ingredient in pot. You can take it on a plane without getting busted; it's legal!"

On the flight back to New York, we each took a tablet, Peter washing his down a few moments before me. After a little while, absorbed in

a book, I vaguely heard him say, "Wow . . . wow." I turned. He was staring out the window. I couldn't tell what he was seeing until a moment
later, when the sky lit up with an aurora borealis. I, too, was reduced to
saying, "Wow . . . wow."

To this day, I don't know if it was real.

I clung to Peter like a lifeboat. The world was changing, too fast for
me to keep up. King was dead. Bobby Kennedy had been assassinated.
Dr. Benjamin Spock was convicted of conspiracy to abet draft evasion.
There were half a million troops in Vietnam, and the Chicago Democratic Convention saw my friends mauled and beaten by rioting police,
in full view of the national networks. Nixon and Agnew were running
for the presidency, and I thought they'd probably win. Every hero I'd
had was dead.

The war on drugs dried up the borders, and there was next to no
marijuana in the five boroughs. The Mafia moved in with heroin, and
normal people my age, not in the music business, not on the fringes,
started dying. It seemed like death was all around me, so I turned to
music. I was working on songs for my next album, but I hated what I
was writing, and I couldn't seem to break out of the rut.

I grew tired of ads that said, "Live In Concert—Society's Child!" followed by my name in smaller print. I got tired of promoters patting me
on the head and telling me I was a nice kid. It was absurd; I was out there,
making three to five grand a night, but I was too young to rent a car or
make a plane reservation. I was seventeen now. I lived with a man, I ran
a business, but the world still treated me like a child. I was sick of it.

My agent, David Geffen, wanted me to meet some local people closer
to my own age. He was also representing Laura Nyro, and he arranged
an evening out for the three of us. We spent most of it in his limousine,
riding around downtown and smoking pot. I invited Laura to dinner at
our new apartment, promising to cook. On September 24, I opened the
door to see her standing there, clutching a portable television.

"Laura, we have a television here," I said. She explained that her friend Peggy Lipton was starring in a new show called *The Mod Squad*, premiering that night, and she didn't want to miss it. So we watched TV through dinner, smoked some dope, and made our good-byes.

I'd known Laura vaguely from Music & Art, where she was two years ahead of me and had a reputation for being weird. You could hear her coming; she wore a long coat that clanked as the Cheracol bottles hidden in her pockets collided. She'd sip from them throughout the day, her eyes getting duller by the hour. In her bright red lipstick and long black dresses, she looked like a caricature of Morticia Addams, with bigger hips. But she was an amazing songwriter, and I really respected her. In fact, for my next album I'd deliberately chosen Charlie Callelo as producer, based on his work with Laura.

Still, she was strange, and oddly inarticulate for a songwriter. Charlie once called me in a panic and asked me to rush down to a session they were doing. Laura was having hysterics because the band couldn't play what she wanted. I arrived to see Charlie walking out of the studio with Laura slung over his shoulder. She was kicking and screaming and crying with frustration. After we got her calmed down, I asked what she wanted the song to sound like. She looked around the room, pointed to a purple chair, and told me, "Like that. I want it to sound like *that*."

I walked back into the studio, looked at the chart, and told the musicians, "She wants it *legato*. A deep, mysterious *legato*. Not quite *largo*, but *legato*." They got it on the next take, and congratulated me on my translation skills.

After finishing the record, I headed to Spain to score the film *Four Rode Out*. Jean sent her secretary, Frankie, along as my chaperone. Before departing, I hollowed out a tube of Max Factor pancake makeup and dropped some THC in it. I can't believe, now, how stupid that was—I could have gone to prison and still been there today. It's amazing how invulnerable you feel when you're young.

Spain was different. We stayed at the tallest building in Madrid, the Torre de Madrid (Tower of Madrid). It was six stories high. The only words I could remember from Spanish class were *hamo y caso con lechuga y mayonnaisa,* so every day for lunch, I went to the store across the street and had ham and cheese with lettuce and mayonnaise. After lunch, I'd meet with the director, John Peyser, and discuss the score, watching a rough cut of the film through the Moviola projector. I took notes on timing, and started working on guitar parts.

I'd packed the clothing I normally wore, jeans and tights and paisley shirts. One day I went for a walk by myself, without Frankie. She was a conservative dresser, and the locals had probably assumed I was a lunatic on leave from the asylum when they saw us together. Alone, it was a different story. I passed a school letting out for recess, and was quickly surrounded by uniformed children who pointed at my pants, laughing and shouting. The nuns accompanying them glared at me, then made the sign of the cross over their chests. I looked around. All the men were in suits. All the women were in dresses. I was the only female in pants. The children shrieked and hooted until a nun dragged them away.

Peyser introduced me to a lovely young man named Tito del Amo. Four years older than me, his family was amazingly wealthy. For his twenty-first birthday, his brothers had bought him a custom-made Lamborghini. He thought he was dating me, although I didn't realize it at the time, and because of him I actually got to see a bit of the country. Tito took me to a restaurant on the coast, which he said had been built by a top-ranking Nazi's wife after the Second World War ended. The officer had told his wife he didn't think they'd win, handed her a suitcase with a million dollars in it, and told her to build the best restaurant in Spain. Which she did; it was fabulous. We sat in red velvet chairs shaped like thrones. A butler stood behind each chair. Every time I reached for a cigarette, the lighter was in my face before I got it to my mouth. We ate roast suckling pig and admired the view.

I'd never been out of America, and it was strange to be in a Fascist country. I'd paid lip service to my generation's beliefs, saying America was Fascist, but this was the real deal. You couldn't criticize the government; you might be picked up and taken to jail, or even disappear completely. People paused by pictures and statues of the dictator, Franco, and bowed their heads as a sign of respect in case anyone was watching. Everyone had to be on guard, all the time. Tito and his brothers published an underground newspaper, the only one in Madrid. When I made the mistake of saying something about it in a restaurant, he quickly clapped a hand over my mouth and hustled us away.

Tito invited me to see "real" flamenco, and we spent an evening in a tiny cellar room crowded with people and flowers. I'd always thought flamenco dancers were young, beautiful women, accompanied by dashingly virile men who gazed at them with adoration while playing at supersonic speeds. The man who took the stage was venerably aged, with the pounds to match. He settled his carcass into the chair and began playing, never looking away from the guitar strings.

In a minute or two, a middle-aged woman with room to spare walked onstage, shot a contemptuous look at the audience, then began to dance. Just at that moment, my allergies hit. I tried to stifle the sneeze, but it echoed around the room like a shot. The guitar continued, and the dancer stared into my eyes with an intensity that made me understand what a mouse feels when it's cornered by a cobra. Still dancing, she moved downstage, until she was right in front of our table. She snorted, smiled, and spit on my plate.

Spit appeared to be one of the few constants in my life.

When Tito finally asked me to go to bed with him, I realized my mistake. Naive as I was, I'd never really dated anyone. By the time I was old enough, I was famous, and the boys were scared to ask me out. I explained my commitment to Peter as politely as I could, and he shook his head, laughing at my naiveté. Tito continued to be kind, giving me an advance copy of the Beatles' *White Album* when I left.

I started realizing how much freedom I had in America. There was a saying in Spain: "Franco never dies. They keep him in a bottle and take him out for parades." The dictator tried to put himself on a par with God, all-seeing and all-powerful. His face was on every coin, every stamp—it glared back at you as though it disapproved of the money you were spending to send a letter. Books were ridiculously high-priced, so only the wealthy could learn. Side by side with Franco, the Church ruled with an iron hand. No birth control. No divorce. It was awful.

I came back to New York convinced I lived in the best of all possible worlds.

To CELEBRATE our new apartment, Peter and I decided to throw a Christmas party. Dad was supposed to come, and it was really important to me. I hadn't seen him in a while; he was secretive and elusive when I spoke with him on the phone. We were going to hold the party a week before Christmas, because I was slated to perform over the holiday season. I phoned my father the day before to make sure he'd be there, and he assured me he would.

The party came and went. I checked the hallway every half hour, hoping to catch a glimpse of him, but he was nowhere to be found. I was distraught. Maybe there'd been an accident. At about midnight, long after everyone had gone home, I phoned Jean to say I was going to call the police. She told me not to, that my dad was fine. *What do you mean, fine? I asked. How do you know?* She confessed he'd told her he was leaving town, and made her promise not to tell me when or where.

To say I felt betrayed would be an understatement. For months after, I had no idea that he'd moved to California. For years, I didn't know that his girlfriend Natasha's father had met him with a shotgun and told him to get out of her life. That he'd fled as far as he could go without crossing the ocean, and was trying to pull himself together. All I knew was that, once again, he'd deserted me.

I played the Bitter End that Christmas, selling out every show in advance. The dressing room radiator was broken, and the club manager said he couldn't afford to have it fixed. I asked him to buy a space heater, but he was worried about the electrical cost. So show after show, drenched in sweat, I'd make my way from the scorching stage through the overheated club and into a freezing dressing room, where I'd towel down and change as quickly as possible. One night Odetta came to see me and said, "Child, you'll catch your death in here!" She wasn't far from wrong.

I started feeling sick about three days into the two-week run. By day four, I had what I thought was a terrible cold, with a touch of bronchitis. Peter worried over me, but there was little he could do. The show must go on.

Day five was a Sunday, and my doctor wasn't in the office on Mondays. I made an appointment for Tuesday, did my sets, got home, and collapsed in a slumber so deep that I couldn't be roused. Peter called the doctor Tuesday morning, and he made a house call. His immediate diagnosis was severe double pneumonia.

By then I was running a fever so high that the doctor didn't want to risk moving me to a hospital. He gave me a shot, and gave Peter a bunch of prescriptions. For the next few days, they waited for the fever to break, feeding me antibiotics whenever I could be roused enough to take them, or giving me shots when I couldn't. The high fever wouldn't go down, and my breathing became so raspy that the doctor talked about bringing in a full-time nurse and an oxygen tent. I was exhausted from the road and my life in general; I didn't have enough reserves left to put up a fight. And I didn't care. It was nice, just laying there in a daze, looking out the windows at the January sky.

Along with the apartment, we'd inherited a once-a-week cleaning lady; it was a condition of the sublet. She'd been a wealthy woman in Paris who'd collaborated with the Nazis. After the war, she escaped to Argentina. How she'd ended up in New York was a mystery. Her

English was fractured, and she was so belligerent that she scared us. Mort had said, "You pay Susie fifteen dollars a day, plus a steak and a beer. Don't forget the steak and beer!" I didn't realize it then, but that was her only meal of the day.

Susie came into our bedroom that week to find me comatose under the covers, radiator blasting, windows shut to keep out the frigid Hudson River winds. She muttered something in French at Peter and turned off the radiator. Then she walked over to the windows, opened all of them, and piled every blanket she could find on top of me. I was too far gone to care, and I think Peter felt like any change would be better than none.

She stalked into the kitchen and returned with a noxious preparation of whiskey, raw eggs, and a few unidentifiable additions that smelled like red pepper and garlic. Hauling me up to a sitting position, she tried to get me to drink it. When I refused, she squeezed my nose shut with one hand until I had to open my mouth to breathe, then forced it down me. About an hour later, the fever broke, and I started getting well.

"Well" being a relative term. The events of the past few years were catching up. I felt like I had no control over my life. The ups and downs were killing me; there seemed to be nothing in between. The flashbacks had receded, but so had my ability to concentrate on anything. I couldn't remember the last time I'd really enjoyed myself without being stoned. Worst of all, I wasn't writing well. All my life, I'd protected my music. Before I protected myself, I protected my music. Now, even that was gone.

I'd been seeing Gerry Weiss, a Philadelphia therapist, every few weeks, and I was starting to confront things like my folks' divorce and my own career. Gerry kept saying I had to make a real commitment to therapy, and that didn't mean seeing him once in a while when I couldn't stand my life anymore. I didn't want to do that. I just wanted everything around me to stop hurting. Since the world refused to change, I stayed stoned.

I never smoked anything when I was working, though. And I was working a lot. Once I recovered from pneumonia, it seemed like there wasn't time to turn around. Jean and my agents kept me booked up; I made my fourth album between concert dates. Callelo was a terrific producer, and we worked closely together on the song choices. I was very pleased with it when we finished, but couldn't think of a title. I mused aloud for days, until Peter finally lost patience and said, "Janis. What does it matter? Titles don't sell records. Who really cares?" I had my title: *Who Really Cares*.

Peter brought home a book by James Ramsey Ullman called *The Day on Fire,* and it changed my life. A fictionalized account of the life of poet Arthur Rimbaud, it turned my world upside down. Overnight, I became steeped in the mysteries of being an artist. I'd never given it much thought before. I wrote songs, I sang them, I made a living.

Rimbaud saw it differently. To be an artist in his eyes meant making a lifetime commitment to being an artist first. Before you were a wife, before you were a mother, before you were even a human being, you were an artist.

The opening lines of one of his poems sit before me even now, hovering on the wall over my desk:

My eternal soul
Redeem your promise
in spite of the night alone
and the day on fire

I'd finally connected. Someone else felt like I did. Someone else had been an outsider, had tried to fit in, and had failed. Someone else gave words to my feelings, made me aware that out of such torment could come great art. And what a concept, that the artist must remake himself daily, and redefine himself in every waking moment! What a notion, that words had colors, feelings of their own!

I immersed myself in Rimbaud's poetry. The way he played with language fascinated me. The way he'd return to a theme using different metaphors, different visualizations, gave me a motif I could embrace. I began writing songs with the hope of attaining at least a tiny bit of his majesty, but I hated everything I wrote.

I knew something was wrong with me, and in conversations with Gerry, I slowly realized that I'd have to make some major changes if I was ever going to be the person I wanted to be. To be the *artist* I wanted to be. Because being just a person wasn't enough after reading Rimbaud, not by a long shot.

I'd had a lot of success, particularly for someone my age, but it might have been a fluke. Most of the world seemed to think so. Nothing had been as big as my very first record. I no longer had the edge of being a wunderkind. MGM didn't seem very interested in me; even though *Who Really Cares* was the most commercial album I'd made, there'd been little or no promotion. And to be fair, I wasn't much help in that regard.

Rimbaud led me to other poets, and they in turn led me to novelists. I realized that I didn't know anything about literature; I just knew music. That wasn't enough to become what I wanted to become. I felt abysmally ignorant. The more I thought about it, the more I saw that I knew only a couple of things for sure.

One, I was not a great songwriter. Yet. I might never be. I might just keep cranking out albums to make everyone else a living, while my songwriting went down the drain. What was the point of being a songwriter if I couldn't be great? Might as well just be a veterinarian, like I'd originally planned.

Two, something was terribly wrong with me. Something bone deep.

My brains felt like they'd been seeping out of my skull for months. I had flashbacks. I couldn't connect.

Everyone else remembered their childhoods; I just remembered a few scattered frames. Everyone else had feelings that showed on their faces; mine only showed in my voice.

Most of all, everyone else laughed. I'd forgotten how.

SIX

Jesse

And I'm leaving the light on the stairs
No, I'm not scared
I wait for you
Hey Jesse, I'm lonely. Come home

We moved to Philadelphia that August, settling in a garden apartment close to Gerry's home. He'd tried to see me at the office, but every time anyone walked in the waiting room and saw me, it became a mess. I might not be famous to MGM, or myself, but I was still recognizable. Sometimes his other patients would ask for an autograph. Sometimes they'd demand one. Sometimes they'd get in my face and sneer, saying, "Bet you don't feel like a big star now, do you?!" I couldn't fight back; it was all I could do to make myself sit there and wait.

He ran a battery of tests, and when I asked what he'd found, he said, "You don't trust anyone. You're scared of everyone. There's a whole lot going on that you keep hidden. You've done a great job of locking up your feelings, but it's time to let them out."

I don't know that any of us knew just how badly damaged I was, but as the months passed, therapy became a descent into hell. Feelings I never knew existed came rushing up, only to be squashed as quickly as I could get rid of them. I had no mooring besides Peter, who remained patient and loving as I tested him in every possible way.

I bailed on a project to produce my best friend, Janey, and her singing partner, Dennis. I bailed on my tour dates. I bailed on my recording schedule. I walked away from everything. I refused to speak with my family. I refused to speak with Jean. All I wanted to do was hide, and all Gerry wanted me to do was to come out of hiding and be real.

How could I be real? I didn't know what *real* was. I'd thought my family was real, but they weren't. I'd thought my career was real, but it wasn't. The more I thought about things, the more I talked about things, the more confused I got.

I began smoking more dope, keeping myself in a dulled state where nothing mattered. I could sit and watch *Star Trek* all day long, while Peter took photography classes and worked in his darkroom. That got boring after a while, so I took an overdose of Seconal. I didn't take enough, so I tried a second time. Peter came home unexpectedly and rushed me to the hospital, where they pumped my stomach out and sent me home.

I didn't want to die. I didn't even think about dying. I just wanted everything to stop for a while, wanted *myself* to stop for a while. My head was too busy, and nothing seemed to slow it down. I wanted to sleep a long time, so that when I woke up again, everything would be different.

But it didn't work. I was a complete fuck-up. I couldn't even commit suicide right.

Gerry wouldn't give up, even though I told him and told him to just cut me loose. He continued to push, to demand I remember things I'd rather not confront, to talk about them through the waves of silence running through me. He wanted me to feel whatever I felt about them, even when I said I felt nothing.

He told me I had no "affect," that what I felt didn't show on my face.

I told him it didn't show in my heart, either. I explained that I had no affect because I had no feelings. I knew other people had feelings, had facial expressions that reflected them. Sometimes I could even tell what people felt from looking at their faces. I knew other people laughed, and cried, but I didn't. Everyone but me seemed to have those things, so, obviously, nothing was wrong with them. Something was wrong with me. I told him I probably wasn't even human, and asked him to just put me out of my misery.

He told me I was human. He told me it would change, that it *could* change. He broke all the rules for me. Some days, I'd spend the entire session sitting in his lap, and he'd hold me and rock me back and forth while I wept unshed tears and tried to stay grown-up and strong. He'd tell me I had to let myself feel, no matter how painful it was, and he promised that when I reached the other side of the pain, life would be good.

I didn't believe a word of it.

Nevertheless, the feelings were building up, and the more they built up, the more I denied them. I was living on spaghetti and Hunt's tomato sauce, drinking a six-pack of Coca-Cola each day. I didn't care. Nothing tasted good, anyhow.

I began cutting my arms with Peter's shaving blades. When Gerry asked why, I told him I wanted some visible proof that I'd lost my mind. When he asked again, I said it was a blood sacrifice. He told Peter to hide all the knives and razor blades.

My head felt like it was filled with shards of glass that clanked every time I tried to think. My brain felt like a desert floor. Broken crystals lay scattered everywhere, rubbing up against each other if I moved. A lot of the time, I just sat still, watching the flashbacks running in my head. When I wasn't doing that, I'd impersonate a human being, and hope no one noticed how poor a job I was doing.

That January of 1970, I ran away from home. I didn't know why. I just knew I had to get out. I slipped through the door in jeans and sneakers and an old shirt. It was just starting to snow as I walked to the train station, where I pulled out enough money to get me to center Philadelphia. By the time I arrived, the snow was coming down in earnest, so I walked to the only safe haven I could think of: the library.

I'd brought a little notepad and a pen, and I passed the day journaling and jotting down scraps of verses and song ideas. It seemed very peaceful to me, sitting at a big table looking out the window at the falling snow. It was so still in the reading room. My head was silent for the first time in months.

The library closed, and I tucked the pad into a pocket and made my way to the street. I was hungry, so I stopped at a diner to order a bowl of soup, then found myself a quarter short of the price. A man sitting next to me, seeing that I wore no jacket, probably thought I was homeless, and told the counterman he'd pick up the slack. He said something funny, and I laughed, which surprised me. The laugh wasn't pretty; it was the laughter of someone who hasn't laughed in years. But it was laughter.

I'd been feeling really good at the library. I'd forgotten about Peter, frantic with worry and ready to call the police to report me missing. I'd forgotten about Gerry, trying to concentrate on his other patients and stopping every fifteen minutes to check on whether I'd come home yet. I just remembered, for the first time in more than a year, what it felt like to be at peace with myself.

When I walked out of the diner there was snow coming down everywhere, and for some reason my body was feeling the cold. I stood a minute, bewildered, trying to remember where I'd been going. Ah. Gerry's office was somewhere around here. He'd give me a ride home. It seemed like a good plan, but when I reached the office, it was locked and closed. I walked back into the street, strolling toward the car park. Maybe Gerry would still be there.

I spied Gerry's car just as he spied me, and the passenger door opened. I slid in, shivering, and turned to thank him. He was weeping.

Tears were pouring down his face as he grabbed me in a fierce embrace, saying, "You're alive, Janis. You're alive. Oh, thank God, you're alive."

I was baffled. Of course I was alive. If I'd wanted to kill myself, I'd have done it at home.

But he was crying, and that was mystifying. Why would he cry over me? I wasn't important to anyone, not really. I wasn't even a good writer. My father knew I wasn't worth anything; he didn't even think to tell me when he moved. My mother knew I was worthless. I hadn't spoken more than a couple of sentences to her in the longest time; she'd never forgive me. Peter knew I was useless; all I did was mess up his life. Why on earth would anyone cry over me?

And it slowly dawned on me, in the car as we rode toward Gerry's home, that he cried over me because he loved me.

We walked into the house and he asked his wife, Maureen, to make me a bowl of soup. His son, Randy, younger than me and a much better guitarist, sat and told me about his day at school, and a blues singer he'd discovered. Gerry called Peter and told him I was all right, but he'd keep me at his house for the night. Maureen found me some pajamas and I took a hot bath, then stretched out on the couch downstairs while Gerry got a blanket and tucked me in.

The next morning, he sat on the edge of the bed and spooned some cereal into my mouth. Then he took my hands and said, "Look, kid. Let me explain. I'm not going to let you die. I'm just not. But you persist. You're very thorough, and Peter can't be there all the time. Sooner or later, you're going to succeed. I'm not going to let that happen.

"So here's what I'm going to do the next time you act crazy. I'm going to put you in a mental hospital. In a private room. With no guitar. No paper. No pens. No piano. I'm going to put you in the room, and I'll see you once a day. Otherwise, you'll just sit there. No music. No nothing. Got it?"

I looked at him, sure he was joking. He looked back at me and didn't smile. Oh, shit! Maybe he meant it. I couldn't live without any music, without a pen at hand. I'd lose my mind, I really would.

That was the turning point. Somewhere in that moment, I decided to try to get well.

I stayed at Gerry's most of the day, curled up on the couch. When Randy got home from school, I asked him for a favor. He said, "Sure, what is it?"

Teach me to laugh, I said. *You have a great laugh. Teach me how to laugh.*

I reasoned that if I couldn't feel things, I could at least *act* like I felt things. I'd watch other people's faces for cues; when they smiled, I'd smile, too. When they raised their brows, I'd raise mine. It was hard, but it trained me to be observant.

True to his word, Randy taught me to laugh, or, at least, to make a laughing sound. He'd laugh, and I'd imitate him. It was the strangest feeling, but I seemed to recall the muscles of my face moving that way before. I practiced at home, when no one was around, standing in front of the bathroom mirror and staring at my face as the sound echoed around the room. And one day, while I was practicing, my expression struck me as funny, and a giggle escaped before I could stop it. I was amazed.

Gerry saw me every day, five days a week. Weekends, I hung out at his house, playing guitar with Randy or listening to music. Gerry was an audiophile, and he had an astoundingly diverse record collection. We listened to everything but pop music—jazz, classical, African, anything and everything. He fed my soul with the music, and he fed my body with the gourmet meals he cooked to relax.

I was out of money, so Gerry carried me. He did almost everything a therapist isn't allowed to do, seeing me for free, holding me, having me at his house, making me a part of his life. If Randy was his son, I was the next best thing to a daughter.

And he saved my life. I began trying to be a partner in my therapy, instead of fighting it. I began telling Peter how I felt about things, instead of hiding them. And I started working at my writing, seriously, for the first time since I could remember.

I knew I had no craft, so I worked out a plan. For a month or two, I would write a song a day. Didn't matter if they were bad songs; no one was going to hear them. I needed to learn my craft, and that meant practicing it.

I'd also make myself listen to music at least two hours a day. I couldn't go to clubs yet; it was too painful when people asked, "Are you still a musician?" or "I thought you were dead!" But I could listen to records, and I did, feeling like I was ten years old again, discovering a whole new world.

After weeks of writing a song every day, I would cut it down to one every other day. Then one every third. When I got to one a week, I'd begin to relax, and eventually only write when I felt like it. That was the plan.

In between songwriting and listening, I read omnivorously. Peter brought me books on Buddhism, poetry, cultures. I read Ezra Pound, then everything he recommended. I discovered T. S. Eliot and Diane Wakowski. I realized there was a host of artists out there who lived their lives and weren't crazy. They had normal lives, and they saved the drama for their work. It began to seem doable.

Jean came down to tell me that MGM wanted to drop me or get an album out of me. There was no middle ground. We'd long since realized that Verve Folkways had been formed as a tax loss for the company; the more money it lost, the better tax benefits MGM received. That's why they'd released "Society's Child" three times with no protest. When the record became a moneymaker, it was a real accounting nightmare, but they'd adjusted. Now they wanted to turn a profit.

Leaving MGM would be like leaving home all over again. I'd always been there; I didn't know any other companies. Someone suggested

Columbia, but Mitch Miller was head of A&R, and he detested rock and roll. He thought it was a fad, and he refused to sign any pop singers. Jean couldn't see any alternative but trying to make my present deal work. Everyone else thought I was gone for good. They wouldn't make an investment in me.

Record companies don't understand what they mean to their artists. They really don't.

So I went to New York and met with the newest president of MGM, Mike Curb. The company had been sold twice in the few years I'd been there, and gone through five presidents during my tenure. The instability hadn't done my career any good. When she told me who the new guy was, I asked Jean if this was the same Mike Curb who'd had a group called "Up with People," and she said yes.

Ecchh.

I wasn't real thrilled. In fact, it was contempt at first sight. Curb was everything I detested. He made music I loathed. Even his smile annoyed me, with those big, healthy, whiter-than-white teeth. He belonged to a white bread world, with white bread music. But he was the president of my record company. And I was running out of money. I needed to make a record.

I sat in Mike's office, nervously shaking my foot. I looked him in the eye; he looked at some spot just above my head. He smiled. I tried to smile back. What the hell, at least his suit fit well.

Mike leaned toward me, and said in a confidential tone of voice that he wanted me to make "family friendly" music. I grimaced and asked, "Who in their right mind wants to be *friends* with their family?!"

He thought Jerry Ross should produce. For incentive, he told me Ross had produced "I'm Your Venus." I kept my mouth shut over that, and gave him a tape of some new songs, including one I was really proud of called "Jesse." It was the first song I'd felt good about in three years, so it meant a lot to me. Mike promised to pass the tape on.

A few weeks later, still feeling pretty fragile, I went up to Ross's office. He sat behind the desk and opened his mail, never looking my way, while he told me about his fabulous career and his fabulous self. At the end of the half-hour monologue, I asked if he'd listened to my tape. Yes, he said. Did he want to produce me? He shrugged, shuffled over to a shelf, and handed me a stack of LPs, saying, "Here's some records. Go home and listen to them, because then you'll know how to write."

I'd been taught that my record company was my home, and in some small corner of my heart, I clung to that. When my parents broke up, there was still MGM. When my life went south, there was still MGM. And now, after I'd worked so hard to become a good songwriter, I'd expected them to welcome me home with open arms. Instead, they weren't listening.

So I went back to Philadelphia and stopped eating. Just stopped, cold. I'd promised Gerry not to cut myself or overdose, but he'd said nothing about food. I drank Coke like it was going out of style, but I couldn't stand putting anything in my mouth. For my eighteenth birthday, I ate half a cupcake.

I also stopped talking. What were words worth, anyway? I refused to speak on the telephone. I mumbled to Peter. I waited anxiously for my sessions with Gerry, then sat in silence. He sighed and waited, reminding me there was another world right in front of me. I'd felt it, for a few months, and I could feel it again. I just had to let go.

My weight dropped, from 105 to ninety-five to ninety pounds. Peter took me to Grand Manan Island, where his parents had a home, to get away for a while. Gerry worried about what would happen if I was away from everything familiar for two weeks, and gave Peter some Thorazine to knock me out completely if I started getting crazier.

I spent the time feeling pretty peaceful, reading and walking along the rocky beaches. It's no wonder I felt peaceful. I was taking 150 milligrams of Valium a day, just to survive. Gerry didn't like it, but it seemed to be the only way to keep me from trying to kill myself, short of locking me in a padded cell.

When we got home, my weight had dropped to eighty-two, and there were bruises up and down my legs from vitamin C deficiency. Gerry spoke to Peter about hospitalizing me, force-feeding me, any option but watching me starve myself to death.

And then I got lucky, as funny as it sounds. I was laying on my back in bed one night, feeling my heart beating through my back against the mattress, and I got hit with an excruciating stomach cramp. It eased up eventually, but it scared me. The next morning, the same thing happened, and Peter noticed me doubling over. He called the doctor, who diagnosed a severe case of gastroenteritis, brought on by poor diet, stress, and drugs.

His prescription? Complete bed rest, and nothing but water for a while. No drugs, no Coca-Cola. Just water. Then a few days of Jell-O, a few days of tapioca, and slowly, I'd be allowed to return to a normal diet.

The pain was so severe that I listened to him. And sometime that September, as I forced down the tapioca and tried to get used to a world without crutches, Jimi died of an overdose, and I decided to live.

SEVEN

Stars

People lust for fame. Like athletes in a game,
we break our collarbones and come up swinging
Some of us are crowned. Some of us are downed.
Some are lost, and never found.

Gerry made it his personal mission to put weight on me. He was a true gastronome; he loved food. When his family went out to dinner, I went, too. He took me for sushi in New York when there was only one place in the entire city serving it. He introduced me to Chinese gourmet cooking, feeding me black bass with bean sauce instead of the spareribs and fried rice I'd known. When Gerry decided to go to San Francisco and eat at a restaurant he favored there, he took me along the same way he took Randy. We went to Washington, stayed at the Watergate, and ate at *Sans Souci*.

I began gaining weight. Gerry cooked for me, spending hours preparing chili while I sat on a stool in the kitchen and dreamed aloud of writing the song of songs, something that would affect the entire world. I'd been reading Rilke, and fallen in love with a line of his: *I don't want to be a poet. I want to change your life.*

It bothered Gerry that I kept going back to the music business. He worried for me. "That business eats people alive," he'd say. Better I become a therapist. I had the talent, the smarts, the empathy. If he had five or six people like me to train, he could change the world.

"It's not my calling," I'd say. "If I had one big hit record, *I* could change the world."

I spent the next couple of years growing up, and growing into myself. I worked when I could, but my immune system was still shot, so I had to take it easy. Peter and I went to Marin County to record *Present Company* for Capitol Records, who'd taken me in when MGM dropped me. I looked on it as a transitional album. Most of it was bits and pieces I'd written at the library that day.

We drove out, leaving a week early so we could play tourists. It was a glorious feeling, being on the open road with no agenda. Despite all my touring, I'd never seen much of the country, and I was hungry for new places. We stopped everywhere to look at the sights and visit friends along the way. I couldn't believe how good it felt to feel well.

When we got back home, I realized I didn't know anything about microphone technique. In the years I'd been away, the technology had changed, and I wanted to catch up. I called a friend at Bell Sound Studio and asked if I could apprentice for a while. I went there a couple of times a week, sweeping the floors and wrapping cables, emptying ashtrays and making sure all the equipment was properly stored. In exchange, after the work day was done, an assistant engineer and I would lay down a guitar track, then I'd stand in the control room and sing into an expensive Neumann microphone, watching the VU meter carefully. If it went into the red, I was singing too loud. If it went all the way to the left, I was too soft. I learned to judge how far back or forward my mouth should be from the mic, so I could sing without needing a limiter. Listening to my voice playing back through good speakers, I also learned to adjust it so it sounded like the voice I heard in my head.

In December, Jean invited Peter and me to spend Christmas at her mother's home in the English countryside. We decided to go to Europe for a few weeks and visit friends as part of the trip. Because I was still underage, I needed a parent's permission to travel overseas. I wasn't sure where my dad was, so I got in touch with my mother. It was awkward talking to her on the phone, asking for a favor. It was doubly awkward because she sounded so happy to hear from me.

Mom came down to Philadelphia and stayed for a long weekend. When I saw her again, the pain we both felt at our separation was second only to the joy we felt at being in each other's arms again. We talked, and talked, and talked. For the first time, we met as adults. I was twenty now, with a lot of issues resolved. Chief among them was blaming her. I'd slowly begun to understand what it had cost my mother, who'd never known anything but life with my grandparents or with my father, to leave it all behind. She'd never had a home of her own before. She'd never made friends on her own. She'd always had family around her. The decision to leave hadn't been made lightly; it had been made in an agony of guilt and remorse.

And it was hard. She couldn't get a credit card on her own; she had to have one in her husband's name. After the divorce, she still couldn't get one, because she was divorced. My grandparents never stopped blaming her for the split. The world never stopped blaming her. And she never stopped blaming herself.

There were bright spots. Women's Liberation was at its peak; Mom watched Gloria Steinem and Bella Abzug tearing things up, and she marched along with them. She joined a consciousness-raising group, gamely exploring herself with a speculum and trying to figure out why her life didn't exist without a man in it. She'd gone into therapy, and was beginning to see that as difficult a child as I might have been, I was the only thing I could be. She adored Eric and me, and for the first time since the divorce, I let myself feel it and be nurtured by it.

I left for Europe with a light heart. Peter and I were amazed at the differences between America and England, and at the things we'd been taking for granted. Our first night in the UK, I got up at midnight, jet-lagged and wide awake. I went into the parlor to watch television. There was none. Oh, there was a TV, but there was nothing on. The next morning I flipped the dial around and discovered there were only two channels in all of England.

We went to Germany to visit my friend June, who turned out to be in Kitzbühl, Austria, so we took the train there and stayed with her. Then we all went back to Berlin, and she took us to the American Consulate cafeteria for a real hamburger. Nixon stared down from the wall as I relished the taste of something familiar.

We had a little money left over after Germany, so we went to Paris. We'd both been dreaming of it since reading *The Day on Fire*, and it was everything we'd hoped. Travelers Aid found us a cheap walk-up, with a tiny charcuterie below. The lady who ran it took pity on us, thinking we were students, and saved day-old bread and yogurt to sell us at half-price. Our room was tiny but efficient, with a bidet in the bathroom that I mistook for a footbath.

We walked the streets, stumbling over famous sites like Notre Dame and the Eiffel Tower. We went into a bookstore and asked if they had anything in English about Arthur Rimbaud. *No,* the owner said, *but if you like Rimbaud, you should read Jean Cocteau. He's not that famous yet, but he will be.*

I spent most of 1971 writing, trying to take small gigs to pick up the financial slack. It was hard getting booked; no one wanted a twenty-year-old has-been who'd lost two recording contracts in a row. But some people were astonishingly kind. Mike Douglas heard that I was working again, and issued an open invitation to be on his daytime talk show. I did it every few months, and started getting my bearings back.

Once, the other performer was Jerry Lewis. He'd just finished a diatribe about "Spare the rod and spoil the child," insisting that his father had beaten him, and it had made him what he was. I knew what he was; I'd seen him popping pills backstage until his eyes were practically bugging out of his head. We got into an argument over obedience and discipline that almost turned into a fistfight, until Mike got between us.

I called the Main Point, which had been the first out-of-town club to book me years before. It had always felt like home; small, intimate, and welcoming. Jeanette MacDonald, the owner, made the brownies they served herself. She agreed to have me in for one show, just to see how I was doing. It was odd, being onstage after two or three years away. The audience, mostly curiosity seekers, seemed to like some of my new material, which reassured me immensely.

I asked Jean whether she could get me some more work, and she managed to book a small run in southern California. I put together a two-piece band, and we drove out to a club in Escondido. My pay was supposed to be three hundred dollars for the week. After my first show, I asked for an advance. I planned to pay each band member seventy-five dollars, keeping the same amount for myself and using the rest for expenses.

The club owner didn't have any cash, even though the shows were sold out. He explained that he'd already put it in the night-deposit box. I responded that he was supposed to give me half my fee up front, and I wanted it before I'd go on again.

The next afternoon I went to his office, and he gave me one hundred fifty dollars in cash. I asked for the rest of my fee, or at least an advance on it. The band were getting nervous; I needed to pay them. He refused, saying he'd pay me the rest when I finished out the contract.

I checked my wallet; there was a single twenty-dollar bill in it. I went back to the hotel, paid the band members, and added up my options. I'd be there for another six days. There was a Taco Bell across the street, next to a Sizzler steak house. If I ate two tacos for breakfast with no drink, skipped lunch, and had the Sizzler $1.99 special for dinner, I could squeak by.

So I just shrugged my shoulders, got through the shows, and forced down the special every night. I remember it distinctly—a thin piece of steak with too much salt, a small baked potato with ersatz sour cream, and a limp piece of broccoli that had seen better days.

That first night, I was so grateful to have anything that I wolfed it down in a couple of minutes. The second night, I soaked the potato in the meat juices to make it more palatable, and got it all down. By the third evening, I was wishing for anything but steak and baked potato. Liver, a radish, anything. By night six, it was all I could do to get it down.

I'm still grateful for the food, but I've never eaten at a Sizzler again.

After we got home, I went back to writing with a vengeance, practicing guitar for hours on end and listening to every new album that came out. One afternoon, I put on an LP someone had sent me by Don McLean. I was listening with half an ear when a song called "Vincent" came on. It drew me in, and before I knew it, I was fully involved.

The song ended. Everything in my head stopped, and I approached the record player cautiously. The song couldn't possibly be that good, that heartfelt. It was everything I'd been reaching for. I must have misheard it.

I listened again. And again. And again. It was indeed that good. In fact, it was the finest song I'd ever heard. I must have listened to it thirty times, marveling at the concise imagery, the way the chorus embraced the listener by speaking directly and openly of the narrator's feelings. I'd never heard anything like it.

And when I'd memorized the song, the arrangement, the guitar part, I walked into our living room, grabbed a guitar, and wrote:

Stars, they come and go
They come fast or slow
They go like the last light of the sun,
all in a blaze
and all you see is glory
But those who've seen it all,

they live their lives in sad cafés and music halls
They always have a story

I continued writing, sitting cross-legged on the ugly green shag rug I'd insisted we buy, while Peter, unaware of the monumental thing happening inside me, worked in his darkroom. I wrote, using everything I'd learned in therapy. I wrote about things it humiliated me to talk about—the mortification I felt when I realized I'd lusted, not to be an artist, but to be famous. The shame I felt when television directors would ask me to "Move, damnit!" and my body would freeze because I was convinced it was so ugly. My fear that I'd wind up a complete has-been, never getting to see the inside of a concert hall again. I told my story, told it honestly and bravely, without feeling sorry for myself or blaming the world. And it was glorious.

A friend once said to me, "We all need to tell our story, and someone needs to witness it." I think that's the noblest thing I've ever heard. Whether you're the storyteller or the witness, it's noble. With "Stars," I told my story, and later on, the audience of listeners became my witnesses.

I wrote for two hours, finished it, then went to bed. The next morning, I sat down and played the song to myself. Something was wrong. How could I ask an audience to understand a song that began with the chorus, whose opening lines were "Stars, they come and go, they come fast or slow"? I needed the listeners to connect, and connect immediately, both to me and to the song. They couldn't do that if they didn't know me. So I wrote what I thought of as a preamble:

I was never one for singing
what I really feel
Except tonight, I'm bringing
everything I know that's real
Stars, they come and go . . .

When I finished, the song was everything Gerry had drilled into me. To be real. To be truthful. To confront the events of my life honestly, embrace them, and walk through the fire to the other side. I was cleansed.

When I sang it to myself a second time, I remember thinking, *Now . . . Now I'm a* real *songwriter. Today, at this moment, I have written a great song. I am not a fluke. I've written two great songs, "Jesse" and "Stars." I am a real writer.*

It changed my life, that song. Everything was wrong with it. Regardless of the preamble, it really began with the chorus instead of the verse. There was no constancy; the lyrics changed each time a chorus came around. The verses were all different lengths, with different rhyme schemes. There was a bridge that came out of nowhere. At the end, there were actually two bridges, linked together by a chorus. And it was more than seven minutes long. I didn't even know if you could *write* a seven-minute song that would hold an audience.

But it had magic to it. There was something incantatory about the melody, something that felt older than I'd ever be. It felt good to sing. It felt *right*. It was a real performer's song, one any entertainer could relate to. And even now, "Stars" is my most recorded song, kept alive by people as diverse as Mel Tormé and Cher.

IT WAS TIME TO JUMP-START MY CAREER in a big way, and I knew it. No record company would have me, but Jean thought if I could make a couple of commercial-sounding demos, we might be able to change their minds. I called Carol Hunter and asked if she wanted to produce two sides. I flew out to Los Angeles and we went into the studio for a few days.

At the tail end of the session, after the musicians had gone home and only the engineer, Carol, and I remained, I did a quick worktape of "Stars." I'd sung it for Jean the week before, and she'd begged me to make her a copy. I couldn't understand why. It was too long to interest anyone.

I wanted to cut something commercial, something that would give me a chance at a record deal, not a seven-minute dirge. There was no point.

Besides, I was determined not to sing it onstage. It was too personal, too painful. I'd never be able to look an audience in the eye again. I thought that if I ever made it back to concert halls, I might sing it for the first and only time as my encore at Carnegie Hall, then leave the music business forever.

That worktape was so pure, so artless, that we wound up using it on the album. There's a guitar flub on the next-to-last bar, but since the guitar and vocal were recorded at the same time, we couldn't fix it. You can still hear the mistake if you listen to it now.

I booked a full weekend at the Main Point, mostly to prove I could. A gentleman named Burt Haber, who had a publishing deal with the company he worked for, Frank Music, was there to see the opening act. When Burt heard "Jesse," he flipped. So did Sal Ingeme and Don Colberg, two promotion men from CBS who happened to be there that night. Jean got copies for both, and Burt took the song to his boss, the legendary Frank Loesser.

Frank had written Broadway musicals longer than I'd been alive. His *Guys and Dolls* had won eight Tony Awards. He had a small but vibrant publishing company, and was very choosy about who he signed. We met, and he made me an offer I couldn't refuse. He'd pay me a minimal amount, barely enough to get by, but Burt would work his butt off trying to get my work recorded by other artists. Frank would also throw in a tiny office of my own, with an upright piano in it, so I'd have a regular place to work when I visited New York. Even better, he'd allow me a reversion clause; at some point, I would own my songs again.

I signed.

Meanwhile, Sal and Don began bothering the higher-ups at CBS. They thought I belonged on the label, and told anyone and everyone so. Clive Davis was head of the company at the time, and totally uninterested in me, but they persevered. Their persistence would pay off, but only two years later.

I needed an attorney, and I wanted to hire one on my own this time. I asked around and wound up calling Ina Lea Meibach, who I'd originally met when she worked for Johanan and his partner, Paul Marshall. I'd walked into their office for a meeting, a cocky sixteen-year-old, and spied a woman with bright red hair wound in a tight bun. I immediately said the dumbest thing possible: "Hi! Nice to see a new face. Whose secretary are you?"

Ina, one of the first female attorneys to graduate from New York University, cum laude no less, was not amused. Now, five years later, she agreed to represent me. It was one of the smartest things I ever did. She was my attorney, friend, and advisor for the next two decades, always brilliant, always caring.

I went home to Philadelphia and Peter, but I was restless beyond words. I'd be twenty-one in a month, but I'd never cashed a check or made a bank deposit. I'd never even gotten my own mail; it went to my accountant, Sam, who I'd hired when I was fifteen, or to my manager. I saw other people my age driving themselves around, handling their own lives, and I felt like an idiot.

The two weeks I'd just spent in L.A. had been a revelation. I'd stayed with Carol, then my friends Hedge and Donna, who'd cut my song "He's a Rainbow" the year before. There were fruit trees everywhere, and while it was freezing back home, the sun crept over Los Angeles each morning and hung there all day long. We went to the beach, and I loved it. Best of all, I only knew three or four people in the whole city. It felt like I could start over again, clean, without encumbrances.

I decided to go back in May for a few months. I discussed it with Peter, and it seemed like a good idea, but as I was packing he came in, sat on the edge of the bed, and began to cry. I asked what was wrong and he said, "I just don't think you'll ever be back." I snorted and told him to stop being a jerk, but he was right. I didn't know it then, but I never would go back.

Before I left, I finished a song called "Thankyous." It was an homage to my family, opening with:

Papa gave me music, mama gave me soul
Brother gave me reaching out to hold

and ending with:

Thank you for loving me
and letting it show

I went up to New York to visit Mom, and while she was standing on her bed taping a photo to the wall, I pulled out my guitar and sang it. When she turned around to look at me, her face was heavy with tears, and we collapsed in each other's arms.

We were family again.

Carol found me an apartment in her courtyard complex, and I arrived with a small suitcase and my father's Martin guitar. That guitar was the most important object in the world to me. Dad had bought it just before I was born, from a woman who found it in her attic after her husband died. My father paid twenty-five dollars for it, and it was the best-sounding Martin I'd ever heard. Gary Davis liked to borrow it; so did Jimi. A big New York session musician had offered me $5,000 for it back in 1966—it was that good. I'd written my first songs on it, done my first shows. Dad gave it to me for my sixteenth birthday, and I cared about it more than any object before or since.

I rented some modest furniture and a cheap upright piano, and prepared to live as an adult. The first problem I encountered was transportation; I couldn't afford to buy a car, and I couldn't pay the stiff rental fees Hertz and Avis charged. Someone suggested I go to Rent-A-Wreck, so I hopped on the bus and wound up in a parking lot full of dented cars. I went to the office and was met by Dave Bundy, a jovial guy with piercing blue eyes, who said he'd let me have a sorry-looking Mustang convertible for the incredibly low price of two hundred fifty dollars a month. When I pulled out my wallet, he said, "No, no. No deposit. I trust you. I've looked at your eyes."

The car was absurd. Pepto-Bismol pink, with a V-8 engine that revved up to sixty in seconds. If I floored the gas pedal, the front end would actually lift off the ground. I loved it.

The next problem was income. I had my small stipend from Frank, but nowhere near enough to live on. I asked around and began doing lead sheets for other people, listening to their songs and copying the melody and chords onto onionskin with India ink and a Rapidograph pen. It was tedious work. If I made a mistake, I had to start all over again, or carefully cut out the offending bars with a razor, then tape new onionskin onto the page and rewrite them. The paper was so thin that I could tear it in half just by writing too hard. But it paid.

I supplemented that income with commercials, when I could get them, and learned to put on a bright fake smile as I sang, so the final take would sound happy. The Sands Hotel loved the way I sang *"Quel fromage!"* brightly and cheerfully at the end of one ad, and used me for several more.

I got hired to sing the first Egg McMuffin radio spot for McDonald's, which was thrilling because it paid well. I spent the morning running scales to loosen my throat, and arrived at the studio ready to sing. Walking into the control room, I counted fourteen people in addition to the engineers. The storyboard people. The lyric writer. The melody writer. The arranger. The advertising agency head. The McDonald's head. Too many heads.

We spent forty minutes going over the "feel" of the commercial, so they could all relax and believe "Waking up in the morning" was the most important line I'd ever sung. Then I went into the studio and began to work.

I earned my money that day, believe you me. I sang the sixty-second piece over and over again, while they all gave me different directions between takes. "Can you sound happier?" "Can you sound more interesting?" "Can you sound more American?" "Can you sound more morning-y?" It was crazy-making.

Finally, after I'd been singing for a few hours, I took a break and went to the bathroom. When I walked back into the studio, an agency person hit the talk-back button and said into my headphones, "Janis . . . Can you make it just a little more *eggy*? We think that'll solve it."

Eggy. What the hell was "eggy"? I panicked. I really needed this commercial. I needed the money. I needed the credibility. What on earth was I going to do?

I looked up at the control room. Everyone was waiting. *Can you turn the lights down?* I asked the engineer. The lights went down. I slowly turned and walked over to a wall, then stood in front of it for a few minutes so I'd look deep in contemplation. Finally, I went back to the mic, said, "I think I've got it now," and sang it exactly as I'd been singing it for hours.

The control room were thrilled with the new interpretation.

DONNA INSISTED I CUT MY HAIR, saying I looked like a leftover hippie reject, so I got a short Afro that seemed to suit my new life better than the long hair of my "Society's Child" days. She and Hedge also bought me a membership to their gym, the Sanctuary, and I began working out every day. Between lead sheets and workouts, I lived with a small transistor radio stuck to my ear, listening to Top Forty radio.

I was entranced with Los Angeles. At that time, you could buy a nice house in the Hollywood Hills for around forty thousand. Rents were absurdly low, especially compared to New York. And people thought about their health, physically and spiritually, in ways I'd never encountered. Soon I was doing cantaloupe fasts, enjoying the new body my exercise routine was creating, and discovering how much fun it was to feel pretty. I hung out at the Bodhi Tree bookstore, where a picture of Satchitananda hung on the wall, and no one minded if I read the lost books of the Bible or metaphysical tomes for a few hours without purchasing anything.

I was content, living alone and writing. I'd started working on a song called "Applause, Applause," and heard horn and string parts in my head. I had no idea what to do with them, so I decided to learn to orchestrate. I was so ignorant, I didn't know you could purchase a score and learn from it! Instead, I bought a record called *Instruments of the Orchestra,* a book on orchestration, and recordings of Stravinsky's *Rite of Spring* and Bernstein's *West Side Story.* I loved both scores, and reasoned that if I could write them out myself, I'd end up learning to score.

It was a back-assed way to do things, but it worked. I'd go to the gym early in the morning, come home and write for a few hours, make myself a light lunch, then try to figure out what instruments were doing what, and copy the parts out. I lived on one chicken and two trout a week; both were twenty-nine cents a pound, and about all I could afford in the way of protein. I'd roast the chicken, eat that for two or three days, then use the bones to make soup. I could throw some vegetables into the soup and eat for another couple of days. Then, to break things up, I'd have broiled trout for a day or two, and start the cycle again.

Carol brought me to a little songwriter's group led by Len Chandler, and I sang a few new songs. Len went around town telling people I was now a writer to be reckoned with, and had written a song called "Jesse" that would make them shrivel up in envy. Herb Gart, Don McLean's manager and an old acquaintance of Jean's, was shopping a tape of it in the hopes of getting me a record deal, to no avail. As with "Society's Child," everyone said they loved the song, kept the acetate, and refused to sign me. I wasn't terribly bothered; I was happy in my little courtyard, sitting on the front stoop, strumming my Martin and making up songs.

At least, I was happy until I looked up one day to see my father walking out of an apartment on the other end of the complex. He didn't see me; he was busy talking to the young woman I'd met four years earlier. Later that day, I knocked on Carol's door and said, "Um, excuse me, but I thought I saw my dad coming out of an apartment here today." Carol had the grace to look sheepish as she explained that he lived there, too. She hadn't wanted to tell me. But wouldn't it be a nice idea to go over and say hello?

"No," I said. Out of the question. No way was I exposing myself to being torn up again.

"Eric's there," she said.

Oh. That was different.

The next afternoon, I knocked on the door and spent a few hours catching up with my kid brother. After bouncing around between my parents for a couple of years, he'd decided to grow up. He was staying with Dad until he could get a job and afford his own apartment. Dad was living with Natasha, and they were all having a lot of fun together. Why didn't I come to dinner?

Instead, when he got home from work, I asked my father out. We went to a Chinese restaurant on La Brea and grudgingly discussed where we'd been over the past four years. He'd run to Los Angeles, dead broke, trying to get away from Natasha and his feelings for her. It hadn't worked; she'd tracked him down and made her way out there. Done was done. He loved me dearly, had missed me, and hoped we could be close again. Meanwhile, who was I to judge anyone else?

I thought about that carefully. This was a whole new ball game. I had my mother back in my life. I wanted my father, too. So we agreed to try to see each other as people, and get along.

I had other things on my mind. There was a beautiful young instructor named Beth at the Sanctuary. We'd taken a liking to each other from the first, and begun hanging around after class, talking and cutting up. She was four or five years older than me, with long, streaming hair, and a dancer's lithe body. I thought she was beautiful, the ultimate earth mother.

One day, she asked to see me after class. We sat on the stairwell, and she said, "I had a dream about you the other night." No one had ever dreamed of me before. I fell for it, hook, line, and sinker.

Soon we were spending every available minute together. My body became incredibly toned as I worked out two and three times a day. We met on the stairs. We met in our cars. We met for lunch. I couldn't understand why she'd never have dinner with me, or why she always got so nervous watching the clock. It didn't matter—I was falling in love. It was puppy love, desperate love, can't-get-enough-of-you love all rolled into one.

About mid-July, she told me her birthday was coming up the next month. Did I want to come to dinner then?

Did I? I not only wanted to come to dinner, I wanted to *be* dinner.

I offered to take her out for her birthday instead; I had spare money in my pocket, because I'd been accompanying Hedge & Donna on the piano at their shows. Beth declined; she wanted me to see her home. I was delirious at that.

It felt like my entire life was finally on track. I was writing a lot, getting to the point where even I couldn't keep up with myself. Melodies and lyrics ran in my head all day and all night. At lunch, I'd grab a napkin and scribble a melody line. In the car, I'd pull over to jot down a lyric. I spent long hours at the piano, working on my songs and arrangements. I was writing most of my next album, struggling to capture the feelings on paper, sometimes turning out three or four songs a week.

I finally liked what I was writing. The girl I loved seemed to love me back. Herb and Jean were sure we'd have a record deal any day now. My family loved me. And the Philadelphia Folk Festival had asked me to perform, not as a headliner, but in an evening slot nonetheless. Life was good.

I flew into Philly and stayed with Peter for a few days before the festival. I tried to be honest with him, but there's no doubt that I left him badly. I couldn't tell him I no longer loved him, because I did love him, with all my heart. It just wasn't the forever kind of love we'd both yearned for when we met.

I didn't have words for what was in my heart, so I settled for half-truths instead. And sometimes, lying by omission is just as bad as an outright falsehood. To this day, I want to apologize every time I see him, for causing him such indelible pain, for not being the person I'd promised to become.

And yet . . . and yet. We were so very, very young when we met. Now, five years later, I was just beginning to feel like a real writer. And Peter, well, Peter was taking the most incredible photographs. He had an extraordinary talent for capturing a person's candid soul, without ever seeming to get in their way. I could see from the way his eyes lit up when he talked about photography that at last he'd found what I'd always found in music—a home that transcended any dwelling, a mistress who'd be there when marriage failed.

We laughed a bit, we cried a bit, but most of all, we tried not to hurt each other any more than we already had. I asked if he'd shoot my next album cover. He said he'd think about it. We found ourselves talking more about the past than the future, and I finally went off to play the festival.

I was scared, no doubt about it. It had been four years since I'd faced a large crowd. With my short hair and trim, toned body, I looked completely different. And I was determined not to sing "Society's Child" for a long, long time. Backstage, I sat and talked with the other performers, meeting up with old friends like Steve Goodman and David Bromberg. Most of them didn't recognize me, or did a double take. I couldn't confess how worried I was. Philly had been my home for almost four years, and in some ways it always would be. There's little worse than failing on your home turf.

I labored over my four-song set list and decided to go for broke. Instead of opening with an up-tempo, familiar number to catch the ear of the milling crowd, I'd do the unthinkable—I'd open with "Jesse," a ballad no one but a handful of Main Point regulars had heard. With one brave choice, I hoped to capture the hearts of two thousand strangers, at least long enough to get through the rest of my set.

I walked onstage with all the fake confidence I could muster, and sang the opening lines. Much to my surprise, the audience quieted down immediately, seating themselves on the grass and paying full attention. Off in the distance, by the food stands, I could see kids and dogs playing Frisbee. But everywhere I looked before me, people were paying attention.

"Jesse" received thunderous applause, and cries of astonishment. No one knew where I'd gone for those four years, but they sure as heck knew a great song when they heard one, and I was welcomed back into the fold so vociferously that my show ended with the longest standing ovation of the evening.

When I came back for an encore, someone in the audience yelled, "Janis! Where have you been?" and I decided to sing "Stars." A folk audience was probably the only audience with enough patience to sit through it, and it seemed only fair to answer the question.

After the show, Bob Dylan came over to meet me. He'd become a recluse after his motorcycle accident, avoiding touring and festival crowds. Somehow, they'd sneaked him in, and no one but a few performers knew of his presence. He shook my hand and said "'Stars' . . . great song. *Great* song." I rode back to the hotel on his lap and he made an inarticulate proposition, which I declined in favor of going back to Bromberg's room for a late-night jam.

I FLEW BACK TO LOS ANGELES just in time for Beth's birthday. She seemed nervous that morning, edgily looking around to make sure no one was near, then whispering that she had to speak with me privately. I nodded and walked her to the stairwell, then shut the door behind us. She fidgeted for a few moments, saying at last, "There's something I have to tell you."

"What is it?" I figured she would say she wasn't a virgin, or she'd slept with someone else at the gym before.

Instead, she took a deep breath and said, "I'm married."

I stood there, a confused look on my face. How could she be married? She didn't wear a ring. She'd been necking with me for weeks.

"Uh, what exactly do you mean by 'married'?"

"Well, not exactly married. He's my fiancé. I love him, and we're going to be married."

I scratched my head. This was getting a little peculiar. "If you're living with someone, why do you want me?"

She explained. They'd been together for a while, she and Tino. They both had very sensuous natures. They liked exploring. They wanted to explore me.

Like a submarine? I thought. *How strange.*

I thought again. My friends always said I was too prudish; they'd worried over how long it had taken me to lose my virginity. I'd never slept around like so many others I knew; people raised their eyebrows when they found out I'd only had sex with Peter. Everyone but me seemed to take it in stride. People went to orgies, people slept with lots of other people, one after the other, and no one seemed the worse for it. Besides, if I didn't go along with it, I'd lose any chance with her.

So I said *yes,* not thinking about the husband-to-be, just focusing on Beth. Somewhere in the background of the conversation, my foolish heart was saying, *I'm so fabulous anyway, he can't possibly hold on to her. How could he compete with me?*

It was antipathy at first sight. Her boyfriend, Tino, was polite and cordial, carefully avoiding any personal conversation. We sat and played chess while Beth made lamb chops. I beat him on the first round, much to their surprise. He was, as he told me afterward, grand master class, so playing against an amateur had thrown him. "Your moves had no logic," he said. I agreed, though silently. Most of life had no logic, so what did it matter?

He was a large man, two decades older than me, with the body of someone who'd done a lot of strenuous athletics in his youth. He smoked Gaulois, spoke with a Portuguese accent, and seemed very out of place in Sherman Oaks. "He's a writer," Beth told me, "but don't say anything about it. He's also a count, though he doesn't use the title. Don't say anything about that, either. He's very private." Private to the point of paranoid, it seemed to me, but I was centered on Beth.

Their apartment was small, three tiny rooms and a kitchenette. We ate off the coffee table, sitting on the floor. I was still feeling blindsided by Beth's afternoon revelation, and it all seemed very strange. The conversation was stilted; every other sentence coming out of my mouth seemed to take Tino by surprise. I was pretty open after the years with Gerry, and startlingly honest. I thought everyone else was open and honest, too. This was California, after all.

After dinner, Beth disappeared into the bedroom while Tino laid down the ground rules. Sex only. No love. No sex with either of them unless the other was present. I didn't listen to most of it; I was busy daydreaming about Beth in the other room. After a while, Tino said, "Shall we?" and we went to bed.

It was weird.

It was way beyond weird.

I wanted to be with Beth, but here was this other person. And although I wasn't very experienced, I knew three bodies couldn't fit together the way two bodies could. There was always an elbow in my eye, or a foot on my nose. I felt like I was in a petting zoo. After a while, I faked an orgasm, said I was tired, got dressed, and went home.

I knew I didn't like a ménage à trois. I'd done it once before, back when I was doing a lot of dope, and Peter and I had gone to bed with a mutual friend. It wasn't fun then, and it wasn't fun now. But it was the only way to get to Beth, so I decided to play it out and see what happened.

Tino was from Portugal—Madeira Island, to be exact. He'd traveled all over Europe and attended La Sorbonne and L'Ancienne Comédie Française, finishing both with perfect scores. He'd come to America for graduate school, but stopped two semesters short of a degree. He worked as a waiter in a fancy French restaurant called Robaire's, and he was the most intelligent person I'd ever met. He was also an incredibly Eurocentric snob. I would say something, and he'd shake his head and say, "You are so American. Janis, you *are* America."

One night, he was watching a documentary about World War II and invited me to watch with him. "Why should I?" I asked. "I already know how it ends." He didn't think it was funny.

Back at the health club, Beth and I stole time. We'd meet on the stairs and in back rooms to neck, but she worried constantly about Tino finding out. It made me edgy—why was she so concerned? How could he find out, unless she told him? Besides, we were in love. It was obvious to anyone with half an eye, and I figured it would become obvious to him as well. Then he'd do the gentlemanly thing and bow out.

We talked about our lives, our dreams. We lied a lot, kept a lot hidden, exaggerated just enough to make ourselves look good. We were really young.

One evening before dinner, Tino sent Beth away and said we needed to have a talk. "This just isn't working out," he told me. "We're too different. It's nothing personal—it just isn't working out." I was stunned. It was the last thing I expected.

Tino continued. "I know you understand." Then he patted my hand and said, "Of course, we can still be friends."

Still be friends? Why would I want to be friends with this son of a bitch? All I'd wanted in the first place was Beth. This big bruiser was just an impediment. I stumbled to my feet as he invited me to stay for

Janis with her Zaddy on the farm, around 1951. *(Uncle Bernie)*

Deep in thought outside Philadelphia, 1968. *(Peter Cunningham)*

With Odetta in 1972 at the Philadelphia Folk Festival.
(Peter Cunningham)

Mock-up for the *Stars* album cover shoot, in my
living room, using a cheap piece of material
for the background. *(Peter Cunningham)*

In the studio, overdubbing a shaker on the *Between the Lines* album.
We couldn't afford extra musicians, so I wound up doing
a bunch of percussion. *(Peter Cunningham)*

On tour in 1975,
and finally able to afford
good clothing again!
(Peter Cunningham)

Mom and me shortly before she took her last steps.
(Peter Cunningham)

With Joan Baez, doing a benefit show in 1994.
(Jane Cleland)

With Melissa Etheridge after she interviewed me for an *Advocate* cover story.
(Judy Wieder)

With Odetta, Helen Reddy, Jewel, and Judy Collins, performing at Madison Square Garden in 1999. *(Nancy Picconi)*

Dolly Parton and I after we finished the vocals on "My Tennessee Hills." *(Tina Abato)*

On the front porch in 2005, ready to begin work
on *Folk Is the New Black*. *(John Leonardini)*

Bruce Springsteen and I, and DJ
Ed Sciaky and Billy Joel, backstage
at the Academy of Music in Philly,
1974 or 1975. Bruce and Ed had
come by to see the show.
(Peter Cunningham)

Backstage at the
Ryman Auditorium
with Chet Atkins and
Garrison Keillor, 1997.
(Barbara Short)

In 2000 I did more than 200 shows—the first time in my life. Here's me at a festival, working out on the guitar.
(Tina Abato)

Working on a song in 1972, after my Martin was stolen.
(Peter Cunningham)

With Chick Corea. Need I say more?!
(Stan Schnier)

Mel Torme and I, singing "Silly Habits" together for
his special, *Mel Torme and Friends. (Stan Schnier)*

dinner. I tried to maintain some dignity as I declined, and he said again, "We can still all be friends, Janis."

"I wouldn't be friends with someone who used me like this," I said through gritted teeth. He looked amused as I walked out the door.

I had no idea what a broken heart felt like, but this seemed like a pretty good start. I spent the next weeks in the depths of despair. Gerry had worked so hard to get me to open up, and I had no defenses to deal with what had just happened. Mom was coming to visit, so I cleaned the house and spent my time writing in my journal. I didn't go to the gym. I didn't work on songs. Nothing seemed to matter. I'd hit something I'd never felt before, and I couldn't understand it. Where was love supposed to go when it had no home?

Then I started getting angry. How could these people do that to me? I blamed it all on Tino. Beth was beyond reproach here, a victim. I liked victims. I could rescue them.

Mom arrived, all smiles, and immediately asked what was wrong. I couldn't talk to her about it, or, at least, I couldn't explain it in detail. What was I going to say? "Mom, see, I was in love with this girl. The girl I loved was living with the man she's going to marry. I slept with them both. At the same time. Then they kicked me out." Really. How many shocks could I lay on my mother at one time?

Besides, how could Beth not love me enough to leave him? Impossible. I must have done something wrong somewhere along the line, something they'd misunderstood. Tino said, "It's nothing personal," but it felt very personal indeed. And here was my mom, trying to make it better, when all I wanted was to soak in my misery. She pushed and pushed, and finally got out of me that there'd been someone, and now there wasn't. She was wise—she left it alone.

One day, Tino called. He asked if I'd meet with him, and keep it a secret from Beth. No problem, I was never going to see her again. My mother glared at him as I got into his car.

He told me Beth was very upset. Very hurt. She couldn't stop crying.

He hated to see her this way. He'd like me to come back. But no love, just sex. He was willing to try again, for Beth's sake. We could make it a surprise, me just appearing one night out of nowhere. Beth would be so happy.

"I am not a birthday cake!" I yelled, surprised at how angry the offer made me. A few weeks earlier, I might have jumped at it. But I wanted no part of him, and if that was the price for Beth, I wanted no part of her, either.

A few mornings later, Beth called. She was leaving Tino, she'd be at the bus stop, please pick her up. I slammed into my car and drove there. Nothing and no one. I waited thirty minutes, then drove home, feeling dead inside. This was some kind of bizarre game to these people. Unfathomable.

Just when I thought my life couldn't get any worse, it did. Mom and I went to the beach the next afternoon, and when we got home, the apartment had been ransacked. Clothes were strewn everywhere. The rented television was gone. The Gallagher guitar I'd bought on time a month before was gone. I stumbled through the rooms, searching for my Martin. When I realized it was gone as well, all the breath got sucked out of my body. I'd written "Society's Child" on it, and "Jesse," and "Stars." It was the only tangible thing in my life that meant anything to me, and now a stranger held it in his arms, while mine were empty.

Weirdly enough, the credit cards and cash I'd hidden in my underwear drawer were still there. I called the police, who said they'd been trying to catch a ring of guitar thieves—this was probably them. There was a good chance the guitar was already gone, taken out of state to be resold somewhere else. I shouldn't expect to see it again.

I sat down on the living room floor and bawled my head off.

EIGHT

This Train Still Runs

Times when I tried to jump the track
Weight of the world upon my back
Still, after all is said and done,
This train still runs

Mom went back to New York, and I went back to the gym. I avoided Beth like the plague, but I must admit that I took pleasure in how bad she was looking. I was looking pretty good myself, getting on with life and doing a great job of ignoring her. Even when she bumped into me here and there, trying to make conversation, I refused. A broken heart was bad enough; I didn't have to add stupidity to the list of my faults.

One day Beth cornered me and begged for a chance to talk. She was leaving Tino. He scared her—she'd have to leave suddenly and secretly. He had hit her.

I'd never met a woman whose boyfriend hit her. I didn't think that happened in middle-class families. I thought it only happened to people who lived in shacks, couldn't read, and drank a lot. It was a brand-new concept.

I couldn't imagine someone hitting Beth. The past months forgotten, I turned back into Sir Galahad. Of course she could come live with me. I'd help her sneak out. Did she have any money?

She had a little saved up, but her salary had always gone to Tino. She had a cigar box with some silver dollars in it, but taking it would make Tino angry. She didn't want to make him angry.

Beth moved in a week later. I was delirious with joy, but worried about how my family would react. By then my father, brother, and I were all living in different apartments in the same courtyard. We could see each other's doors when we looked out the window. It was strangely reassuring, having that much family around, within earshot but separate.

Just before Beth's arrival, I strolled over to Eric's place. He was working full-time at a local hardware store, and when he'd discovered there was an employee discount, he'd decided to paint his apartment. There were only certain colors available at cost, so everything in the bathroom had been painted dark purple. Everything. Including the inside of the toilet bowl. It was disconcerting.

"Eric, I'm in love," I told him. "She's moving in."

My brother looked pleased. "Jan, that's great!"

I grimaced. "Yeah, but I don't know how to tell Mom and Dad."

Eric's eyebrows furrowed and he asked me what the problem was.

"She's a *girl*, Eric! For Pete's sake! I'm a homosexual. If I tell them, they'll think it's their fault."

He looked at me disingenuously and said, "But, Jan . . . it's not a fault."

I was surprised and pleased. My kid brother had nailed it on the head. I walked over to Dad's place that night and told him and Natasha. Dad grinned and said, "Great! When are you bringing her over for dinner?"

His reaction made calling my mom less worrisome. The next morning, I got hold of her at work and told her I was in love. My exact words were, "Mom! I'm in love. She's great, you'll like her."

There was silence on the other end. Then my mother's voice said in a strangled tone, "Honey, how nice for you." I waited for the rest. "Janis, I need to think about this a little. I'm happy for you, but I need a little time to adjust."

The next time we spoke, she seemed fine. I didn't know she'd hung up the phone and immediately dialed my Uncle Bernie, a psychologist who'd run a clinic for sexual deviants in Pittsburgh a while back. He saw everything from gay people to child molesters and necrophiliacs. I guess she thought he'd have an expert opinion, so she called and told him there was an emergency, come to New York right away.

Bernie arrived to find my mother pacing up and down in the living room, shaking her head. She told him what had happened. He asked about her best friend, a gay man named Rod. Was Rod well? Oh, yes, Rod was doing just fine. Hmm. Was Rod sick in the head? Of course not, he was a normal guy, just gay. Hmm. Did she think I'd gone crazy? Of course not! No child of hers was crazy. Quite the opposite.

With that, he smiled and said, "Then what's the problem?"

Beth moved in. She worked at the Sanctuary all day while I wrote songs. Herb was still looking for a deal and getting nowhere, but Roberta Flack wanted to record "Jesse," and asked my publisher to put it on hold. The problem was, she wouldn't be going into the studio for another year. I began running out of money, loath to take time off from writing to do lead sheets again. We lived on Beth's small earnings and nurtured ourselves on love. It was about as clichéd as you could get; it was great.

I drove people crazy with the amount of time I spent writing. The whole courtyard could hear it when I played. One day, I was working on the piano part to a song called "Dance With Me," playing it over and over again while I struggled to make it perfect. A couple of hours into it, Natasha burst through my door, shouting, "Are you *ever* going to stop playing that piano piece?! It's driving me nuts!"

Sal and Don had been pushing Clive Davis to give me an audition, and he finally said yes. He was a great song man, and I respected his ears, so I was positive that with pieces like "Jesse" and "Stars," he'd finally see what I could do. I arrived in New York full of hope. Clive had passed on me twice already, saying I wasn't hungry enough, and the material wasn't there. Now I wasn't just hungry for a contract—I was starving.

Don met me in the lobby and took me to a conference room. It didn't hold a lot of chairs, so he suggested I sit on the table. I tuned nervously, running over my instructions from Jean and Ina. *Don't talk to Clive. Don't look at him if you can avoid it. Concentrate on the rest of the room. Sing your songs, then wait for him to say something.* Clive was head of the biggest record company in the world. He was known for his ability to pick talent, and his incredible ego. Years later, when his autobiography came out, street word was it should have been titled *How I Invented the Music Business.*

After ten minutes or so, Clive came in, trailing a group of men behind him. He sat down without looking at me. After he sat, everyone else sat. Then they looked at him for the next cue.

Clive glanced at me. All heads swiveled in my direction. Clive nodded. The rest of the room nodded. I started to sing.

As I sang, I looked around the room for a reaction. Any reaction. There was none. Everyone was busy looking at Clive, and Clive was stone-faced.

I finished "Jesse" and waited. Nothing. Don made circular motions with his finger, telling me to do another song. I did "Thankyous" to no visible reaction. Then I did "Stars," which I was sure would find its way into their hearts. Nothing.

I laid the guitar down on the table beside me. Clive stood up and walked out of the room, never looking my way. Everyone else filed out behind him. Not a word was said. I was completely freaked.

I went downstairs to a pay phone and called Ina to tell her how it went. When she came on the line, I began crying. Through my sobs, I hiccupped, "I felt like a piece of meat, Ina, like a piece of meat! He inspected me to see if I was good enough for his table, then he left. I am *not* a piece of meat, I'm *not*!"

Clive passed, and Herb gave up on the United States. He had a close relationship with Alan Hely of Festival Records in Australia. He'd be flying there soon with Don McLean for a concert tour. He'd bring my tapes.

Jean called later that month, ecstatic. Festival had agreed to bankroll an album, in exchange for the worldwide rights. I needed to move back East, choose a producer, and get to work. There was no time to lose.

Herb stopped by on his way back to New York. I played him a new song or two, and he particularly liked one that started out "Would you really come and live with me?" He asked what the title was, and I told him there wasn't one. I couldn't decide on any single line that represented the entire song. I handed him my notebook, opened to the ninth page, so he could see for himself. Laughing, he said, "Just call it 'Page 9.'" I thought it was funny, and thanked him for the idea.

Then I told him I had a problem. A big one. He and Jean wanted me to move back East, and I had no money. No money to move, no money for rent, no money, period.

Herb sat down and pulled out his checkbook. He wrote one and handed it to me, saying, "Move back. You can't do what you need to do here." I looked; it was for $10,000. Gaping, I tried to thank him. He just waved an arm and said, "Someday you'll do this for someone else. Pay me back when you can."

That was it. No receipt, no note, just my word for surety. I felt like a million bucks.

I called Brooks Arthur, who'd engineered "Society's Child." He'd worked with Janey & Dennis after I'd bailed, and they spoke highly of him as a producer/engineer. Brooks was interested. Once he heard the material, he was very interested. He owned 914 Sound Studio, in Blauvelt, New York. He lived nearby, and found us the top floor of a house a few miles away. Our landlady lived below, a lovely woman who burned acrid incense on Sunday mornings that would float up through the heat registers and infest the house for days.

With the money Herb loaned me, we flew into New York and spent a couple of weeks with Mom so she could get to know Beth. I worked at my Frank Music office each day, spending evenings catching up with old friends and family.

Peter and I had worked hard to remain friends, connected by our memories and a mutual love of music. He called and said I had to see a new act playing at the Main Point in Bryn Mawr, and invited Beth and me to stay with him for a weekend. Since my old friends Aztec Two-Step were opening, it was fine with me. The three of us piled into a car and drove out to Bryn Mawr, and I watched as Bruce Springsteen did a three-hour show. Peter was more excited than I'd ever seen him, saying, "This guy is going to be as big as Elvis! Just as big as Elvis. You wait and see!"

After the show, we chatted, and it turned out Bruce was also from Jersey, not all that far from where I'd lived. He, too, would be recording at 914 that summer. As our recordings progressed, we developed a nice pattern. He worked nights, I worked days, and we would meet when the time overlapped, walking across the parking lot to the diner for my dinner and his breakfast.

Brooks brought in Ron Frangipane, a brilliant arranger who'd studied one-on-one with Aaron Copland and Stravinsky before graduating from Eastman. I shyly gave him the score I'd done for "Applause," and asked him to look it over. He was surprised, asking where I'd gone to school. I hadn't, I explained, and told him how I'd taught myself.

He read the score, put it down on the table, clasped his hands behind his head, and said, "Let me get this straight. You learned to score by listening to two pieces and scoring them yourself?" Yeah, I answered. His eyes went to the score, then back to me. "You've never conducted an orchestra?" Heck, no. I'd never even seen one except on TV.

Ron leaned back in the chair and laughed. Then he patted the seat next to him and we looked at the score together. "Only a couple of minor problems," he said. "Here, where the French horns hit a high note. You have to give them room to get up there, a running start." I looked at the part, then added two bars before it so they could climb up to the note. Ron nodded and pointed to another page. "Here, the piano part. You're going to have a hard time finding a pianist to play this on first sight." No problem, I assured him, I'll play the part.

He looked at me. I looked at him. We both leaned back and laughed.

I HAD A BUDGET of $30,000, but that wasn't enough to hire a forty-five-piece orchestra, or to pay Brooks and Ron and the studio at their going rates. Ron worked for next to nothing, and Brooks worked for nothing. That meant we couldn't record unless the studio and they were free, which was rare. Ron and Brooks needed to take as much work as possible to subsidize my record, and the studio needed paying customers. So we recorded when we could, all summer and through the fall. Sometime halfway through, Herb sent the rough mixes to Alan Hely and begged for another $10,000 so we could use an orchestra on "Jesse" and "Applause." Alan gave it to us.

Brooks was a patient teacher, and a hard taskmaster. Ron and I were in charge of the musicians; Brooks and his assistant, Larry Alexander, were in charge of the engineering. When it came time to overdub the vocals, though, Brooks was the only one whose voice was heard. He pounded me to put more emotion into my voice, to take chances with my phrasing. I'd adored Billie Holiday for most of my life, and I'd picked up a lot from her. My phrasing was more jazz than pop, back of the beat instead of on top of it.

Brooks wanted me on top of the time; that would give the vocal an urgency it needed. He hammered me, saying, "You've got great songs. Now you need a great record."

Dad drove in from L.A. with my car, our furniture in tow. We'd just cut "Jesse," and knowing he was a master whistler, I'd written a part for him. He was thrilled to be in the studio. It took an hour to get him calmed down enough to whistle the part, but he hooked it perfectly the first time. We celebrated by eating lamb chops Brooks's wife, Marilyn, grilled for us all.

Brooks knew I was running out of money, and had decided to feed us whenever possible so we could save a few dollars. I was over there a lot, listening to the masters with Ron and working on arrangements. Marilyn made sure I went home fed, with leftovers she said they couldn't use.

When it came time to finish the record, I got to play engineer. We'd recorded on sixteen tracks, which had fantastic quality, but it was pre-automation, so Brooks needed more hands. He divided it up; he took the vocals, Larry took the rhythm section of bass, drums, and percussion. I got everything else—strings, keyboards, guitars. It was a fantastic, monthlong lesson in really tuning my ears to hear the subtleties. When we finished, we played the entire album back for ourselves, then had steak to celebrate.

Months passed, and Jean started trying to book some dates. My agency, William Morris, had a huge roster and a lot of clout, so I began getting gigs as an opening act. They paired me with anyone and everyone who'd have me. I did a few dates with a group called America, who were riding high at the time. It was a living, and I could pay my band, but I got tired of drunken audiences who'd heckle me because they'd paid for America and had to endure thirty minutes of opener before the lead act came on. I never met the other band; they stayed in their dressing room, playing poker.

One night, someone threw a bottle onto the stage. I glanced at my drummer, who shrugged his shoulders. Another bottle followed, narrowly missing the bass player, who stepped behind his amp and continued playing. I looked at the drummer again. He was crouching low over the snare, hiding behind the cymbals. I went into a solo, walked over to him, and said as another bottle flew by, "Dibs on the space inside the bass drum." Oh, the glamour . . .

We were talking to CBS again, but Clive still wasn't interested. Then, much to everyone's surprise, Clive was fired. Charles Koppelman, a friend of Brooks's, was brought in as interim president. Brooks and Jean met with Charles, who liked the record but didn't think there was a hit on it. He proposed a bet. CBS would fly me and my band down to Nashville, where they were holding their annual convention. If I could hold an audience of drunken promotion men and sales managers, and get an encore, he'd negotiate with Festival and buy my contract.

We flew down on a frigid morning toward the end of January 1973. The stakes were high; I knew exactly what I stood to lose if I failed. I'd brought my road drummer, Barry Lazarowitz, along with Richard Davis, a great upright player and bass chair of the New York Philharmonic. Richard, who'd spent years on the road accompanying Sarah Vaughan, was a sea of calm. His Buddhist chanting left the air around me filled with peace.

I, on the other hand, was a nervous wreck. As journalist Bob Sarlin later wrote:

> It was a difficult show, performed before a bunch of semi-sober record biz types, and Janis was clearly terrified. By the time she took the stage, those in the first few rows could see her knees knocking.

I decided the only thing I could do was to be open, and vulnerable, so my first words to the audience were something like, "Good evening. I hope you're having fun. I'm absolutely terrified." By the end of my half-hour set, they were jumping up on tables to get closer to the stage. When I closed with "Stars," there was complete silence, then pandemonium reigned.

CBS bought the rights to everywhere but Australia and New Zealand, and gave me a small advance. With it, Jean and I went shopping at Saks Fifth Avenue. I found an outfit we both liked, cotton lace-up pants and T-shirt with a short jacket in the same color. We bought five of them, in different pastel shades, for seventy-five dollars apiece, and I'm embarrassed to say that I spent the next couple of hours at home, changing in and out of them and admiring myself in a mirror. It had been so long since I'd been able to afford good clothes!

The advance was barely enough to cover the clothing and equipment I'd need for touring. I hadn't earned much the year before, making only scale for the sporadic recording sessions. We couldn't afford the Blauvelt house, and it didn't make much sense to stay there when I'd be on the road, so we moved in with my mother. It was humiliating to be supported by her again, but I told myself it was only for a short while, to tide me over until I could start touring full-time.

Stars came out that February, to gorgeous reviews. As with the Philly audience, no one knew where I'd been, and no one particularly cared. I bought a used station wagon and began touring with Beth and a two-piece band. By the time we'd loaded the equipment and ourselves into it, there was no room for the bass drum. Since I was smallest, I'd endure the long drives with it sitting on my lap.

CBS pushed a single, which went nowhere, but the album created a lot of buzz. And Roberta Flack had finally released her album, with "Jesse" as the first single. It hit Top Ten that summer, increasing my credibility. I was still fighting marquees that said, "Presenting Society's Child—Little Janis Ian!" but at least I had work.

The Bottom Line, the first truly state-of-the-art club in America, opened that February 15, and I attended, along with Mick Jagger, Bette Midler, Charles Mingus, and a host of other celebrities. There was an incredible jam session with Dr. John, Stevie Wonder, and Johnny Winter. Sometime during it, a very drunk young man came over and asked Beth to dance. She politely refused, but he persisted. I noticed a couple of Hell's Angels looking our way, and told the guy to cool it or there'd be trouble. He insisted she dance with him and grabbed her hand, pulling her from the seat.

Before I knew it, he was on the ground, I was pushing Beth behind me, and three Angels were stomping him. The music was so loud that no one heard, so I rushed over and got Allan Pepper and Stanley Snadowsky, the venue owners. Somehow, they got the Angels off, and escorted the bloody fool to the street.

Jean suggested we take a vacation, saying, "You won't get another chance for a while, so take it now." I didn't understand what she saw coming, but we took off for an inexpensive hotel in St. Lucia. It was difficult; we were a couple, but outside of my own family and our closest friends, no one knew it. Both Jean and Ina said it would be death for my career if the relationship was made public, so I kept my mouth shut. They were right; you could still be institutionalized in a lot of states for being gay, and you were subject to arrest and prosecution in many places. When asked if I was dating anyone, I truthfully answered "No." I wasn't dating; I was living with someone.

At the hotel, our unmarried status caused major problems. You either had a male companion, or you were looking for one. Men began leaving their cards in the room door, and sending flowers. It would have been laughable, except they were very determined, and the entire time strangers followed us around, making lewd comments and sucking noises when they got nowhere with their requests. We were relieved to get home.

I had the full CBS machinery behind me now, and their press people had a field day. How many times do you get to promote someone who'd been a star at fifteen and a has-been at seventeen? I did interview after interview, glad of the chance.

Cool things started happening. Leonard Cohen asked me to sing backup on his new album. Hearing it had gone well, a session singer I knew called to say she was going to be doing backup vocals for James Brown in early March; did I want to be the third singer? You bet!

We arrived at the session to find James already seated next to the console. He smiled and gestured toward the microphone, so we filed into the studio and arranged ourselves. The first song was "When the Saints Go Marching In." The track and lead vocal were already done; all we had to do was make up a three-part backing vocal to go with it.

We began singing, but after half a take the tape stopped rolling. James came in, looked us up and down, then said, "Ladies. If I wanted black chicks, I'd a hired black chicks. Now, do it again, and this time, sound white!" It was the strangest vocal direction I'd ever heard, but apparently we "sounded white" to his satisfaction, because he used us on another few songs.

I had plenty of downtime, and I spent most of it with a guitar in hand. One afternoon, I was sitting at my mother's dining room table, idly plucking a Brazilian samba feel as I read *The New York Times*' Sunday magazine section. Beth was off at lunch with Tino; to my consternation, she was still very attached to him, and they met any time he passed through. I couldn't understand it, even though she told me she'd exaggerated to impress me. At the time, I resented it deeply. I didn't realize how deep the hooks go, in a battered woman.

Anyway, I was alone in the apartment, absentmindedly playing a little samba part on the guitar while I read an article about debutantes. The woman who'd written it was talking about her coming-out party, how excited she'd been before it, how flat she'd felt in the aftermath. The opening line was "I learned the truth at eighteen."

Interesting line, I thought. *Might be a song in there somewhere.* I hunted around for a melody to go with my samba lick, and tried the line. Nope, it didn't scan. I needed another syllable.

I learned the truth at seventeen, I sang to myself. Something in me clicked, turned over, examined the line, and I got a chill up my spine. I continued to play as I read more of the article. She'd been elected queen of her class, and thought that would solve all her problems. It didn't.

What rhymes with seventeen? I wondered. *"Beauty queen,"* of course. I grabbed pad and pen, then wrote the first four lines:

> *I learned the truth at seventeen*
> *That love was meant for beauty queens*
> *and high school girls with clear-skinned smiles*
> *who married young, and then, retired*

I stared at the paper. How could I write about high school girls, or prom night and homecoming queens? I hadn't had any of those experiences. I thought about that for a while. There were plenty of other school things I *had* experienced. I knew what it was like to never be asked out on a date. I knew the sinking feeling when everyone else in class came in to find a valentine on their desk, and yours was empty. And I sure as heck knew what it was to feel clumsy and ugly. I could write this song, I was sure of it.

The chords and melody felt familiar from the first. In fact, I got so worried I'd unconsciously lifted someone else's work that I called a friend with an encyclopedic memory for pop music and sang him a verse, anxiously waiting until he said, "Nope. Never heard it before. Pretty, though."

Writing "At Seventeen" took a long time. I went carefully, afraid that if I rushed, it would lose its intensity. I didn't care much whether I told the truth, but I wanted it to be *truthful* to my own life. As I began tossing in lines like "Those of us with ravaged faces, lacking in the social graces," I became increasingly shy about singing it to anyone. The song was really personal to me, now. I couldn't see facing an audience, singing that line, then watching them search my face for pimples and scars. I was so short, they might laugh when I came to the line about never being chosen for basketball. At best, I'd look like a fool. At worst, they'd think I was whining.

By the time I finished the second verse two months later, I'd decided I'd never sing it in public. It was just too humiliating. I was sure no one else felt that way. Everyone else was more popular, more socially adept, than I'd ever been. No one would relate to it; they'd probably laugh.

Decision made, I could finish the song in peace. But I'd said all the embarrassing things I wanted to say, and the song was still a full verse short.

I let it go for a few weeks, then had an idea. Why not involve the listener? Why not suddenly look at it from a different point of view entirely, and bring them in on it? So I started my last verse by assuming that out there, somewhere, there was at least one other person who'd been through what I'd been through:

To those of us who knew the pain
of valentines that never came

The song ended with:

Repenting other lives unknown
that call and say—Come dance with me
and murmur vague obscenities
at ugly girls like me, at seventeen

Ah. Resolution, finally. I'd called myself "ugly." No one would dare laugh at that. And by using "ugly duckling," I felt I'd given the song some hope, because the ugly duckling always turns into a swan.

I knew I wrote sad songs; that was what I seemed to do best. But I also knew my songs had hope and redemption in them. I'd worshipped Billie Holiday for decades, feeling like we were linked by our birth dates. Mine was April 7, 1951, and hers was April 7, 1915. I'd read an interview where she'd been asked why she always sang such depressing songs. "Depressing?" she said in surprise. "Depressing? Baby, my songs always have hope!" When I read that, I wanted to yell, "Yeah! Me, too!"

I hit the road hard. It was a small group, just Beth, my drummer, a bass player, and our tour manager, Patti Rix. There weren't any other female road managers out there, to my knowledge, but Patti was bright and personable, and did a great job. Once in a while we'd run into a problem when someone didn't like taking orders from a woman, but Patti stood her ground and always prevailed.

It was rough, touring without a hit. I played wherever I could, small clubs that quickly learned to leave "Society's Child" off the marquee. I felt it was imperative that I not become a nostalgia act, and refused to sing the song again until the mid-nineties.

Once you left the major cities, the road was an unkind place for a group of traveling musicians. We learned to keep a contract on the top of our luggage at the back of the car, so when we were stopped by the police and hassled, I could show that I earned enough to hire a lawyer and fight any trumped-up charges. It also gave us a reason to be carrying a lot of cash. Otherwise, we could be accused of drug peddling and held up for days.

Jean called to say that Charles Aznavour, the famous French singer and songwriter, wanted to translate "Jesse." Before he began, though, he wanted to speak with me. On a sunny April day, I made my way to his suite at the St. Moritz hotel. He was nothing like I expected. Short, barely taller than me, with a lithe, elfin body, he sat me down and explained what translating a song is really about.

"See, here, my Janis? This line, 'We lay by the hearth.' There is no French equivalent, nothing that conjures up the image you use. I will have to change that word, that concept, that line. And 'There's a hole in the bed where we slept.' Also untranslatable. So, my Janis. You cannot insist that your songs be translated accurately—it will not work. If you want to hear your songs in other languages, you must first find a great lyricist, then let them do the work freely. Because we must translate the *intent* of the words, not the words themselves."

It was a fantastic lesson, one I've returned to many times since.

With the record getting press, my gigs were improving, and my fee went up. I still couldn't play concert halls, but I went back to the Main Point for a sold-out run, then to Max's Kansas City for a series of sold-out nights in New York. Max's was the hippest place to play, and just getting in there meant everything had changed. All the waitresses were gorgeous, wearing black miniskirts, black sweaters, and fabulous shoes. I felt like a plucked fruit tree.

Walter Yetnikoff had been brought in some time before to run CBS, and we enjoyed each other immensely. He was a *landsman,* a poor Jewish kid from Brooklyn, so we had a lot in common. We'd sit in the executive dining room next to his office on the highest floor of the "Black Rock," CBS headquarters in New York, quietly served by a personal waiter who brought dishes created by Walter's personal chef. It struck us both as funny. There we were, two Jewish troublemakers, used to fighting tooth and nail for everything we got, dining on asparagus spears flown in from Paris that morning. We couldn't believe our luck.

In May I played more major markets—Philadelphia, Boston, Washington. CBS was spending money on me now, sending me on a press run of Seattle, Los Angeles, and San Francisco with a reporter and two promotion men at my side throughout. It was strange in San Francisco. I went to a radio station, accompanied by five or six CBS people and the reporter. I was itchy; I'd been sitting in cars and planes all week, and needed to move around a bit, so I decided to take the stairs. The moment I said it, everyone else decided to take the stairs, too.

It startled me. I could see that things were changing fast, but this was a graphic illustration. From now on, I'd have to consider my actions more carefully. I didn't want someone taking the stairs because I did, then dropping dead of a heart attack!

I said good-bye to the journalist and crew the next morning, then flew up to Seattle on my own. The local CBS promotion man, Danny Holiday, met me at the airport, and we drove back to the city in his convertible. He was amiable and chatty, occasionally patting my thigh to make a point. It made me uncomfortable, but I didn't want to offend him or get in trouble, so I stayed silent. At the station, he continued to be physical, taking my arm, putting a hand on my shoulder. When I went into the studio alone, I breathed a sigh of relief, telling myself I just had to get through the interview and back to the airport.

As I left the studio, the program director told me what a good job I'd done. Danny laughed, patted me on the ass, and said yeah, I was great, wasn't I? As I walked past him, he reached out again and pinched my butt.

I had no idea what to do. I'd never been around a business associate who touched me inappropriately. He was a promotion rep, in charge of my career for the entire Northwest. I excused myself to go to the bathroom, and felt tears welling up in my eyes. I wasn't sure if they were tears of rage, or tears of shame.

I called Jean from my hotel room later that night to tell her what had happened. It was a very big deal to me, but she made light of it, telling me to grow up and get over it. This sort of thing happened all the time, it was no big deal. I gave a mental shrug and tried to forget it. Maybe I just hadn't been around enough.

Walter and I had lunch the following week, and he asked how the trip had gone. I carefully told him about every market but Seattle. When he asked how that went, I stammered, then started crying. He patiently got the whole story out of me, then turned dark with anger. "Why didn't you say anything right away?" he wanted to know.

"I didn't know what to say. I didn't want to risk making him angry at me. Maybe he'd go off promoting my record," I answered.

"Excuse me a moment," he said and stepped out to confer with his secretary. When he returned, he leaned forward and said, "Janis. That's not going to happen at this company anymore. We've seen enough of that. It's over. He's being fired."

I couldn't think of anything to say in response, except that it wasn't *that* big a deal. Surely not worth firing someone over.

Walter looked grim. "Like I just said, that will not happen here anymore. And don't you *ever* think you have to put up with it to get our support!" He went on to explain that I didn't have to be scared of offending the people who worked at CBS. If anything, I needed to understand that they were scared of *me*. If I had a complaint against someone, *they* would get in trouble. I was generating income for the company now. I was an important member of the CBS family. I didn't have to put up with anything like this, ever again.

We finished lunch, and I went home to do some hard thinking about our conversation. I was now in a position where a few words from me could make terrible trouble for someone else. It was a novel concept.

NINE

At Seventeen

It was long ago, and far away
The world was younger than today
when dreams were all they gave for free
to ugly duckling girls like me

I entered 1974 with a vengeance. Hard as I tried to pace myself, and keep the lessons of my "Society's Child" days in mind, the thrill of having enough work to feed us and move up a bit in the world was too tempting. I stayed on the road the first eight months of the year, opening for bigger acts whenever I could. My favorite by far was Billy Joel, who had a terrific band and was always down to earth and fun to be with. As the year progressed, we began trading opening and closing slots.

Touring with the support of a major label changed everything. The CBS people were thrilled with me; I worked as hard as anyone they'd ever promoted. In return, their promotion and publicity people worked their asses off. We were still in a station wagon, but now we could afford decent motels, and the bass player and drummer didn't have to share a room. I wanted to keep it that way.

I'd begin my day with a 6 A.M. local television news show, then do radio until one, when I'd get a half-hour lunch break with a station manager. On to phone interviews until four, when I blessedly had to be at sound check. A quick sandwich after that, then change into my performance clothes and do a show. Afterward, there was usually a meet and greet with the local distribution people and their families, then back to the hotel for a shower and some sleep. It was grueling, but it was also exhilarating.

We began recording *Between the Lines* that summer, with the same team we'd used for *Stars*. Even though *Stars* had gotten good reviews, it didn't have a hit single on it, so our budget was still nonexistent. With three artists recording around the clock, 914 was running 24/7. Bruce Springsteen recorded at night, I worked the morning shift, and Melanie took the rest.

I loved recording, putting what I heard in my head into the grooves. But as the album progressed, I began feeling like all anyone did was criticize me. I understood why; everyone had a lot riding on this album. That didn't make it any easier to bear.

Jean had been loyal to a fault, not pressuring me to tour when I was developing as a writer, standing behind me when I insisted Peter shoot the *Stars* cover. But after years of living from hand to mouth, she was determined that this time, we would succeed. She worried that if my second album didn't have a hit single on it, CBS would drop me. To that end, she was vocal in her opinions. She didn't like "Watercolors," she didn't like "The Come On," she didn't understand why they were on the album. She wished I would write a few happy songs and cut them, instead.

Herb Gart was also vocal; his reputation as executive producer was on the line. Ron had done a wonderful Dixieland jazz arrangement of "Page 9," and we'd also cut a very simple demo of it. Herb insisted we use the demo arrangement. We fought over it for weeks. I'd also wanted to continue my tradition of naming the album after what I, as a songwriter, felt was the best song. I wanted to call the record *Watercolors*; he wanted *Between the Lines*. Herb fought me right up to the day before the cover was to be printed. By then, I was so tired of the wrangling that I gave in.

Brooks, too, had a lot to prove if he wanted to become known as a producer instead of an engineer. So I was constantly told, "The rough vocal was better," or "I wish you would get back that bittersweet quality." In retrospect, he made me a far better singer, but on my third day of "At Seventeen" vocals, trying to pump more energy into my voice, I had my doubts.

After we shot the cover, I heard, "It's too 1940ish . . . it's too mysterious . . . I wish you would glamour yourself up a little. . . ." After shows, I heard, "I wish you'd smile more," "I wish you'd dress differently," "I wish you wore more makeup." I'd go to bed each night with "I wish you would . . . I wish you would . . ." ringing in my ears. I'd canceled my vacation, forced myself to go into the studio each morning knowing that everybody was depending on *me* to feed them for the next umpteen years, and it still wasn't good enough.

But the album . . . ah. The actual album was great. I knew it, knew it the first time I listened back to some rough mixes. We were on to something here, something extraordinary. Brooks wanted to make an album that would beat Carole King's *Tapestry*. I wanted to make an album of songs for the ages. When I realized how special it was, I went to him and said, *Brooks. What we have here is so unusual, so amazing—we've captured the times, caught the musical and political spirit of these times. That's something* Tapestry *doesn't do. We should stay in the studio another month, keep going, make the next album right now. Please, let's do that.*

We couldn't. We'd miss the CBS first-quarter deadline.

When I'd finished writing "At Seventeen," I'd called Jean to say, "I think I've just written a hit single." I knew in my bones it could be a career song for me. I could hear the entire arrangement, how I wanted it to sound and feel, in my head, and I was determined to translate that to tape.

We cut it on September 17, 1974. I'd thought about the session carefully. I was worried that the jaded New York session players wouldn't bring enough heart to the record, so I brought in a very young guitarist, David Snyder, on second rhythm guitar. He'd never been in the studio before, but I reasoned that his enthusiasm would make up for his lack of finesse. I knew I wanted to play the key nylon guitar parts myself, but confined myself to rhythm guitar for the session, overdubbing the nylon later. Brooks always told me, "You have to play on your own sessions, because that's part of where the heart of the song lives," and I took him at his word.

There were a number of guests at the session that day, including my manager, Jean. At one point, she started flipping out, taking me aside and angrily saying, "You're ruining this song! There's nothing commercial about what you're doing!!"

In a way, she was right. I was cutting it the way I heard it in my head, simply, with a long instrumental at the center. But in a bigger way, she was wrong. I was cutting it to be true, not to be slick. I wanted the track to serve the song, rather than the other way around.

Jean kept complaining every time she could get hold of me, and after the third or fourth "You're ruining this song!" I turned and said, "Look, Jean. This is music, not business. This is *my* bailiwick, not yours. If you don't like the way I'm doing it, you ought to leave." She stayed.

I was making enough money to afford a place in New York, and Beth and I moved into a two-bedroom apartment at 10 West Sixty-sixth Street, just down from Lincoln Center. We felt rich, living in the city. Gene Simmons and Isaac Asimov were our neighbors, Central Park was a few yards away, and I had a dedicated writing room again. I did as many shows as I could cram in, determined to begin stock-piling cash against a rainy day. I never wanted to be scared about money again.

We played Asbury Park with Loggins and Messina, and I learned something about how to conduct myself if I ever became the lead act again. My band had been on the road for weeks, living off sandwiches while we opened for bigger stars. When we got to the venue that afternoon, we saw half a dozen Weber barbecues being fired up. We looked at one another, shrugged our shoulders, and made our way to the opener's dressing room. More sandwiches.

We were just about to eat when we heard loud voices raised in argument next door. The promoter was trying to contain himself, saying, "We didn't buy steaks for the opening act—we bought steaks for you and Jim and our own crew."

Kenny responded, "You have enough steak to feed an army. What were you going to do, take the leftovers home? Feed Janis's band along with ours!"

The promoter, fuming, said, "No way. No way I'm wasting steak on an opener."

Kenny shouted, "Fine! Fine!! If you won't waste steak on the opener, we won't waste a great show on a stupid promoter!" and stalked off.

We had steak for dinner that night, and I've rarely felt more grateful toward another performer.

Lines came out in March 1975 to glowing reviews. Herb had come up with a brilliant promotion plan. Instead of releasing the obvious single, "At Seventeen," first, we'd release "When the Party's Over." He reasoned that radio people would listen to the album and begin playing "the right single" instead, feeling superior to the record company. He was correct.

He also came up with a beautiful advertising plan, though it would be considered payola today. Our sixty-second radio spots had "At Seventeen" playing for the first fifty seconds; then a neutral voice said, "'At Seventeen,' by Janis Ian. From the album *Between the Lines*. Available now." People would hear the spot and call the radio station, wanting to hear the rest of the song.

The record started gaining national momentum. My audiences got bigger. I began headlining at colleges, then small theaters. I split cobills with everyone from Steve Martin and David Steinberg to Kris Kristofferson and Neil Sedaka.

By the end of August, the single was Top Ten, and the album would soon be gold. I remember the first time I realized things had changed. I was walking from my dressing room (the boys' locker room) to the venue (the gym), talking to my road manager. When I looked up, there was a battalion of students lining the walls on either side of the hallway. I walked between them, remembering how scared I'd have felt if this were the "Society's Child" days. Instead, people were saying things like, "I can't believe I'm this close to her!"

As I walked up the steps to the stage, I heard the most incredible roar coming from the audience. And I hadn't even sung a note!

So, we graduated, from the station wagon to a van to a tour bus. I spent the rest of 1975 in transit, answering the same questions over and over again, trying to keep some semblance of reality in my performer's life. There's nothing like talking about yourself to make a performer happy, and that's what I did for most of that year. It sounds like fun, being the object of interest, but after the fiftieth interview it gets old. I started counting how many times a reporter would ask, "Which comes first, the words or the music?" but stopped when I reached two hundred. I'd never realized how boring I could be.

That fall, I played twenty-four shows in eighteen cities in thirty-three days. The routing was awful. David and Hal were no longer my agents, and the new people didn't care how much time or money I lost getting from place to place. They'd send me from Pittsburgh to Ottawa to Miami without a second thought. Jean and I discussed it, and when my contract was up, I left to go with Ed Rubin and Magna Artists, who made sure things were done with a bit more intelligence.

The Tonight Show booked me for September 24, midtour. Johnny Carson was really sweet, telling me he'd missed me and inviting me to sit and chat. Because I was on tour, CBS sent their private plane so I could make the show and then my next gig. We flew over the Rockies in a thunderstorm, and I thought, *Please, God. Not now, when I finally have a shot. Not now!* as lightning flew all around us.

After *The Tonight Show,* my career exploded. Suddenly every television show in the country wanted me. I couldn't walk down the street without being stopped. I learned to take the back table in restaurants, facing away from the door so no one would notice me. I couldn't go shopping for myself. Things moved so fast that I barely kept up.

On October 11, I flew from Los Angeles to New York to be part of the first *Saturday Night Live.* I arrived at LaGuardia, sporting a temperature of 103 degrees and a throat full of sandpaper. I didn't even think about canceling. It was the first live entertainment show on television since *Ed Sullivan* went off the air. Everyone was nervous enough, so I kept my mouth shut and did my job.

Walking across the studio during a break, I noticed a papier-mâché mountain. A pig and a frog were talking to each other above it. Curious, I stopped and listened to the conversation, then walked around the back. There was a tall, skinny fellow named Jim Henson there, having a conversation with himself in two voices. I shrugged my shoulders and walked away, thinking, *What on earth have I gotten myself into now?!*

The next week, trying to walk around a piano and get back to my guitar, I fell off a stage in Atlanta. I'd been wearing prescription glasses for years, but didn't think they looked good onstage, so I was blind as a bat up there. I fell right into the audience, bouncing off someone's chair, then hitting the floor on my shins and ankles. I crawled back up and continued the show, went to my room and iced my legs, then finished the week's touring before seeing my doctor. When I finally hit his office, he read me the riot act. I had massive bruising on both legs, I'd sprained my ankle badly, I could have gotten phlebitis, what on earth was wrong with me?! He put me on crutches for the next two months.

Limping down Fifty-seventh Street a little while later, I ran into Bruce Springsteen. He was on the cover of both *Newsweek* and *Time* that week, much more famous than I was, but he sweetly turned and

said, "Hi, Janis . . . you probably don't remember me. We worked together at 914 Studios a while back." He was dead serious when he said
it, too. His genuine humility overwhelmed me.

I was loving my life, and having a good time with the money I was
earning. One day, I decided to buy Beth a really nice watch. I walked
into Cartier, one of the biggest jewelry stores in New York, and began
looking around. After a few minutes, I noticed several men in dark suits
surreptitiously looking my way. *I probably don't look like I belong in here,
in my boots and jeans,* I thought. I flashed a Rolex watch I'd been given
by a promoter toward the salesperson. It was no help. The salesperson,
assuming I couldn't afford to buy such expensive trinkets, didn't bother
coming over.

I walked through the store to the elevator and up to the next floor.
The security people followed me, no longer bothering to hide their suspicions. When I finally got someone's attention and asked to see a
watch, the two men flanked me on either side, never taking their eyes
off the jewelry. I moved on until I reached the manager's office. Walking past his secretary, I marched into the office and said, "I was about
to spend somewhere in the neighborhood of five thousand dollars in
your store this afternoon. However, after being followed around like a
criminal for half an hour, I'm going to Tiffany's and giving them my
business!"

I bought two Patek Philippe watches at Tiffany's that day.

It was fun, suddenly being famous and having extra money to spend,
but I was getting nervous about recording. Between shows, press, and
meetings, I was trying to write my next album. We'd planned to start
the following spring, after I'd taken two months off to create the songs,
but CBS wanted to move it up six months. I went into the studio feeling like I didn't have enough good material. I'd never been able to write
on the road; I wrote my best when I was home with nothing to do, bored
out of my skull. I liked a few of the songs well enough; I was particularly

fond of one called "Love Is Blind," but it worried me that my follow-up to a monster hit record might not be as good as it ought to be.

Brooks and Jean kept telling me the songs were fine. I couldn't understand why everyone was pushing so hard, but I thought, *I'm exhausted. I'm probably just not seeing clearly.*

Decades later, Brooks confessed that the record company called him daily for progress reports, insisting I finish the album so they could release it and satisfy their shareholders. He wasn't happy with it, either, but he had to keep them satisfied. No one wanted to rock the boat.

It's a terrible thing, when you're an artist who's suddenly successful, and the people around you lose sight of the very thing that made you so.

Ron Frangipane and I spent most of August working out arrangements and scoring them. Our January 1 deadline looked easy at first, but events conspired against us. Brooks had sold 914, so we went to the CBS studio complex. Because of union rules, we couldn't work with our talented second engineer, Larry Alexander. We had to use a CBS engineer instead, and working with unfamiliar equipment and people slowed us down. To make matters worse, many of the players we'd been using weren't available. I'd told them all I wouldn't be recording again for a year, yet here we were, just a few months later, asking them to clear time.

Equipment broke down; because we were tied to union-ruled CBS Studios, we couldn't just go somewhere else. The new second engineer was great, but he wasn't used to the way we worked. Most of all, I was booked, and booked. We worked around it as much as possible, but in the end we were really up against a wall, and we all felt like there was a gun at our heads. The sessions were rushed. The songs felt unfinished. I was trying to record while doing a million other things, and every part of my work began to suffer.

December arrived, and the album, now titled *Aftertones*, still wasn't mixed. With the exception of Christmas, we were in the studio every day that month, pulling fourteen- and sixteen-hour shifts. I did a dozen shows as well, and woke each morning wanting to cry from fatigue.

I had a sold-out show at Carnegie Hall scheduled for December. It was the most thrilling evening of my career to date, and I prepared for weeks, adding extra pieces to the band, rehearsing until we were sated with it. To walk the same steps Edith Piaf walked, to occupy the same dressing room Billie Holiday had prepared in, was the stuff of dreams.

A few days after the show, I was doing something unprecedented, throwing a party for everyone at CBS and paying for it myself. I wanted to thank them all, from the mail room people who forwarded my fan mail to Walter and my promotion team. I'd hired the penthouse suite of an expensive hotel, complete with indoor pool. The prospect of Carnegie and the party kept me going. I'd planned both to a tee; nothing could possibly go wrong.

A reporter from the *Village Voice* had accompanied the tour for a few days in November, interviewing me in hotel rooms between gigs. I wasn't happy about it; the whole thing gave me a bad feeling. I argued with Jean, saying my hunches were usually right, but she insisted that the *Voice* was going to do a standard profile, putting me on the cover, and the press would be good.

The Carnegie show was everything I'd dreamed it would be, but two days later, Peter called to say he'd just seen an advance edition of the *Voice*. The title of my article was "Janis Ian Comes Out From 'Between the Lines,'" and it focused heavily on my sexuality. The writer, Cliff Jahr, seemed to be making a career out of outing people; according to Peter, he'd already exposed Elton John and David Bowie. At least I was in good company.

I freaked. From everything I'd been told, this would spell the end of my career. It might lead to criminal charges in some states. I could be committed to a mental institution in others. Radio wouldn't play my music. CBS could drop me because of the standard morals clause in my contract.

I got into bed, pulled the covers over my head, and stayed there until Beth yanked them off and sternly told me to get on with my life.

I had a meeting with Ina that afternoon, and she greeted me with anger. Here they'd all worked so hard, invested so much time in making me a household name, and now I'd ruined it all. She thought I'd planned the whole thing, to "come out" at the height of my career. She'd cried when she read the article. I was throwing a party for CBS that night, in the executive suite of the Plaza Hotel. How could she face them?

In my heart, I agreed. My relationship with Beth was open insofar as friends and family were concerned, but most of my business associates knew nothing, or preferred not to ask. Now the whole world could read about it.

But I refused to take the blame. I heatedly told her that over the past year, I'd done more than two hundred shows, *and* written and recorded a new album. I had no stomach for this kind of drama. If Jean had listened to me in the first place, the article would never have been written. I was done with being polite, I was done with being agreeable. My new record would matter far more than which side of the sheets I slept on.

As the weeks passed, it turned out I was right. Though the *Voice* article was read by New Yorkers, the rest of the country ignored it. And fortunately for me, the press ignored it, too.

THE BAND AND I were now touring in a luxury bus, with our own sound and lighting system. Some things about it were great; we could get a decent night's sleep, showering at the venue, then crawling into our bunks after rehashing the show. My tour manager, Patti, didn't have to drive everywhere, and I didn't have to pack and unpack every day. Twenty hours in a bus will try anyone's patience, though, and tempers began fraying.

We were also getting spoiled. People were falling all over themselves to keep me happy, and that was worrisome. A writer can't write about life if they're not living it, and I felt like I was losing my "street creds." Backstage, there was caviar, pâté de foie gras, and champagne. The band was overworked and overpaid. Flung into a surreal situation where the only people we really interacted with were one another, for three and four months at a stretch, the sniping began. The drums weren't loud enough. The bass was too loud. The food and hotels weren't good enough. The money wasn't good enough.

I ignored it. I had no time to think. In January 1976, I was nominated for five Grammy Awards. CBS was ecstatic; I was one of only five solo female artists to receive that many nominations at once. My companions in that honor roll were enough to make anyone's head spin: Ella Fitzgerald, Olivia Newton-John, Barbra Streisand, and Aretha Franklin. A feeding frenzy ensued, with me the main dish. I concentrated on getting through the days, and enjoying what I could.

I was immensely flattered to be mentioned in the same breath as Ella. From the time I could remember, jazz singers had informed my style. Much as I loved Baez, I'd always known I wasn't born with the kind of instrument she had. My own voice wasn't exceptional in any way but one; I had good pitch. Otherwise, there was nothing much to recommend it.

Like me, my favorite singers had one thing in common—none of them were born with beautiful voices. They'd had to *make* themselves great singers. In fact, I've often wondered whether that's why most people who are born with beautiful voices are not, by and large, extraordinary singers. They may become great *vocalists*, sure. They may *sound* pretty. But the *grit*, the *steel*, the *nuances* that make for great interpretation . . . well, they're usually not found in pretty voices. They're found in people like Billie Holiday, Edith Piaf, Ella Fitzgerald.

My mother was an absolute jazz freak. We used to love going out at night together, hanging around the Blue Note and other jazz clubs, listening to Sarah Vaughan and other greats. Mom loved it when we'd go backstage after a show, and Sarah or Nina Simone would greet her by name. One of the proudest moments of her life was the day I made the cover of the venerable jazz magazine *Downbeat*. I strived to become the kind of singer those women were, though I felt about as far away from my goal as the moon.

I had a night off sometime that February; I'd spent the day doing TV and radio, and when I finally got back to the hotel around six that evening, I decided to spend a quiet night alone in my room. I took a luxuriously long shower and slipped into a robe. Room service delivered a light dinner, and I settled happily in bed with the tray in my lap and began flipping through the television channels.

I heard Ella Fitzgerald's voice coming from the tinny speaker and stopped there, waiting for the picture to clear. It was a talk show, though I can't remember whose, and after Ella finished singing, she made her way to the dais for an interview. I was reaching toward the room service cart for some salt when I heard the host ask her if she'd been enjoying anyone else's music lately.

"Well, yes," she said, "I think Janis Ian is the best young singer in America today."

Whoosh! I knocked the salt across the cart and onto the floor. My body followed, landing in a heap by the side of the bed. I righted myself and sat staring at the screen, through the rest of her interview, through the commercials, and on into the next segment. I literally fell off the bed in surprise. *Ella Fitzgerald knew my name!* Not only that, *she'd heard my work!* I held Ella in the highest esteem, and here she was on national TV, holding *me* up to the world.

Unbelievable.

THE GRAMMYS were a few weeks later. I flew my mother and father, as well as Ina and Jean, in for the ceremony. I bought everyone gifts: expensive inlaid belt buckles for the band, a good watch for Dad, a beautiful opal necklace for Mom. It was little enough to pay them back for years of support. The band had worked for next to nothing; Ina and Jean had worked for nothing. It was time to reward that.

What an amazing evening it was! I'd been at the ninth Grammy Awards in March 1967, when "Society's Child" was nominated and Arlo Guthrie joined me onstage to present one of the awards. I remembered how few people were there, and hearing one of the organizers say, "If we could only get some radio coverage . . ." Now, the Grammys were big business.

CBS flew me in from Salt Lake City on their private jet, and I sang "At Seventeen" to a crowd of people who'd last known me as a sixteen-year-old wunderkind. When I finished, the applause went on so long that they had to cut to a commercial.

I was on top of the world. Joan Baez presented one of the awards; when she opened my envelope, she grinned and said, "That's my girl!" I had the opportunity to thank Ella for her kind words, and she led the standing ovation when I won a Grammy. It was the first time I'd met the music industry as an adult, and I kept thinking of Sally Field's words: "You like me . . . right now, you like me."

I had come home.

I'd lost Record of the Year to the Captain & Tennille, which was all right because I liked them. Song of the Year went to Stephen Sondheim's "Send in the Clowns," which was all right because it's a great song. Album of the Year went to Paul Simon for *Still Crazy After All These Years,* which hurt a bit because although we hadn't made as commercial an album, Brooks and I thought *Between the Lines* was a landmark record, one that would endure. But we won Best Vocalist, back when the awards weren't so diluted and there was only one "Best Vocalist" instead of "Best Latin Vocalist," "Best Rap Vocalist," "Best Vocalist From Another Planet." And we won Best Engineered Pop Album, so Brooks finally got his Grammy.

TEN

Love Is Blind

Love is blind
Love is only sorrow
Love is no tomorrow
since you went away

The next two years went by in a blur. *Aftertones* came out in March of '76 to surprisingly good reviews. It went gold within weeks, so I guess the shareholders were happy. With two hit albums in a row, Jean was busier than ever, and she started to drink heavily, sometimes to the point of incoherence. It was no use phoning her after business hours anymore.

I asked Ina, "Why would someone work so hard for so many years, and just when we're at the top, start blowing it?"

Ina cocked her head and responded, "When you're at the top, the only thing you can see is how far you can fall."

I toured, and toured, and toured. By the end of April I'd covered the whole of the United States and Canada, every major and secondary market. I put my foot down, refusing to replay all those markets in the same year. Instead, I asked my agency to book me into tertiary markets, the places no one else bothered playing. Small towns, small halls. We'd make less money, but at that point, I didn't care. I really wanted to see my country, and I did. We'd roll into town on our bus, and the locals would proudly show me their new high school gym, or tell me stories about the town's history. It was great.

We played Louisiana, near the heart of Cajun country, and got invited to a local bar after the show. The place was full of musicians, and for two or three hours we struggled to keep up with the fiddlers. Between songs, the owner served up delicious sausages from the bar. We ate our fill, and asked for more. He shrugged and made a call. A few minutes later, an ancient woman staggered through the door, back bent under a huge tray of sausage. I realized everything I'd been eating was homemade, and asked the owner what went into them. "Oh, dem *boudin*, maybe possum, maybe 'gator, maybe rat. Who know? Who care!"

We had the next night off, and a bunch of us went to see Elvis. It was sad. The last time I'd seen him, I was with Carol Hunter at the taping of his black leather TV special, back in 1968. He was magnificent, and I came away a fan. Now he was a pathetic, bloated wreck, even forgetting the words to "Love Me Tender." Scotty Moore had to bring him the lyric, and Elvis could barely read it, let alone sing it. I whispered to someone, "He's stoned—look at him! High as a kite!" The woman behind us slugged me with her purse, saying, "Elvis doesn't do drugs, shame on you! He's a personal friend of President Nixon's, you know!"

I was rarely home, and when I was, I worked full-time on outside projects. Beth was wonderfully supportive, but she had no life outside of mine. She came on the road with me. She stayed in the hotel room with me. At home, she spent all her time with me. It got wearing, and I tried to encourage her to make some friends outside my circle, or even within my circle. I didn't know it then, but I was sealing the relationship's doom.

I went back to Europe in May, still trying to crack the market. I'd argued about it for weeks with Jean, telling her I was so tired that the only way to wake me most mornings was for Beth to shove a wet washcloth on my face. I hadn't had a day off since the previous Christmas, and was starting to feel like I had no center. I said Europe could wait; Jean said CBS Europe couldn't. If I didn't take advantage of their enthusiasm now, I might lose the territory forever. So off I went.

It should have been fun, going there on the record company's dime, and parts of it were. I ate dinner alone at the London hotel every evening. The wine steward, realizing I didn't know a Cabernet from a Pepsi, took pity on me. He served up the wine from everyone's leftover bottles after the restaurant closed each night, trying to educate my palate. There's nothing like comparing wines side by side. I got to try out truly great vintages, like the 1945 Château Mouton Rothschild, the '59 Château Margaux, along with Haut-Brions, Latours, Pomerols. After the wine, he'd give me port, and toward the end, he'd sneak small tastes of vintage brandies in as well. It's a wonder I woke lucid enough to work the next day.

Still, I was lonely. I missed Beth, and my family. I missed the friends I had, especially Peter and his wife, Janet. I even missed my band. I knew no one in England, and no one knew me. I was virtually unknown outside the United States, and coming off the highs of the Grammys and platinum albums, I found it humiliatingly depressing. I know it sounds absurd, but when you go from playing sold-out houses with roaring crowds to quarter-houses filled with the merely curious, it's disappointing. You feel like you're starting all over again.

Also, European TV was still operating like we did in the fifties. Everything had to be lip-synched, rather than sung live, which made me look stupid. When you've been performing a song live for months, your phrasing changes, and there's no way to keep from mismatching your original. It just looks silly. And they still thought it was great to shoot singers in "interesting locations," so I spent a peculiar day at the Tower of London, accompanying Shirley Bassey as she sang "Jesse."

After a grueling time in London, I went on to the Netherlands. The promotion schedule there was so rough that I began referring to myself as "a performing monkey." We hit Amsterdam at 6 A.M., and I was in a TV station by seven. I worked straight through until midnight, then got up at five to do it again. The local CBS staff took me out to dinner on my last night, and I fell asleep into a plate of lobster.

Unbeknownst to me, Jean and Ina were renegotiating with CBS. When I got home, they took me out to dinner and proudly announced that I had a new deal. I'd be guaranteed a quarter-million-dollar budget per album; anything I didn't spend, I could keep. In addition, I'd receive a million-dollar advance.

I tried to look grateful, but I wasn't so sure. A million dollars was an absurd amount of money to pay someone who'd happily be doing it for free. I was earning more than enough without it. In return, I was promising to give CBS seven more albums in seven years. There was no way I could keep up this pace.

Ina had also negotiated that ownership of all future masters would return to me eventually. The newer ones would revert completely, and I'd own the first three everywhere but North America. While this was stunning news, I wished I'd been consulted. I'd have preferred to take no money, and own all of them worldwide.

Still, none of us had ever seen a million-dollar check before! Ina photocopied it for us. I still have my copy, which is a good thing, because I sure haven't seen one since.

We began work on *Miracle Row* at the end of September. I took the title from a song I'd written while staying with my mom. She lived in a Puerto Rican neighborhood, and I'd fall asleep each night to the sounds of bongos and Celia Cruz floating up from the streets. It was a vibrant, tactile district. Daily life was played out on the tenement stoops; women gossiped, men showed off, and kids played stoopball against the battered buildings.

Brooks and I had agreed to part ways; we'd used up whatever tolerance we had for each other trying to finish *Aftertones*. With my new status, I insisted on producing this album, and asked Ron Frangipane to coproduce. I also insisted on staying in New York for most of the recording process, instead of touring intermittently. I'd been living there for two years, and still hadn't been home long enough to figure out where the local grocery store was.

Besides, I was getting wary of touring when other people controlled the budget. I'd just done fifty shows in nine weeks, grossing more than $250,000, yet I wound up $60,000 in the hole. Jean and Ina shrugged it off, saying, "Nobody makes money on the road, Janis. You make it up on the songwriting and publishing." *Nobody* was a relative term; Jean and my agents made plenty of money from it, since they commissioned on the gross.

I started asking questions, demanding that my tours at least break even. Jean's attitude was that I was still a child, and needed to concentrate on creativity instead of business. I slowly began to see that everyone had a huge investment, both emotional and financial, in my remaining ignorant. I was twenty-five years old, but in their minds, I was still society's child.

By the beginning of 1977, life had settled into a routine. Make a record, tour, stop for a few weeks and write, then begin another record. I had no time to absorb what was happening around me, externally or internally. I certainly had no time to translate it into songs. I felt I'd lost touch with the very things that fed my writing. I wasn't growing.

In my journal, I wrote:

This vicious circle—make an album, release it in time for your tour, so it'll hit and the tour will make a lot of money. You must tour to make the album a hit. Then, if the album's a success, you must release another right away, to capitalize on the success. If it's a flop, you must release another even sooner, to hide the flop. Ad infinitum. Where does one grow, in all this insanity? The distance from song to stage—the inner distance—is too wide. I want my words to leap from the pages like swordsmen. I must learn to think with my eyes again.

But it seemed like nobody was thinking very much; everyone, including me, was just racing to stay in place. I was in way over my head, trying to coordinate the two dozen people who worked for me full-time, and still maintain some semblance of life as an artist. It wasn't working.

A lot of things weren't working. I came around a corner one day and found Peter's wife necking with Beth on the sofa. Surprised and outraged, I demanded to know what was going on. Beth stared miserably at the floor and said, "I don't know. I just know things aren't like they were between us."

How can things be like they were? I asked. *We finally have some money. We're finally living in New York. You can buy all the clothes and jewelry you like, and make no mistake, you're a really good shopper!*

"I'm not sure I like being on the road . . . and I'm having feelings for other people."

Well, that was obvious enough. I scowled. *How could you do this with Peter's wife?*

Again she said, "I don't know." I was losing patience.

Beth, what do you want from me? Just tell me! I took a deep breath. I didn't want this to escalate into World War III. Hands on hips, I waited for her response.

"I don't know. . . ." she said again.

I shrugged my shoulders and left. If she didn't know what she wanted, how was I supposed to know? And if her not knowing meant she played around on me, well, that wasn't acceptable. Not acceptable at all.

To make matters more confusing, my drummer wanted to sleep with me. When I rebuffed him, he went to Beth instead, and told her he wanted a threesome. When I refused that as well, he went after Beth alone, though I didn't know it at the time. I was busy planning a trip to Japan, where *Aftertones* had been No. 1 for months, and the single from it, "Love Is Blind," had already set records for chart longevity. It was amazing to me that I could have success in such a foreign place.

I called Peter, who'd introduced me to Japanese culture and Zen Buddhism years before, and asked if he wanted to come with me. We spent a week planning a ten-page telex of everything we wanted to see. The telex made headlines in Japan; apparently no Western artist had ever bothered taking that much interest in the local culture before. Other performers demanded hamburgers backstage; we were asking for sushi. Other people stayed holed up in their hotel rooms, afraid to walk out into a non-English-speaking world. We had a hit list of places to go, from Kabuki and Noh Theater to the Kiyomizu Temple and Katsura Imperial Gardens. We wanted to stay in a traditional ryokan, and take the bullet train. The press had a field day with our list, reprinting it in Japanese newspapers all over the country.

I rented a house in Connecticut for the summer, determined that Beth and I would have some time alone together. A few weeks before, she'd asked if Tino could stay in the apartment while we were away. "Fine with me," I said, not really caring one way or another. Just after that, she told me she was in love with my drummer. And me. At the same time.

Oh, God, I thought. *I'm right back to square one. Now she's going to say that if I want the relationship to continue, I have to take part in a ménage à trois.* I declined.

"Does he know you feel like this?" I asked. No, no. She swore up and down that he had no idea. Being blissfully, or perhaps willfully, naive, I believed her.

I threw a big party on the Fourth of July, inviting all my family and friends to stay the weekend. None of us had ever been in such a setting before; the house I'd rented sat on five pristine acres, surrounded by grape arbors. From the front patio, large enough to seat forty people comfortably, you could see the Long Island Sound. After breakfast, I'd walk down to the private beach, and enjoy hiding in the shelter of the rocks above me.

One day, laying there in the sun with absolutely nothing on, I heard a loudspeaker booming out from the ocean. I sat up, curious to know why a tour boat was in the area, and heard: "This, folks, is the house singer Janis Ian has rented for the summer—fabulous, isn't it, with its own private beach?!"

Tino came up for the party, and much to my surprise I found myself getting along with him. He was funny, and charming, kissing the ladies' hands, and entertaining us with stories of life in France and Portugal. Beth was thrilled to see us getting along; I think it made her feel less guilty about what was going on with Barry. Because something was definitely going on. A couple of weeks into our vacation, when she'd made up an excuse to go into New York five days out of six, I finally asked her to leave. "Go find out if he wants you," I told her, trying to be noble. "If he does, I won't stand in your way."

Gosh. How stupid can you be?

She came back a few days later, despondent. Barry wasn't responding to her overtures; he wanted to keep his job. We spent a glum week avoiding each other, rattling around in the big house that now felt like a mausoleum.

I think one of the most confusing—and painful—things in the world is when your partner tells you they love you, and they also love someone else. When they beg for a chance to explore those feelings, saying they just need to "get it out of their system," and they fully intend to come back to you, in the end.

It makes you feel desperate, and hurt, and confused. Most of all, it makes you feel like you're not enough.

Two weeks before we were due to leave for Japan, Barry came over for dinner with Jean, Beth, and myself. Over drinks, he casually informed me that if I didn't double his salary, he wasn't going to leave with the rest of us. I looked at Jean, then took her aside. *Let's fire him now*, I said. *Let's fire him now; we can find someone else.* No, she insisted, the work papers are done, the flights are booked. She didn't think I needed the pressure of breaking in a new drummer. So we doubled his salary, after he extracted our promise not to tell the rest of the band.

The band were definitely getting strange. We'd been at a party, and when I'd opened a closet door to get my jacket, I'd found Barry and Stu, my bass player, hiding in the corner. They hastily wiped their upper lips and laughed, saying they'd just needed to discuss some business. It didn't occur to me that they were doing cocaine, and were unwilling to share their stash.

I went to Japan a few days ahead of everyone, walking off the plane and into a press conference with 136 reporters and 35 photographers. I was astounded; entire school classes had been given the morning off so they could come to the airport and greet me. The conference went on for three hours, until I finally pleaded exhaustion and went to my hotel. The most amazing part was the quality of press—not just the entertainment sections, or music magazines, but serious journals and periodicals that targeted intellectuals, artists of all types, and scientists.

Apparently, I'd made a dent in the national consciousness, which was beyond me to explain. "Love Is Blind" and *Aftertones* both struck some deep chord in the Japanese psyche, resulting in my record occupying the top chart position for more than a year.

From my point of view, even though my home life was falling apart, the trip was great. I went everywhere I'd asked to go, accompanied by our Japanese tour manager, Masa Kajimoto. Masa was about my age; his father was the leading classical impresario in Japan, just as my promoter, Tats Nagashima, was the leading pop promoter. They'd traded sons for the work experience, with Tats's son Tommy going to work with Masa's father, and vice versa.

Thanks to Masa, I learned more about Japan than the average tourist, but he irritated me beyond belief in the beginning. He kept taking me to fancy Kobe steak restaurants and ordering American food; I kept wanting to eat Japanese food in local restaurants. I finally broke free of his grip one day and walked up to a traditional-looking eatery, knocking on the door. Someone opened it, saw me, and slammed the door shut in my face. I turned to Masa, baffled, and said, "Why on earth did they do that? Do they not like Westerners?"

Masa hurried to my side and said, "They are ashamed, because they can't speak English." Then, seeing my confusion, he muttered something in Japanese and testily said, "All right. You want to see Japan, you'll see Japan. Just don't tell Tats."

From that moment on, we had a fabulous time. Masa took me to the student restaurants, where we ate *ocha-zuki,* a bowl of rice topped with tea leaves. If you were a starving student, you ordered that with tea, then poured a bit of tea in the bowl for flavor. We went to Fukuoka and strolled along the canal, eating a local delicacy—soup with live fish swimming in it. We saw Katsura Village, and Kabuki and Noh Theater to my heart's content.

Tats arranged for us to stay at the famous Hiragiya Ryokan in Kyoto for three nights, and Peter and I saw temples galore. I also wanted to look at Shunga, the erotic woodblock prints. Masa's father arranged for us to go to the first floor of an old building, where we had tea with the owner of the gallery for an hour. He grilled me, asking whether I intended to purchase prints for resale in the United States. I promised they would stay with me, even adding that on my death, they would go back to Japan. After another hour, we were invited to the second floor, where we gave our host small presents and had more tea, discussing the various artists I liked. Two hours later, having convinced him of my sincerity, I finally entered the top floor. I stopped in my tracks, staring at four walls of floor-to-ceiling shelves overstuffed with scrolls no Caucasian had ever seen before.

Aftertones reached double-platinum status while we were in Japan, and a celebratory dinner was held in a private room on the third floor of an incredibly ancient Tokyo restaurant, which I was gravely informed had "never had a white visitor before." We were seated on the floor around a long table with ten other people, among them the president and vice president of Sony Records, the two premier songwriters in Japan, the two biggest Japanese performers, the head of their biggest TV network, and the president of my Japanese publishing company.

A whole cask of sake was wheeled in; the label head hammered a spigot into its side, and served us all for about half an hour. After that, a chef arrived with an entire barrel of fresh rice. He made sushi for another hour, and I stuffed myself. Some of it was normal (tuna, eel, cucumber) and some of it was pretty exotic (tuna roe, codfish tongue), but all of it was delicious. I ate more than my fill.

The chef eventually departed, along with his barrel, and I began to look forward to bed, only an hour's worth of speeches and salutations away.

"Now comes the *real* dinner," said the chef, returning with a large tray holding an enormous lobster. It was big enough to feed an army, at least twenty pounds. I glanced despairingly at Jean and muttered, "I'm full," to which she shrugged and said, "Too bad." I was handed an antique pair of ivory chopsticks and asked to take the first bite.

All right, I thought, *I'll fit it somewhere and not eat for the rest of the year.* I smiled, bowed, and reached for the lobster to start our feast. When I touched it, one of the front claws slowly rose into the air, hovering there for a moment, then falling back onto the platter with a thud. The antennae twitched, and I sprang back from the table, ready to be attacked at any moment.

My hosts roared with laughter and explained that lobster sushi was a great delicacy. Yes, it was technically alive, but they assured me it felt nothing; its back had been cracked and the spinal cord severed. These were merely "nervous twitches."

I sat back down and whispered to Jean, "I can't. It's still alive."

"You must," she whispered back.

"I *can't!*" I whined.

"You *must!*" she retorted. "You represent your nation, your race, your culture, and your profession. You have no choice. You *must* get it down."

I got it down.

There were huge crowds wherever I went; there still weren't many Westerners in Japan, and when we'd travel en masse, groups of Japanese would form around us and stare at our hair and skin. In many places, the only whites they'd ever seen were on TV. One of my crew, Richard, was a redhead, and he got used to little old ladies coming up and plucking a hair from his chest, to see if the color was real.

I went to the public baths in one town, forewarned that they were co-ed. I didn't have a problem with that, but it felt a little weird when a group of people clustered around me, talking and pointing toward my head and groin. My translator explained that they wondered if the hair everywhere on my body was curly.

Despite our success, or perhaps because of it, Jean was drinking so much that she occasionally became an embarrassment. One night, Tats was telling me about a retreat he went to every year, where he lived in a monk's cell for a week and maintained a vow of silence, eating only rice. Jean chimed in with a smile, saying, "Oh, I just *love* primitive people!" I could have fallen through the floor in shame.

Jean did do me one great favor. Beth and I had been sharing a room, as usual, but she wouldn't touch me. On her birthday, I'd given her a gorgeous lapis lazuli necklace, and she hadn't worn it once. I put it down to fatigue, and the strangeness of our environment. About two weeks into the tour, Jean finally sat me down and said, "She and Barry are sleeping together. The entire band is covering for them. They're making you look like a fool."

I was beyond humiliated. And deeply, deeply wounded. I'd been dim enough to think of the band members as my friends. I'd been silly enough to think that, since they'd played with me when there wasn't much money, the dollars didn't make a difference. It would never in a million years have occurred to me that they liked the money more than they liked the truth. I felt used, and abused.

When Beth got back to the hotel room, I'd already packed her things. "Go stay with your boyfriend!" I shouted. "Get out of my room!" She came back a few minutes later, crying. She'd asked Barry if she could stay with him, and he'd said no. Still furious, I called the front desk and arranged for another room.

The rest of that tour is pretty hazy. The last time I'd had my heart broken, it had been by Beth, five years earlier. Since then, I'd lived my life certain that we would last forever. Now it seemed nothing was eternal.

The capper was our first gig back in the United States. I was playing Universal Amphitheater in Los Angeles, when it was still an outdoor venue. I didn't realize backstage had an open bar, but my bass player Stu took full advantage of it. I didn't know anything was wrong until the guitar solo during "At Seventeen," when I heard a male voice booming out of the loudspeakers into the crowd.

"I hate this fucking song," it said.

I looked at my soundman, thinking someone had grabbed his talk-back mic. He shook his head. A few bars later, I heard, "I hate this fucking song. I'm never playing this fucking song again." A few people in the crowd began laughing, pointing at the bass player. Stu's microphone was still on, and he was mumbling into it, while Jean gestured at him from the wings.

I finished the song, bowed, and walked off to see Stu collapsed on the floor, Jean sitting on top of him. Barry and my guitarist, Jeff, were on the floor as well, rolling with laughter. Somehow, I didn't find it funny.

Why didn't I just fire the lot of them? I couldn't, at that point. There wasn't time to find another band, let alone rehearse. So we went on to Australia, which was a huge success. The Sydney Opera House had just opened, and we added a third, then a fourth show to the sold-out run.

Our promoter, Kevin Jacobsen, rented a yacht so we could spend a day cruising Sydney Harbor and celebrate. I spent most of it sitting on the bow, feeling the spray of water on my skin.

I wasn't talking to anyone in the band, and it was pure hell getting up onstage. The camaraderie was completely shot. The band were all doing such massive amounts of coke that none of them trusted one another. The paranoia resulted in meltdowns. Jeff and I had a dual guitar solo on "Let Me Be Lonely." One night he accused me of playing it without a flatpick just to make him look bad. I was confused, saying, "Jeff, you know I can't flatpick! I always fingerpick it. I've done it that way for months." He screamed that I was ruining his reputation, and stormed off.

The paranoia was actually funny sometimes. Because Jeff was going home a few days early, Barry and Stu gave him money to buy cocaine. They made him promise to buy it Friday afternoon and put it in his safe-deposit box for the weekend. They were worried he'd snort it all before they got home.

When we got back, I took some time off to get my mom up to Goddard College. She'd been diagnosed with multiple sclerosis a few years earlier, after decades of tingling and numbness that doctors said was probably psychological. After the diagnosis, she'd fallen into a deep depression. She couldn't work full-time anymore, and she saw her future as a downhill slide. Eric and I convinced her to apply for college, in the hope that it would give her a reason to continue. She was thrilled when Goddard accepted her, not just because she'd finally realize her lifelong dream of attending college, but because they had a program tailored to her needs. She only had to be on campus a week or two each semester; the rest of her work could be done at home, when she felt up to it.

Beth moved out and into a residential hotel, to spend the next few months sitting by the phone, waiting for Barry to call. The apartment was full of furniture we'd picked out together, and it felt desolate without her there. I was surrounded by too many memories, so I went back to the Connecticut house I'd rented. A few days into my stay, I tripped over a hole and sprained my ankle. It swelled to the size of a cantaloupe, and I was back on crutches. I couldn't drive, or navigate the lawn and stairs, so I went home. Tino was staying there again, and I told him if he didn't mind sleeping on the couch, he was welcome for as long as he liked.

I was still terribly hurt, and feeling pretty fragile. Tino made good company, taking me to museums, making me laugh, trying to pull me out of my sadness. One night that November, while he was out, I sat on my coffee table writing a new song. I was really pleased with the first verse:

> *I'm still in love, though I don't care*
> *to let you know there's something there*
> *It doesn't show, but when you're near*
> *silly habits mean a lot*

and I'd gotten as far as half a verse:

> *I've been alone now for quite some time, it's true*
> *but every night when I come home, I'm coming home to you*

Now I was stuck. Just as I was about to put down the guitar and give up for the night, there was a knock on the door and Tino walked in. Motioning him to be quiet, I quickly wrote:

> *I listen for your footsteps*
> *Sometimes I even knock. . . .*
> *Silly habits mean a lot*

I sang what I had for Tino, laughing with the sheer joy of working on a good song. When I finished, he leaned over and kissed me on the lips. Sweetly, tenderly, and completely. I looked at him, shocked. He shrugged his shoulders, and said, "Janis. Beth has been gone for months. You're a beautiful, sexy woman, and you're good enough to have anyone you want. Please tell me this is the right time."

I can't tell you how that surprised me. Not just that Beth's ex was now saying he wanted *me,* but that anyone would think I was sexy. Sexy was a word for Sophia Loren, not me. As to being enough, he was wrong on that count, too. I hadn't been enough for Beth, had I? I was never enough, it seemed. If I'd been enough for anyone, they wouldn't have wanted to share me.

I laughed, telling him he had the wrong woman. I wasn't sexy, and I certainly wasn't beautiful. Maybe pretty, in the right light, with the right makeup.

"No, no, my love. You *are* sexy. You *are* beautiful. You're perfect, truly perfect."

I laughed again, telling him he was blind. Still, it was nice to hear. Some part of me, desperate to feel valued again, responded. I felt a tug on my heart.

So I looked into his eyes, and said, *This is the right time, Tino. This is definitely the right time.*

We spent the night on the living room couch. I remember that at one point, after hours of lovemaking, we watched the morning clouds make their way downstream over the Hudson River. It was bitter cold outside, but I was warm and satisfied. I snuggled into the crook of Tino's shoulder, hiding my face in his chest. Snow was coming, but winter couldn't touch me tonight.

ELEVEN

Fly Too High

Would you believe
I was once gonna be somebody?
Run too fast, fly too high

I t's difficult for me to write about the next few years. There were so
many disappointments, I can't begin to count them. And when I
look back on the time I spent with Tino, I still beat myself up for
staying with him so long.

He was marvelous at first. All through the harsh New York winter, I
felt like summer lived in my heart. Worlds opened before my eyes. Tino
was a fabulous raconteur, and he'd enthrall me with stories ranging from
his childhood on Madeira to retellings of the Greek myths. He seemed
to know everything, from the plays of Tennessee Williams to what the
middle piano pedal did. He'd had a classical education, spoke and read
seven live and two dead languages, and laughed longer and harder than
anyone I've known since.

My mother loved him; she said I'd finally found someone who could
keep up with me. My father was glad to see me happy again. My record
company was thrilled; Walter said, "I knew you weren't really gay."

The gay-straight question didn't bother me at all. It seemed to me that people have a tilt. Some tilt a little harder toward the opposite gender, some tilt toward their own. I saw no conflict in having been in love with a man, then a woman, and now a man. To me, love was love; the rest was immaterial.

I was wary at first. I asked him about the ménage à trois, and he explained that he'd done it to please Beth. Given what she'd just done to me, that made sense, and I accepted it. We talked about drugs; he didn't use them, never had. I accepted that, too. He seemed even-tempered, so I put Beth's tales of violence aside. By the time Tino returned to Portugal for a visit with his family, I was thoroughly in love.

There was new blood all around. I'd hired a different tour manager, Stan Schnier, and fired my old band. They'd actually sat Stan down when he was first brought in, to explain "how things worked." They'd arrange to buy drugs, but it was his job to pick them up. Stan just smiled and told them that as soon as they were paying his salary, he'd be glad to follow their instructions. Then he called me to say they needed firing.

Stan put together a new band, and they learned the show on their own time. I only had to spend a day or two rehearsing. The old band members all called, demanding an explanation. I told them I didn't owe them one, and suggested they sober up long enough to figure it out themselves.

I was still arguing with the record company. I'd thought that with the success of *Miracle Row*, which spawned yet another platinum record in Japan, CBS would let me produce, but the powers that be refused. Jean wouldn't back me up, and Ina told me I was crazy for taking on more responsibility, when I already didn't have enough time in the day.

CBS wanted me to work with Joe Wissert, an emotionally distant man who didn't contribute much beyond making sure we stayed within budget. It was painful, hearing songs that had seemed vibrant when I'd demo'd them reduced to flat, uninteresting recordings. Joe was from Los Angeles, and my album ended up reflecting the current L.A. sound, over-smooth and dulled around the edges. I hated it.

When I heard the mastered record *Janis Ian II,* I wanted to throw it out and start over again. It was too late, Jean said. The release schedule was set, the tour was finalized. Too bad, but there wasn't enough time.

There wasn't enough time for anything. I'd finished my fifth album in as many years, fitting in countless outside projects, from film scores to guesting on other people's records. Mel Tormé asked me to duet on "Silly Habits" soon after I wrote it, and we were nominated for a Grammy for it that next January.

I was still touring upward of two hundred fifty days a year. Despite the lack of another big hit record in the United States, my crowds were growing. I had to hire a full-time bodyguard. I couldn't get to the car after a show unless my crew formed a human battering ram. People shoved pens in my face, nearly poking my eyes out. They'd scream when they saw me, demanding to be noticed. I always wore a scarf after a show, to keep the stage makeup off my clothing. Now I had to knot it so people couldn't grab the ends and start a tug-of-war with my neck. Between all that, I was trying to build a relationship.

Tino and I were sitting around the kitchen one night. He was telling me how happy I made him, and then he said, "But of course, I couldn't marry you."

I looked at him, surprised. *Why on earth not?* I asked.

"Because everyone would think I married you for your money."

Are you telling me you can't marry me because I make a lot of money? I asked. *Why should I be denied that, just because I'm successful? That's not fair!*

He smiled, got down on one knee, took my hand, and asked me to marry him. I burst into tears and said *yes.*

That's when it all started going south.

We stayed in a rental house in Los Angeles that summer, so Tino could spend time with his old friends before moving to New York. We planned to drive back in a rental truck with the four hundred cartons of books he'd amassed.

The drive was horrible. Nether of us realized that there was a time limit on blood tests. By the time we found out, it was almost upon us. We hurriedly packed the truck and took off, with three days to get to New York in time to apply for our marriage license. Tino was impossible, never letting me take the wheel, doing seventy in thirty-mile-an-hour zones, speeding through the small towns. After twenty hours straight, I finally insisted we stop for the night. He fell into bed, covered in sweat, and I asked if he wasn't going to take a shower.

With a look I'd never seen on his face, he sat up, swore at me, and yelled, "This is what happens to *men*! You don't like it, go back to your lesbian lover!" Then, to my amazement, he fell asleep.

I put it down to pre-wedding jitters, just a bump in the road. The next morning, he behaved as though nothing had happened. I didn't realize at the time that he probably didn't remember the incident at all.

I'd purchased a two-floor co-op apartment at the Beresford, a fabulous old building right across from the Museum of Natural History. We planned to move into our new place after getting married in September. I loved it from the start; looking out the living room window, I could see the museum's atelier room. When the light was on, I knew Margaret Mead was working.

The wedding was lovely, and we took off for Japan a few days later. From Japan, I went on to London, then back to the United States for two shows at Lincoln Center. On to Japan again, and shows and more shows.

Tino began chafing under my continued absence; how on earth were we going to have children if I was never home? We were in agreement about children; we both wanted lots of them. We'd already decorated a second bedroom for our first child. I'd gone off my birth control pills right after the wedding. I'd even gotten pregnant for a heartbeat, miscarrying toward the end of the second month. My gynecologist assured me that it was common to miscarry a first pregnancy, and Tino and I were positive that with time, we'd have the big family we dreamed of. So I decided that in 1979, I'd stay home as much as possible to work on it.

I had plenty of projects at home, more than I could handle. Barbra Streisand called one day. It was odd, talking to someone bigger than life. I picked up the ringing phone, heard a voice say, "Hi, it's me," and immediately knew who it was. That's *real* fame.

She told me she was doing a remake of *A Star Is Born,* one of my all-time favorite Judy Garland movies, and needed music. Was I interested?

Was I ever! I was thrilled. We spoke about the film for a few minutes, I took some notes, and then she said, "So when you get an idea, call me and we'll talk about it."

I was puzzled and said, *Why would I want to do that?*

She explained. "So I can have some input."

I was more perplexed. *Why would I need input? I'll be writing the songs.*

Streisand hesitated, then said, "Well, so we can work on them together."

Now I was really confused. *Why would I want to work on them together? You're a singer and actress; I'm a songwriter.*

I really didn't mean to offend her. It didn't occur to me that she might want to be in on the writing, might consider herself talented in that area. To me, she was a fantastic singer, and a wonderful actress. I was just a songwriter trying to do my job.

Needless to say, I didn't end up writing the songs. It was a long, long time before I worked on another major film.

I had a headache after our conversation, so I went into Tino's bathroom in search of a Tylenol. Rummaging through the drawers, I happened on some Valium. Not just a bottle, but bottles and bottles. By the time I'd finished counting, there were twelve packed containers sitting on the counter before me, each holding a hundred pills.

What on earth would anyone need with twelve hundred 10-milligram Valium? I went into the bedroom and looked down at my sleeping husband. It was only eight o'clock, but he was already fast asleep. He got up early to write, sometimes at three or four in the morning, and I was used to his being dead to the world when I got home from the studio. I'd envied how quickly he could doze off. Now, I realized he always slept like the dead . . . or someone stoned out of his mind.

The next morning, I confronted him. The last thing I wanted was to be married to an addict. He explained that he'd started using Valium when he was going through exams at UCLA, so wired that he couldn't sleep. "But that was decades ago!" I said. "You can't stay addicted to this stuff. I've been there—it's no good!"

With head bowed, he promised to stop. And for a few days, he really tried. But, as had happened when I'd stopped all those years ago, he couldn't sleep. When he finally drifted off, hours after getting into bed, he had crushingly vivid "Valium dreams" that woke him over and over again. And so, having said he'd thrown away the pills, he just hid them somewhere out of sight, and continued washing down 30 milligrams a night with his beer at dinner.

Another album was due, and I'd finally convinced CBS to let me produce again. My tour manager, Stan, thought I might have a chance at a hit if I did some cowriting.

He set up an appointment with his old friend Albert Hammond, and we met one blustery morning in my Midtown office. Albert was wonderful; he had a track record as long as your arm, and he'd cowritten with enough "newbies" to know how scared I was. He took me out to breakfast, carefully avoiding any discussion about writing. When we got back upstairs, he strummed the beginning of a melody and said, "I have an idea for a title—how do you like 'The Other Side of the Sun'?"

I was already hearing words in my head that fit the melody he was playing, so I grabbed a guitar and sang them back to him. Within a few hours, we'd finished what would be the kickoff for my next album, and a European hit.

Stan asked if there was anyone I wanted to work with, and I immediately said, "Giorgio Moroder and Nile Rodgers." I'd loved Nile's work with Chic, and their single "Le Freak" was one of my favorite records. Giorgio had made amazing records with Donna Summer, and I loved those, too. Unfortunately, both men were far too busy to make time for me.

Ina and Jean met with Walter to see if there was anything CBS could do to help. Yes, there was. Giorgio, as it happened, wanted something from them. In return for whatever it was, he would work with me. Better yet, he would write with me.

A week or so later, I received a cassette in the mail with a demo track and vocal line, played by an electric piano. I loved the feel immediately. Instead of pushing me straight into disco, which would never have worked, Giorgio had created a thumping jazz-based track, a swinging shuffle that featured Steve Madaio playing some of the coolest trumpet I'd ever heard. I was thrilled.

I wrote a lyric about the gay men's bathhouse scene in New York. Some time before, my friend Bruce Mailman had asked if I wanted to invest in a new concept he had for bathhouses. He and our friend Billy Nachman were going to build something different from the seedy, rundown places gay men had traditionally frequented. This bathhouse would be the ultimate bathhouse—chic, more in keeping with the times. Gay men were out and proud now; there was no need for them to skulk around in back rooms anymore.

It sounded like a cool thing, so I agreed to put $50,000 into the St. Mark's Baths. Over the next few years, the other investors and I more than quadrupled our money. I didn't know when I bought into the baths that it would trigger a rupture with Tino that would end in violence.

The Baths opened on February 18; Tino and I and our friend Joseph

Piazza went to the party. Joseph had been cutting my hair since I was seventeen, and we were very close. A gay man himself, he marveled at what Bruce and Billy had wrought, commenting that it was about time men could enter a bathhouse without feeling like they were committing a crime.

The bathhouse was gorgeous, with three floors and a rooftop deck, black deco tiles and soft lights, and more than one hundred fifty private rooms. I'd never seen anything like it, and Joseph was soon explaining things I'd rather not have discovered.

The Baths, and the way men used them, really brought home the difference between the sexes to me. Personally, I think most women have to be taught to have good sex. For men, sex is always good, or at least physically satisfying. Not a lot of work has to go into it. But for women, with their hidden crevices, nooks, and crannies, until you're familiar with your *own* body and what *you* like, it's impossible.

Our culture doesn't help. Being able to say, "a little higher," "a little harder," doesn't come easy to most of us.

Joseph and I prowled around until well after midnight, drinking champagne and having a high old time. When we were ready to leave, Tino was nowhere to be found. We searched every nook and cranny, but no Tino. Finally, an hour later, I decided to go home. Joseph walked me to a taxi, looking worried, saying, "He wouldn't have just skipped out on you, would he? That's not like him. I mean, he's probably not feeling well or something. Don't worry about it."

I wasn't worried; I was furious. Bruce was a close friend; we had dinner together regularly. Joseph was one of my most intimate friends, and a regular visitor in our home. Tino hadn't just walked out on me; he'd walked out on them as well.

At the least, he could have said good-bye, I thought to myself as I rode the elevator up to our apartment. *At the least, he could have apologized for leaving early.*

I stepped into the bedroom and angrily shook Tino's shoulder. He was asleep, but I was mad enough that I wanted to have it out with him before I went to bed myself. There was no response, so I shook his shoulder again.

Wham! The back of his hand hit my cheek, spinning me across the room and onto the floor. I sat up, dazed. There he was, angrily moving toward me. I scuttled backward and he stopped. Then he calmly got back into bed and said, "Don't ever, *ever* wake me again." And with that, he was asleep.

I was thunderstruck. No one had ever hit me before, least of all in the face. Oh, my parents had spanked me now and then, usually with a slap on the wrist that was more humiliating than painful. This was a brand-new experience.

I stood up, trembling all over. I was shocky; my jaw was beginning to hurt. This was the man I wanted to have children with?

I couldn't think of anything except my mom. She'd know what to do. I grabbed a change of clothes and made my way to her apartment, ringing the doorbell until she woke up. The story tumbled out as she got a cold compress for my jaw. Her mouth was set in a grim line when I finished, and she calmly suggested I try to get some sleep on the couch.

The next morning, I woke to the sound of my mother's voice. She was on the phone with Tino, yelling at him. "We don't hit in this family, Tino. I don't give a good goddamn what *your* family or *your* culture find acceptable—we don't hit. And let me tell you, if you lay a hand on my child again, I'll kill you. I swear I'll kill you. Just stay away from her!"

The phone landed in its cradle with a crash. I sat up, gingerly rubbing my jaw. My mother came into the living room and sat on the edge of the couch as I began to cry.

I don't know what happened, Mom. I don't know what happened. What did I do wrong?

My mother took me by the shoulders and glared. "You did absolutely nothing, honey. Absolutely nothing . . . That son of a bitch had no right, no right at all. What on earth was he thinking?"

I had no idea what was going on in Tino's head, but I did know one thing. There was no way I'd stay with a hitter. No way.

I called Tino a few hours later. He was contrite, apologizing up and down, swearing it would never happen again. I'd woken him up out of a sound sleep. He'd barely realized it was me when he lashed out.

I didn't care what his excuses were. I told him he had two days to clear himself, and everything that was his, out of my apartment. I'd be staying with my mother and working in the studio. I didn't want to see him again, ever.

I went to the studio that morning feeling breakable. Tino was a big man, 185 pounds to my 95, a foot and three inches taller than me. I realized how lucky I was that he'd hit me with an open hand; his closed fist could easily have broken my jaw.

I was relieved to see one of my engineers, and when he asked how the opening had gone, I burst into tears and blurted out the whole story. I finished and sat back, expecting him to be outraged. Instead, his reaction puzzled me. He said, "Janis, this happens in families . . . sometimes it happens. The important thing is, do you love him, and does he love you? If you both still love each other, you should try to work it out."

Now, of course, I know a bit more about battered women. Now, of course, I know that once someone's crossed that line, they never take the line seriously again. But in 1979, all I knew was that my dreams of children and marriage were going up in smoke.

Tino didn't call, but when I left the studio that evening, he was waiting with a bouquet. I had no idea how long he'd been standing there, but I ignored him and went back to my mother's home for the night. The next morning, he was there when I left, standing on the sidewalk in the February cold, tears in his eyes, with another bouquet. When I left the studio, there he was again.

When I went back to my apartment two nights later, his bags were packed. I sat across the table from him and listened to him beg. He was sorry. He was miserable. He couldn't live without me. He needed me, and I needed him. Couldn't he have just one more chance?

He looked so dejected, so sincere, that I said, *All right. We'll try again. But understand. Two things will destroy this relationship—you wanting a ménage à trois, and you hitting me. If the first happens, I'll cut you out of my heart. If the second happens, I'll cut you out of my life.*

He agreed, unpacked, and turned back into the sweet, supportive man I'd thought I'd married. At least, for a while.

In her book *Men Who Hate Women and the Women Who Love Them*, Dr. Susan Forward says that men like Tino are chronically angry and depressed, but they present well. That's because when they fall in love, they don't feel depressed anymore. Somewhere inside, they equate the new feeling of lightness with you, as though you magically pulled them out of the hole they were living in. They only revert to their true selves six to twelve months later. When the depression returns, they blame you. You fixed it before; why don't you fix it now?

I wish I'd read the book back then.

I flew to Los Angeles to record with Giorgio. It was a completely different experience. To Giorgio, the beat was the thing. The track came next, then the melody. The lyric, and the singer, ran a distinct last.

I went in and sang the vocal through to warm up. When I was done, Giorgio leaned into the talk-back mic and said in his thick German accent, "Very good. Thank you."

Wait a second! I said. *I'm just warming up!*

"Oh." He consulted with the engineer. "Okay. Take two."

I sang the song again, and again he said, "Very good. Thank you."

I laughed and walked into the control room for the playback. When it was over, I said, *Do you always work this way?* He looked puzzled.

You know, do you always give the singer a track, then have them sing it once or twice and kick them out?

Yes, he always did. He looked at the voice as just another instrument.

But, Giorgio, what about the lyric? I asked. *What about art?*

He thought for a moment, then smiled. "Art . . . yes. Once, I did art. . . . Now I make money."

I didn't know it then, but Giorgio had just given me my first international hit.

I flew back to New York and got my period midflight. Alone in the tiny bathroom, I started to cry. I'd been trying to get pregnant for more than a year, with no success. Every month, my heart would sink. Every month, I'd have to tell Tino I'd failed again. I knew that wasn't rational, but it felt like a failure.

I'd seen my gynecologist, who ran a few tests and told me to relax. I'd seen my family doctor, who'd suggested I stop touring for a while. *That's what I'm doing,* I told him, *but it's not working*. He laughed and told me to stop stressing; it would happen sooner or later. It was looking to me like later.

I spent the summer recording my next album, *Night Rains*, with Ron Frangipane coproducing again. We had two standout commercial cuts, "The Other Side of the Sun" and the Moroder cut, "Fly Too High." There was good news all around on that song; it would be the lead track in an upcoming film called *Foxes*, directed by Adrian Lyne and starring Jodie Foster. Another song, "Here Comes the Night," was the title song for *The Bell Jar*, a film about the life of poetess Sylvia Plath, starring the incredible Julie Harris. Knowing so many of the songs were already going to be heard, whether the album was a hit or not, reassured me enormously.

I'd brought in a new engineer, Leanne Unger, to record and mix the album. Between Leanne and Ron, I felt like I was finally working in a fully supportive environment. In the end, it was the best recording experience of my life. I was determined to do two things with this record: have a hit, and prove to CBS that I could produce.

Within that framework, I was also determined to have fun. I was enjoying playing around with the structure of songs, with the very concept of what a "song" was. I'd been hanging around the New York loft scene for years, and I'd seen Luciano Berio and Cathy Berberian performing passionate and barbaric pieces. I'd watched Liz Swados stand in the center of a loft, doing her bird songs. I'd had a violent argument with another musician over a Lou Reed song I loved, which consisted of a single lyric line. I wanted to stretch.

On the previous album, I'd cut a song called "Hopper Painting," which Ron and Richard Davis said was some of the finest truly American music ever made. I'd written it with the intention of not having any static chords; in other words, the chords under the vocal line could change every time I played it.

I had a song called "Jenny" for this album, written when my cousin Jamie was born. It consisted of just one verse and one chorus. I thought it would be interesting to see what would happen if I combined my traditional chords with a nontraditional ear, and went with whatever happened.

Stan knew Chick Corea, a pianist I'd met briefly. I asked if Chick might be willing to play the piano part as a duet, and we met at CBS Studio B, one of the few large rooms in town that had two grand pianos and a live echo chamber. The engineers placed the pianos face-to-face, and Chick and I sat down and played, with me singing live as we went.

I'd always been fortunate enough to attract great musicians—my recording history reads like a hall of fame, with Richard Davis, Ron Carter, Steve Gadd, Chet Atkins, Victor Feldman, and a host of other great players working by my side. But I'd never dueted with anyone before, and Chick gave me a great opportunity to watch a master at work.

He was an incredibly generous player. I don't know how to explain it to someone who doesn't play, except to say that he made me shine. He made me look better than I was. Somehow, he managed to take my piano part and enhance it, until I sounded like I played as well as he did. When we listened to the playback, I laughed at one line he'd played and said, "Nice one, Chick!" He turned and smiled at me, saying, "That's your line, Janis."

We cut most of the record at the Hit Factory, then a funky midtown studio with great acoustics and good vibes. I walked to work from my Eighty-first Street apartment each morning, cutting through Central Park in the staggering summer heat, stopping to watch the street musicians and acrobats. We worked at a fairly leisurely pace all summer and into the early fall, while I tried to relax and get pregnant. Every month, Tino would look at me hopefully. Every month, I'd give him the bad news.

And my time at home was coming to an end. There was a huge promotional tour planned for November, twenty-one nonstop days in Europe. As of February 1980, I'd be touring again for five months, doing fifty-six shows in fifty-four days in thirty-nine cities across the United States, plus Israel, Ireland, Belgium, Holland, England, and Japan. I wasn't going to be around much to help with a pregnancy.

TWELVE

Arms Around My Life

I have waited for so long,
I've forgotten what it's like
to feel somebody's arms around my life

Tino and I spent January of 1980 with his family on Madeira Island. Though I came to love them, misunderstandings were legion at first. Because I hadn't worn a veil in my wedding pictures, they thought Tino had converted from Catholicism to Judaism. Because my wedding dress wasn't entirely white, but studded with pearl gray, they thought I'd slutted around. Or so Tino said. I spoke no Portuguese then, and it was hard to tell whether he reported the conversations accurately.

Tino had never fussed over the way I dressed, but he was suddenly worried about the impression I'd make on his family. He insisted I wear dresses all the time, and high heels. I realized all the women there dressed that way, but it was crazy-making. On top of not speaking the language, I couldn't even look like myself!

I tried to lose myself in work, writing songs for an ABC-TV Movie of the Week, and lyrics for two melodies by Teo Macero that would become part of a film called *Virus*. After Madeira, I flew to L.A. for the recording sessions. Teo and I were both excited to be working together, and he was expecting great success in Japan. He was right—both songs went No. 1 on the charts there, giving me four hits in a row.

I took the red-eye back to surprise Tino, who wasn't expecting me for another day. I sauntered into the bedroom, wearing jeans and a bright Hawaiian shirt, happy to be home. He woke up smiling, took one look at my clothes, and started to berate me. "How can you possibly wear something like that? Don't you care what people think of you?! Don't you care what *I* think of you? I married a *woman*, not some teenager who thinks a shirt like that looks 'cool'!"

The fight escalated in seconds. Tino said he wanted a divorce. I said, *Fine, just leave me alone.* He said he'd find someone sexier, someone prettier. I kept silent. He said I never knew what he wanted. I said, *I'm not a mind reader.* He said that just proved how shallow my feelings were. "If you loved me, you'd *know* what I want."

A few hours later, he was back to his old self, contritely telling me that New York was getting to him. He missed Los Angeles so much, missed his friends, missed the weather. *I am not moving to L.A.!* I said. *All my business is here. My friends and family are here. No way!*

I spent the next months flying around the United States doing television and radio, then took off for Israel in mid-April. People were urging me not to go; there was a lot of violence, and everyone worried I'd be caught up in it. I felt like we'd played Ireland through the violence, and it had been worth it. This would be, too.

I gave my band the choice of coming with me, or being replaced for the one tour. They all came. It was a great group. Our drummer, Arti Dixson, was a black Baptist. Our guitarist, Scott Zito, was an Italian Catholic. The bass player, John Crowder, was a Protestant from the Midwest. And Stan Schnier, my tour manager, was a Jew, same as me.

On arrival, I was ushered into a press conference, and shown a Jerusalem paper with the banner headline "LOCAL GIRL MAKES GOOD!" It was strange, being in a country where the majority were Jews. I'd grown up in Baptist neighborhoods, or mixed Christian neighborhoods, but never Jewish. There was something simultaneously reassuring, and unsettling, about it.

We were taken to our hotel, the King David, where I was shown into an incredible suite by a David, who'd been introduced to me as "your local guide." It was late, so I turned in. When I woke the next morning, there was David, sleeping on the couch. I looked at him for a minute; his eyes opened.

You're not a local guide at all, are you? I asked. *Why did you sleep here?*

David wiped the sleep from his eyes and explained. Yes, he was qualified as a guide, and part of his job was to make sure I saw as much of the country as possible between shows and press. The other part of his job was bodyguard. He'd recently been bodyguard to David Ben-Gurion, and was now looking after people like me.

People like me? I asked. *What do you mean?*

David looked uncomfortable.

David, is there something I should know?

He asked me to sit down, then said, "I listened at the press conference yesterday. You're a straight talker, so I'll talk straight to you. There have been some threats, kidnapping and the like. Only a few American artists have come here, and of those, not many Jews. You'd be high profile, worth a lot of publicity, and a lot of money. Wherever we go, there will be people watching you, keeping you safe. And I'm sticking to your side like glue."

He stood up and strolled to the gigantic picture window, gesturing for me to come over. I stared out at the desert. I wasn't terribly impressed; the information he'd given me was still rolling around in my head. Then I noticed the light.

It was completely different from any sunlight I'd seen before. Ethereal. Almost tangible. I wanted to reach out and touch it, hold it in my hands, let it wash over me and cleanse me.

I stared at the desert sand. It looked alive, sinuously weaving its way to the horizon. I wondered what lay under it, covered by the ages. This was *the* desert. The desert my forefathers had walked through. The desert my religion had been born in. The desert Jesus had suffered in. Incredible.

All five of us had exactly the same experience, waking up that morning groggy from the flight, looking out our windows, not really seeing anything, then getting hit over the head with it.

We had a fantastic time in Israel. David took us everywhere; even if I had only an hour free, he knew something interesting to see. We went to Jericho, stopping at an Arab friend's home for an expansive Middle Eastern lunch. We went to Jerusalem's Old City, where I distinguished myself by bargaining with a shop owner over a Moroccan hammered plate, finally walking out of the store and down the street as the owner followed me, wringing his hands and shouting, "My wife and children will starve, but all right, all right, you can have it at that price!"

We spent a few weeks in Israel, flying on to the Netherlands and UK for twelve more shows. Then I flew back to New York to fire Jean.

Things had been getting worse between us. She was drinking more, not even waiting for dinner. The record company put in a discreet complaint. Jean insisted she didn't have a problem. She didn't hear herself slurring on the phone, didn't see how strangely she sometimes behaved. I'd plan to have dinner alone with someone from my band or crew, and Jean would ask where we were going, then show up at the restaurant. After protesting that she'd meant to eat alone, she'd inevitably join us. One day, she sat on the balcony of her room and watched my room for hours to see if I was going out. When I did, she caught me at the elevator and joined me. It was all pretty disturbing.

To make things worse, her business judgment was off. She was keeping things from me, and getting way too chummy with my accountant. Just before my London show, she'd casually mentioned that "Fly Too High" was No. 1 in Australia. I'd had no idea.

Why aren't we touring there? I asked. She replied that I'd said I wanted some time off. *For God's sake, Jean, how often do I have a number one record somewhere?! The least you could have done was offer me a choice!*

The next day, I spoke with Ina. My contract with Jean was up in May; she advised me to wait until then. I took Stan aside and asked if he'd be willing to fill in as interim manager. Then I asked Jean to book a tour of Australia. I'd have to pay her commissions on it, but as Ina explained, it would be cheaper to pay her than risk a lawsuit that could go on for years.

Ina asked whether I wanted her to fire Jean, but I said no. My attitude's always been, "You hire them, you fire them." I wanted no one else doing my dirty work.

It was one of the hardest things I've ever done. Jean had been like a sister to me. She'd been my confidante, the person I went to when all else failed. She'd protected me as best she could, from "Society's Child" through my parents' divorce and Beth's deceitfulness. We'd gone hungry together during the lean times, and feasted together when times were good.

She began to cry when I told her I was leaving. She asked me why. I said I couldn't deal with her drinking anymore; I had too much at stake. She promised to stop. I said I couldn't believe her promises any longer. She said she'd just learned she was diabetic. I said I was sorry. She cried harder, and asked for another chance. I told her I just couldn't risk it. The list of missed and almost-missed opportunities was growing daily, and I couldn't afford any more.

My *Night Rains* album was at the top of the charts in Australia, and "Fly Too High" was still No. 1 when we landed there a month later. The previous tour, I'd played to sold-out houses, but I wasn't a huge star. There was also the *Beth & Barry Show* to contend with, which really put a damper on things. This time, free of entanglements, I was determined to have a good time.

The Australian fans were enthusiastic to the point of lunacy. Stan and I had begun sharing two-bedroom suites, because so many people came banging on the door, trying to talk to me. No matter how many aliases I used, someone from the hotel staff would leak my room number, and the banging would begin. At least with the suites, Stan could answer the door. They'd think it was his room, and go away.

One night, after a very late show, I grabbed a robe and went into the bathroom for a shower. I pulled the shower curtain open and found a fourteen-year-old girl sitting in the tub, fully dressed. She'd climbed up the fire escape and hidden there after the concert ended, waiting for me to come back.

I pulled the robe tighter around my body and called for Stan, who was furious. He threatened to call the police, and the girl began crying.

Stop being so silly, Stan, I said. *Can't you see she's terrified?*

I calmly called room service and ordered some tea, then phoned her parents, who were frantic with worry. The concert had ended at ten; they were sure their daughter was laying in an alley somewhere. They arrived to take her home just as we finished our tea and biscuits, and she left smiling.

I did a ton of television the first few days, upping my visibility. And I looked exactly like the album and single covers, upping it still further. It got hard to have any downtime unless I stayed in my room. I couldn't walk around without attracting a crowd, pushing and pulling at me.

Stan came up with a few disguises, wigs and scarves, so I could go out on my time off. I'd started playing an arcade game called Space Invaders in Ireland and had become obsessed, finally winding up rated the third-best player in the country. Stan located an arcade with the machine one night, and we went out to play. I kept getting to the third-from-final level, then crashing. A couple of teenage boys were looking over my shoulder, calling out encouragement. On my third loss, I turned to face them and said, "Okay, if you're so smart, show me how you'd do it!"

They both stared, then one yelled, "It's that chick, the one on TV!" Cover blown, I asked them to show me their tricks. A crowd gathered around us and they showed me a few moves. By the end of the tour, I was rated the third-highest player in Australia, too.

Ridiculous the things that make you happy on the road!

"At Seventeen" had been a hit in the United States, but not anywhere else. Whatever worldwide career I'd had to date was the result of hard work and constant touring. Now "Fly Too High" was No. 1 all over Europe, South Africa, Israel, Australia, and New Zealand. The songs from *Virus* were at the top of the charts in Japan.

I could work all over the world, but there was no more success at home. CBS released *Night Rains* in November, and it got lost in the Christmas shuffle. American radio was resistant to the idea of Janis Ian doing something up-tempo, with a beat. Program directors just refused to play "Fly Too High."

I still felt I'd proved my point. Everywhere but America, something I'd produced had gone platinum and double platinum. I'd done *Night Rains* exactly as I'd wanted to do it, and it's still one of my favorite albums. Unfortunately, CBS didn't see it that way. By summer of 1980, while I toured the world with a hit record, they were busy picking my next producer.

I couldn't believe it. I stormed into Ina's office. *How can they insist I have an outside producer?* I demanded. *I've sold close to ten million records for this company, so why can't I do what I want to do with my music?*

She explained. There were changes at CBS. The company was only getting bigger, and people like me were getting lost in the shuffle. She told me to see this as an opportunity. Charles Koppelman would be working with me, through a satellite group he'd brought to CBS called the Entertainment Company. I'd be moved from the CBS promotion and publicity departments to Charles's.

I liked Charles a lot, but I trusted him about as far as I could throw a piano. Still, at least he was sober. Things could be a lot worse. Friends of mine were losing contracts right and left, as the music industry began shoving cocaine up its collective executive noses. The higher the position, the more white dust was scattered around the office. People were on a coke power high, paying outrageous sums of money in bidding wars for artists who might never have another hit. I looked around at what was happening to people like Walter, once my close friend, now a spaced-out cokehead, and I wondered if I even wanted to keep making records.

Koppelman put me with Gary Klein, a very nice guy with the backbone of a noodle. We decided to record in Los Angeles, starting in January. Gary lived there, and Tino would appreciate three months in L.A. So I rented a house in the Hollywood Hills, and we began. I had a crackerjack band, some good songs, and a lot of faith.

I needed the faith, because things with Tino had gone from bad to worse. He complained constantly about New York. He loathed my friends and family. He was only back to his old self when we stayed in L.A. I started thinking a move there might be the only way to save my marriage. So in February 1981, I purchased a large house in Hancock Park, and leased the New York apartment out.

I saw a local fertility specialist, who ran some tests and put me on monthly shots of Clomid, to make sure I ovulated regularly, and pregnant mare's urine (go figure). The regime definitely worked; once a month, I'd be hit with excruciating pain that made me fold over in my chair. But it would all be worth it, if I could just have a child.

The fertility specialist assured me that any day now, I'd turn up pregnant with twins. Or triplets. Or more. It was all very hopeful for a while.

The only problem was Tino. At first, happy in Los Angeles, he'd wanted more sex than ever. But when I began timing my cycles and checking my temperature, asking him to perform on schedule, he lost all interest.

He wouldn't discuss it. He wouldn't see a counselor. He just stopped wanting me. We went from constant sex to zero sex, almost overnight. It was awful.

When someone you love and desire stops wanting you, no matter what the reason, you take it personally. It hurts. Every time they show their lack of interest, your vulnerability increases. I tried to tell myself it had nothing to do with me, that it was his depression, his anger, his fear, but I felt even more like a failure.

I had no one to talk to about it. It's typical of an abuser to try to remove everything familiar from your life, and Tino had succeeded in spades. All my friends were in New York. My family was on the East Coast, except for Dad, who was living miles away in Berkeley. Stan was supposed to move out when we did, but he'd changed his mind. I literally knew no one in Los Angeles but my agents, and Tino. It was scary, and lonely.

I worked steadily on the new album, *Restless Eyes*, but I wasn't enjoying it the way I'd loved making *Night Rains*. Gary couldn't make decisions, which drove me up the wall. If someone asked for an opinion from the control room, his solution was, "I don't know. What do you think? I know—let's have lunch!" I finished my last album for CBS with a sense of relief.

When I played it for Koppelman, he said, "I love this record. Just love it! Get me the artwork and let's go." I began putting together the credits, and when I was done, I cross-checked them with Gary. My understanding had been that the credits would read:

Gary Klein, producer
Charles Koppelman, executive producer

"No, no," Gary said. "Just 'Gary Klein, producer.'"

Are you sure? I asked him. *This is the way Charles's projects are always credited.*

"Absolutely positive."

I still wasn't certain, so I asked again. Had he cleared this with Koppelman?

"Yep. Spoke with him twice, the last time just yesterday. You know, he wants me to start taking a little more credit for myself."

The artwork went in, and I heard nothing more until a week before the album's release. A friend at CBS called to tell me Charles had gone apoplectic when he'd seen the credits. He'd called Gary on the carpet, and Gary said I'd insisted they read that way. My friend said Koppelman had pulled most of the publicity budget, basically withdrawing the company's support. So much for my chance of having another hit . . .

Lack of support regardless, the tour was a sellout, from Amsterdam to Tokyo. Tino came on the road for long stretches, and when he did, touring turned into a nightmare. When he wasn't depressed, he was raging—at me, but also at anyone else around me. He'd become insanely jealous, accusing me of sleeping with, or at least wanting to sleep with, everyone in my band and crew. I tried to keep him away from my staff. That way his rage stayed focused on me.

When Tino wasn't on the road, he'd call four and five times a day, and the conversations would always end with him telling me how much he wished he didn't love me. I was a fool, half a woman. I couldn't even get pregnant, that's how worthless I was. My body was ugly. I walked badly. I didn't even know how to sit like a lady. He was going to find someone else, wait and see. I was probably fucking around out there on the road anyway, why should he bother being faithful? All performers were alike—he'd slept with enough in his day to know that.

I tried saying, "I'm not going to listen anymore," and hanging up the phone, but that just made him madder. He'd call the tour manager, demanding I be brought to the phone. At home, he was drinking more, doing more Valium. Most nights, he was barely coherent, eventually lurching upstairs to fall on the bed and pass out.

I received an offer to tour in South Africa, and decided to go. After thinking a lot about cultural boycotts, I decided I didn't believe in them. It seemed to me that by staying at integrated hotels, playing integrated theaters, and taking an integrated band with me, I'd be doing more to end apartheid than I would just staying home.

I offered my band the same choice I'd offered with Israel: anyone who didn't want to come didn't have to—their job would be waiting when I got back. To a man, they said, "I'm in!" Arti Dixson, my black drummer, was particularly excited; he spoke about "returning to the homeland," and seeing where his roots lay.

The tour laid out like a dream. We'd be playing eight cities, staying in each for half a week. We wouldn't have to tear down the equipment every night, or travel every day. We could get a feel for the place and its people.

I turned down Sun City. Plenty of performers had played there, including Elton John, Rod Stewart, and Linda Ronstadt. Plenty of black performers had played there as well. I turned it down even though they offered me twice what the entire tour was making, because it was a segregated facility. I wanted to come out of this feeling clean.

My mother saw it differently. When she heard what I was doing, she called once to yell at me, then stopped speaking to me. I could talk myself blue in the face trying to explain my position; she didn't care. I was breaking a boycott, and that was that. It took a full year for her to calm down.

South Africa was a revelation. Our first day, a few of us sat on a Johannesburg bench and watched the people come and go. It felt like we were in *National Geographic*. Women without blouses walked by, their breasts swinging heavily in the sun. A young girl with rings around her elongated neck strode past, almost loping. A man with his ears distended from the weight of jewelry hanging from them sat on the bench opposite us and casually read the morning paper.

People were getting on the buses, black and white, sitting next to each other, chatting. We were stunned.

Dixson and I went exploring. Wherever we went, people would ask, "What tribe are you from, man?" He didn't know, and didn't care. He'd thought all blacks were brothers, united in their color. He was learning otherwise.

The hills around Johannesburg were filled with bodies, hundreds of them a month, all victims of tribal warfare. That had nothing to do with apartheid, nothing to do with white racism. It had to do with tribalism, and it depressed us all. In a grim foreshadowing of the genocidal practices in Rwanda, neighbor was killing neighbor because an accident of birth had brought them onto opposite sides of the tribal conflict. It was horrifying, and sobering.

From South Africa, I went on to meet Tino in Madeira. He was in an expansive mood, and our sex life started up again. We returned to Los Angeles a few weeks later, with me determined to make the marriage work. I decided to stay in L.A. the rest of the year, hoping Tino's good mood would continue.

Once we got home, I received a letter from the United Nations, telling me I was blacklisted for performing in South Africa. I was forbidden to work with union members. No television, no radio, no recording. I couldn't work in England, either; I was blacklisted there as well. The U.N.'s official position was that there was no blacklist, just a list of performers they "hoped would change their minds." Bullshit.

I got on the phone with someone and explained my position. They offered me a way out—if I'd say I hadn't known South Africa practiced apartheid, and promised not to go back, I would be forgiven.

I can't do that, I told him. *First, I'm not that stupid. Second, I don't believe cultural boycotts work. And last, I can't promise not to go back.*

My name wasn't lifted from the blacklist for years, but I was in good company. They'd even blacklisted some South African performers for playing in their own country!

It was strange, not having any touring commitments. After the schedule I'd been keeping, it was doubly strange to wake up in the morning with nothing to do. I didn't even have to pay bills, or balance a checkbook. Sam Weintraub, my accountant since I was a child, handled the business end. All my money went to him, and outside of checking my monthly statement, I didn't have to think about it.

I'd been very careful with my money this time around. I hadn't forgotten the "Society's Child" days. When Ina told me CBS was going to cut a million-dollar check, I'd bought some books on investing and economics. The next weekend, staying on Fire Island with her and Bruce Mailman, I'd read them cover to cover. I'd drawn up a financial plan for myself, and stuck to it. I'd diversified what I had, cautiously playing the stock market and getting lucky over and over again. I owned rare coins, instruments, jewelry. I had a large pile of cash socked away in long-term treasury notes. I owned the New York condo, two rental houses in Westport, and four houses in L.A. Now that I had some time off, and could take a closer look, I slowly began to realize how well I'd done. It gave me pause.

I'd been touring and recording for ten years straight, one project after the other, and I had no outside interests. I also had no friends. I'd lost touch with everyone in New York, and I'd been out of town or in the studio ever since we'd moved to L.A. I took stock of my life, and suddenly saw that I needed to *get* a life.

The house had a huge living room, and I realized I could finally indulge a lifelong dream and buy a grand piano. With Chick's help, I decided on a Bösendorfer, and went to Dave Abell's to find one. He had more Bösendorfers than anyone in the country, but none of them was right. For more than a year, I went there every time a new one arrived, trying them out.

Finally, I found the perfect piano. Even Abell said it was the best Bösendorfer he'd ever seen. I took it home and sat in front of it for an hour, just touching the keys, not playing yet. When I finally hit a few notes, the sound thrilled me. It was the piano equivalent of Dad's Martin. Perfect bass, perfect treble. Unbelievably beautiful.

And unbelievably honest. It showed every single flaw in my playing. I plowed into a Bach prelude and was dismayed at how bad I sounded. I phoned Chick in tears. *How can I call myself a pianist? I sound horrible!* He reminded me that I'd never had a decent teacher, and suggested I start lessons. Dave Abell recommended Leonid Hambro, Victor Borge's accompanist. I began lessons right away, learning the basics, improving my technique, and glowing with pleasure as I improved.

I also wanted to feel more comfortable in my body onstage, so I went to David Craig, who specialized in teaching movement. After a short conversation, he smiled and said, "I can do nothing for Janis Ian. Nothing. But you should study with Stella Adler."

I asked him why. "Because she's eighty-three years old, and everyone should study with Stella Adler once."

That May, I interviewed for a spot in Stella's beginner's class. Looking at the schedule, I also saw she offered a class in script interpretation, which I thought might be helpful when I was writing for films. Before I knew it, I'd signed up for all the other courses, and committed to spending four nights a week there, three to five hours a night.

I took my seat for the first class with little idea of what to expect. I thought Stella would probably be a little old white-haired lady, tottering about and offering words of wisdom in a high, wobbly voice. Boy, was I wrong!

When Stella's assistant, Irene Gilbert, announced that class would begin in a moment, the room went still. A tall woman with a blond bouffant entered, wearing a red gown that showed off her ample cleavage. On her feet were bright red "fuck me" pumps. She moved to center stage, turned to face the class, and said, "Good evening. From this moment on, you will call me Stella, because we are all actors here." Then she blew us a kiss.

It sounds tacky, that she blew a kiss, but it wasn't. Somehow, it was graceful, and inviting. Stella was the most elegant woman I'd ever seen. Her voice was elevated, accentless. She was as articulate as a poet. She carried herself like a queen, but a queen without the props. No tiara, no throne. Just a wooden chair, and a small table where she laid her purse.

She didn't need props. She *was* the prop. Her body, her voice, her gestures were all props she used unmercifully, to teach us, goad us, and lift us beyond where we thought we could go, into a universe where we were no longer Americans—we were citizens of the world. She told us that if we worked hard, and were talented, we would become more than nobility. We would learn, not the base nobility conferred by an accident of birth, but the nobility of merit, of achievement in the arts.

I fell in love. I suddenly understood why young men ran off with old women. At that moment, I would have done anything on earth for Stella, and I feel that way still.

Stella opened worlds to me, and I embraced the actor's community and tools with fervor. She would spend an hour breaking down a title, until "cat on a hot tin roof" became more than just a phrase. She'd challenge actors to change on a dime, shouting, "Now, do it faster . . . faster!! All right, stop. Stop! Tone it down. Don't get muscular. Use your head, not your memories. Use your imagination!"

Stella could be quite intimidating, larger than life. She thought part of her job was to separate the wheat from the chaff, and she had no patience with the chaff. She'd actually fished a dime out of her purse one night and told the actress onstage, "Use this dime to call your mother. Tell her to come and pick you up, because you have no business in the theater."

Another night, I watched an actress argue with Stella when she was asked to take off her dress. Patient at first, Stella grew increasingly annoyed that the actress wouldn't take direction. Stella wanted her to play the scene differently, break through some of her own defenses. The girl kept refusing.

Finally, Stella said, "Dear. Are you wearing a slip?" Yes, said the girl. "Then take off the dress!" Stella roared. The actress shot back, "Stella, I'm not getting paid for this!"

Stella slowly rose, made her way across the tiny stage, looked the actress in the eye, then ripped the dress right off her back. Oh, and by the way—the scene was brilliant after that.

She scared me even as she enticed me. It was nerve-racking to think of Stella's gaze turned on *me*; I don't mind admitting that now. I worked very hard at not being noticed, sitting off to one side, toward the back. Then one night, Stella began to speak of the artist as a phoenix, constantly dying, and constantly being reborn. She said no one could possibly compensate us for living with that knowledge. She told us that as artists, we were by nature outlaws. And toward the end, she looked straight at me and said, "So when you leave him—as leave him you must—understand that it has nothing to do with you. It has to do with the *artist* in you, that must liberate herself, in order to grow."

I looked at her in astonishment. I knew from Irene that Stella wasn't familiar with my music, let alone my life. She didn't even know my name. Yet somehow, she'd tapped into my life, as an artist and as a woman.

A few weeks later, she was trying to explain onstage rhythm to the class. She employed the Socratic method, questioning various actors and getting no satisfaction. Finally, she pointed at me. I looked around, hoping she was pointing at someone else. Stella gestured again, saying, "You! Stand up. Yes, you!"

I stood, and she asked, "When you sing, do you sing the notes?"

I thought for a minute, not wanting to look like an idiot. *I don't sing the notes, Stella. I sing the space between the notes.*

Stella turned to the class, annoyed. "You see? *She* gets it, and she's not even an actor!"

With that, we became friends. Over the next ten years, we corresponded regularly, and I attended every class I could until she stopped teaching. When I was in New York, I'd escort her to salons, or have dinner with her at the Russian Tea Room. When I finally left Tino, she was one of the first people I told.

I'd had very few female role models; there was no woman to pattern myself after as a professional. When I was coming up, women didn't lead the band, let alone play lead or write all their own material. My role models as an artist were exclusively male—Dylan, the Beatles, Leonard Cohen. Singer-songwriters.

Stella changed all that. She gave me a language for what I'd only felt in my heart. She set me free, telling me it was not only good to be an artist, it was noble. It was necessary. It brought order out of chaos, it served the teeming masses. It made the world tolerable.

It was like discovering Rimbaud all over again, except *this* Rimbaud was alive and available. I didn't want to be like Stella; she made me want to be like myself. Only more. More articulate. More considered. More in control of my body, my life, and my work.

Stella was all about imagination, the more the better. And education. I sought her out one day before class, confessing that my writing was in a rut. I couldn't come up with anything that pleased me; my words were trite, my melodies clichéd. I didn't know what to do, and I felt I was failing my talent.

Stella looked at me for a long time, her eyes searching my face. Her expression passed from curiosity to sadness to understanding, as she grasped my hands in hers, pulled me toward her, and said, "Ah, my dear . . . you have reached the age where talent is no longer enough." Her words struck like lightning. To be true to my gifts, I needed help.

She told me to study with other teachers, and on her recommendation I sought out Nina Foch and José Quintero. Stella sent me to William Chow, also known as Chao Shao Lin, whose father had headed the Peking Opera Company and who now lived in Los Angeles. She said that since there wasn't "a decent fencing instructor left in this town," I should take dance, suggesting Dora Krannig, formerly of the British Royal Ballet, as a fine instructor.

I reveled in the process of learning, and as the months passed, I became friends with Dora and William and the other students. I began spending my evenings at plays and recitals with the actors and dancers I saw all day. Afterward, we'd spend hours debating everything from the quality of the directing to whether Jean Genet's homosexuality had affected, or afflicted, his work. I watched Quintero direct *Cat on a Hot Tin Roof* from the first rehearsal to the last performance. I saw Makarova dance Juliet, transforming herself from child to woman in three measures of music. I heard Eugene Ionesco speak after a performance of his play *Rhinoceros;* there couldn't have been more than forty people in the whole room. I lived and breathed the different forms, and learned to see them all as part of a greater whole.

I was in heaven.

Stella liberated me, and as she liberated me as an artist and a woman, she began liberating me from Tino. I started living two lives again, one with my mentor and new friends, and one with Tino.

My marriage was going down the tubes, and nothing I did seemed to help. Tino was angry all the time. He'd get impossibly drunk; one night, out to dinner with Sam, he actually passed out onto a plate of food. In the mornings, he'd be fine, but as the day wore on, he'd start building up a head of steam. By dinner, he was ready to kill. And I was ready to leave.

I went into the hospital for a laparoscopy that September, making one last attempt to find out why I couldn't get pregnant. It showed nothing wrong, but I knew in my heart that I'd never bear children. It just wasn't meant to be.

The doctor discovered I had a mitral valve prolapse, and a severely irregular heartbeat. She warned that if I didn't start taking better care of myself, the consequences would be dire. Her prognosis scared us both, and Tino cut back on his drinking and treated me very tenderly for the next month. It was the last good month we had together.

I began trying to let go of my dreams. I felt good about my own life, and tried to hang on to that as the relationship continued to deteriorate. I threw myself into my classes, taking private lessons from Dora, enjoying the freedom of practicing art forms I didn't have to be good at.

All my life, I'd gravitated toward fields I could excel in. If I wrote, I wanted to be a great writer. If I sang, I wanted to be a great singer. The drive was natural to me. I'd never done anything I couldn't succeed at before. Now, I'd met my match, and it was more fun than I could have imagined.

When I started taking the ballet barre, nothing went right. Everyone pointed their feet left; my right leg shot out. Everyone plié'd gracefully; I practically fell on my ass. My teacher, Dora, told me later that when I started, she thought to herself, *In twenty years of teaching, this is the absolutely worst student I've had.* It was true, but I didn't care. I knew I'd never be a good dancer, let alone a great one. I was just having fun.

When I got discouraged, one of the other dancers told me, "Janis, hang in there. I know you're tripping over your own feet now. I promise, in six months to the day, your body will suddenly 'get it,' and you'll see a huge change. Then you can start dancing!"

I was seeing the change now. I moved differently. I sat differently. For the first time, I was comfortable in my own skin. Between Dora and Stella, I was becoming the self I'd always wanted to be. It was a visible change, and when I saw Ina that December, she spent half an hour telling me how good I looked.

Tino, too, saw the changes, and they scared him. I stayed away from the house as much as possible, taking classes and spending time with my friends. I was no longer interested in sex; if he didn't want me, I certainly wasn't going to humiliate myself by begging. I'd stopped talking about having children; if he wouldn't adopt, we wouldn't have them. I was trying to adopt the Buddhist attitude of acceptance, and stay on the path.

A friend of mine once told me, "For people like us, the meaning is in the *search* for the meaning." Those words had a profound impact on me, because they explained my life. I don't really care about arriving. I care about what happens on the path I take to get there.

I stepped back and considered my future. Not "ours," but mine. Making records and touring were interfering with my writing. My words weren't leaping off the page anymore; they were crawling. I'd always looked on myself as the guardian of my talent. I'd done nothing to earn it; it was given to me at birth. My job was to protect it and nurture it. That was the prime commitment in my life, to take care of the artist in me, and I wasn't doing my job well.

I called Ina and told her I wanted out of my CBS contract. She argued, reminding me that I had only three albums to go, and I could pocket close to a quarter million for each. I argued back, saying I wasn't willing to spend the rest of my life at the beck and call of promoters and disc jockeys. I was sick of rushing through projects to satisfy shareholders. I didn't want to go on the road anymore. I wanted to spend my life writing, and learning.

She spoke with Walter, and he agreed to let me out, provided I didn't go anywhere else for a while. They drew up the dissolution papers, Ina asking me every day if I was sure. When she finally told me I was free, she waited to see my reaction. I had none. I felt very calm, very sure that I was doing the right thing, walking away from that part of my career. I've never regretted it.

A few days before my thirty-second birthday, Tino sat me down and said he had a surprise for me. He was taking me to the Hotel Del Coronado for a fabulous romantic weekend. He'd already made the reservations; I should pack my bag.

I was thrilled. Tino never made plans like that; I was always the one to find the hotel, make the reservations, arrange travel. This time, he'd done everything. Maybe he was changing. My heart soared.

He continued. We would go to the hotel, unpack, relax. We'd have dinner, then drinks at the bar. It would all be terribly romantic, he said. Terribly romantic.

As part of that romance, he wanted me to find a woman at the bar. Someone we could seduce into having a ménage à trois with us. As a birthday present to me.

Something broke inside when he said that. Something broke, at the bottom of my heart. It cracked and went crashing, split into a million pieces.

I wasn't enough. I'd never been enough, not for anyone. I wasn't enough to keep my parents together. I wasn't enough for Beth to stay. And now, in this living hell, I wasn't enough for Tino.

It has to be something in me, I thought. Every single person I'd been with wanted to share me. Did I pick them for that? I couldn't decide. There'd been signs with Beth, in retrospect, but I'd bought her story that Tino had wanted it. There'd been signs with Tino, too, if I'd believed Beth—but how could I believe her when she'd had an affair with Barry under my nose? It was confusing beyond redemption.

We went to the Del Coronado. I didn't find anyone. I didn't really look. I just began removing my heart from the home it had known for six years. And the more removed I became, the angrier Tino became.

THIRTEEN

His Hands

His hands, they never hit me sober
His hands, they never marked my face
I would rather be blind than see him treat me this way
I would rather be deaf than hear that sound

Whap!
I looked up from the floor into the barrel of a gun. A very big gun. A .45, to be exact. Tino shook his head.

"Why did you make me do that, my love? I don't like to hurt you. Why?"

It was hard to answer. My ears were ringing. My jaw hurt. There was broken glass scattered all around me. After knocking me across the room, he'd flung a bottle of beer at my head. It missed me by centimeters, and shattered on the tile floor.

The blow caught me completely off guard. I'd expected Tino to be angry when I crossed him; I didn't expect him to hold a gun on me.

I sat up gingerly and began gathering up the bits of glass, afraid one of our puppies would stumble into it. I was trembling so hard that I cut myself on a piece. I couldn't get to a towel to wipe up the blood without crossing the kitchen, and no way was I going near him again. Blood dripped from my hand to the floor, staining the white grout. I tried not to look at it. I looked up at Tino instead.

He just stood there, shaking his head. Sorrow lined his eyes. Part of me detached itself from my own pain and watched the interplay of emotions across his face. Through the puffiness brought on by drink, I could see that he pitied me for the stupidity and willfulness that had led me to challenge him.

I moved warily, like an animal backed up against a wall, picking up small pieces of glass and collecting them in my open shirt. He'd torn the buttons off when he grabbed me, pulling me closer to backhand me across the face. I'd flown clear across the kitchen and into the pantry beyond, landing in a heap.

Are you trying to kill me? I whispered, half afraid it was true.

Tino snorted; I could feel his contempt from across the room.

"Don't be a fool. If I'd really wanted to hurt you, I'd have hit you with a closed fist. This was just a slap."

I thought of Tino's six foot one, and my four foot ten. His 210 pounds, and my 95. It was a big slap.

He walked away, saying over his shoulder, "Come with me to the table. I want to talk to you."

He didn't bother looking back to see if I would follow. I did. I sniffled as quietly as I could, trying not to cry, knowing that would just make him angrier. I sat down softly, afraid to attract his attention.

He put the gun on the table, barrel pointing toward me, with his finger on the trigger. I was frozen to the seat, unable to move.

He smiled.

"Here's what I think should happen, my love. We aren't happy anymore. You're going to leave me, I know it, and you'll leave me destitute. That's the way you people are. You'll hire your big fancy lawyers, and you'll get out of paying anything. Don't think I can't see it coming.

"I have a better solution. I'll kill you first. You'll have all the publicity you want, then. You'll sell lots of records. And I'll have all the money."

He lifted the gun, still pointed at me. I moaned in the back of my throat. He looked surprised at my objection.

"What? You don't appreciate my solution? How can that be?"

I asked, quietly, if I could say something. He nodded.

Tino, this is a community property state. The court will give you half of what we have. If you shoot me, they'll lock you up. You won't have a chance to spend the money.

He rubbed his eyes, bleary with alcohol and Valium. "True. Maybe the solution is to shoot you first, then myself."

He brightened up. "That's it! I'll take care of us both, and our heirs will have the money!"

He pointed the gun toward my heart, holding it steady, bracing it with his other hand. He looked at me with pity.

"I'm so sorry, my love. I'm so sorry it worked out this way. If you'd only been . . ."

Tino shook his head as if to clear it.

"Do you have any last words, Janis? Anything you want to confess? Anything you want to tell me?"

Oh, God. Is that what this was about? That he thought I was having an affair? I was quaking so hard that I could feel the chair vibrating under me. I tried to hide the shaking from him. Tears, unbidden, rolled down my cheeks. My nose was running—I didn't dare wipe it.

He winced. "Tears, always tears. Women and tears. I know you're faking it. You have no heart, how can you cry?"

He leaned toward me. The gun moved closer. "Can't you be brave, Janis? Can't you be courageous, just this one time? I'm so tired. . . . Can't you just make it easy?"

Desperately, I suggested he have another drink. He swayed as he stood, and I quickly offered to get it for him. I rose and made my way to the sideboard, pouring a triple Scotch and placing three Valium on the table beside it. The gun followed my every move.

I sat down again, moving at a snail's pace. I was frantic, trying to think through the hammering in my ears. I looked away from the gun, into his eyes.

Tino. My love. I know you've been unhappy. And you're tired. You're so very tired. . . . What you need is a good night's sleep. Take these, drink this. Things will be different in the morning.

He raised the gun again as he washed down the Valium, then twirled it around in his hand. My heart was beating so fast, I thought it would burst out of my chest and solve the whole problem.

Tino finally stopped playing with the .45 and looked at me. His voice was raspy with fatigue. "Yes, my love. I am tired. Tired of you, tired of this life. So very, very tired." He put the gun down and rubbed his eyes again.

I started begging. I begged him to give me another chance. I begged him to give the marriage another chance. I begged him to let me live, just one more day. I told him that if, at the end of tomorrow, he still felt this way, I wouldn't try to stop him. I said everything and anything that popped into my head, short of begging him not to kill me. I knew that would tip the scales in the other direction.

I pleaded with him to think of his adored Catholic grandmother, how he'd never get to heaven and see her if he killed himself. His eyes got misty as he told me how good she'd been to him. Then he remembered that I'd never been as good to him as she'd been, and the barrel was on me again.

We went on like that for six or seven hours, until dawn broke. At some point, I became serene, passing from a state of complete terror into a sea of calm. I was going to die, and that was the end of that. There was nothing I could do about it now.

I looked at Tino, bloated and miserable, and I actually felt compassion for him. I was prepared to die, and he'd be left to deal with the consequences. Or not. I felt sure there was a God in heaven. I knew I'd be meeting Him. The world would go on without me, and that was fine. The only regret I felt was the pain my family would go through.

By morning, I'd managed to get a few more drinks and I don't know how many more pills into him. He was slurring now, unsteady in his movements. It occurred to me that I might get shot accidentally, if his finger slipped. I suggested he go to bed. After a few minutes, he staggered to his feet.

"We'll continue this discussion tomorrow, my love. I'm going to sleep now. Please don't bother me anymore tonight." He took another beer from the refrigerator and made his way to the bedroom, enough Valium in his system to fell a horse.

After I heard him collapse on the bed, I went and washed the tear stains off my face. I looked in the mirror; my jaw was swollen. I could barely see out of my left eye. My hands began shaking again, and I was suddenly very cold. I took a sweater off the rack in the hall and put it on, shoving my fingers under my armpits to try and warm them up. I was exhausted, and not thinking very clearly, but I knew I couldn't stay in the house any longer.

I packed a bag, got in my car, and drove to Dora's house. She'd never liked Tino; he scared her. One day she'd told me there was always room in her home, if I ever wanted to get away. Dora opened the door and greeted me, exclaiming over my face. "What happened?" she asked. "How did this happen?!"

I couldn't really explain it. How had things gone this far? It made no sense to me.

We sat at the kitchen table and talked. No, I didn't think Tino would be coming after me today. And anyway, he didn't know where Dora lived. I'd fed him at least a hundred milligrams of Valium, on top of most of a bottle of Chivas. I was hoping he'd sleep for hours. I was hoping he'd overdose and die.

"He's crazy, Janis," Dora said. "He's insane. Completely insane."

I automatically began making an excuse for him, saying, *He's only hit me twice, in seven years* . . . I stopped myself short. Even I could hear how bad that sounded.

Dora was right. Tino was crazy. Not crazy as in, *When he has a few drinks, he puts a lampshade on his head and sings* Annie Get Your Gun. Not crazy as in, *He's kind of cute when he gets angry.*

No. Tino was psychotic. If he hadn't been when we first married, he was now.

Did I really think he was going to kill me? Yes. When someone's that stoned, that angry, that sad, there's no predicting what they'll do, except that it will be the one worst thing they can do in that moment. They may live to regret it, but you won't be around to see their shame.

And yet, sitting there at her table, I mourned the end of the marriage. I'd wanted it to work. I'd tried to make it work. Some part of me still loved him deeply, and I didn't want to let that go, even at the risk of my life.

I don't think anyone who hasn't been abused can understand what I'm saying. Abuse changes you, on a core level. I'm sure many women, reading this, are thinking, *How could she let it go that far? That would* never *happen to me!* Oh, the arrogance of certainty.

I thought I was exempt, too. I wasn't like "those women." Those women, battered women, were stupid. Uneducated. Ignorant. Poor. I was just the opposite. I had everything going for me—success, brains, money. And still, I was seduced, and reduced, until after seven years with him, part of me honestly thought I was stupid, uneducated, and useless.

It took me decades to understand how it happened, and even now, I don't really get it. Tino's decline was a slow slide, made up of tiny changes that barely registered on my busy life. He always had a logical-sounding explanation for any strange behavior. His obsession with keeping his dressing room door locked was explained by telling me he'd never had any privacy as a child, so it was paramount to him now. His obsession with guns, carrying one in his waistband from waking to sleeping, was explained by his concern for my safety. It all sounded reasonable at the time.

I *wanted* it to sound reasonable.

I'm not sure exactly when Tino began to lose his mind. It's funny how these things happen; in retrospect, you can see all kinds of clues, but you can never find the exact starting point. I've thought about it a lot since then.

Over the years we spent together, in what I can now see is a predictable pattern, his craziness escalated, from little things that only affected him to global configurations. We went from his wanting me to call when I'd be out late, to his wanting a flowchart of my movements through each day. From his being jealous of the time I spent with my friends, to his accusing me of whoring with them.

Eventually, we went from his love for me, to his obsession with me. He needed to control every second of my life. On some level, he'd elevated me to an impossible standard. Then he had to tear me down from the pedestal he'd placed under my feet. Tino needed to annihilate whatever "me" was, by separating me from everyone I knew, changing the way I dressed, spoke, moved, until I became someone more to his liking.

Dora put it best. She said, "Michelangelo sculpted his *David* out of marble. When he was done, he could stand there and admire his work. Tino sculpted his *David* out of you. Only when he was done, you stepped down off the pedestal and walked and talked."

I used to spend a lot of time trying to figure out the reason it ended the way it did. Maybe it was the years of Valium and booze catching up. Maybe it was sheer fatigue, from the weight of the anger he carried and refused to confront. Maybe it was that I couldn't have children.

Maybe, maybe, maybe. It's an unending trail. Maybe he just married me for the money. I hate to think that, but it's a possibility. It certainly didn't hurt to have an attractive, successful woman on his arm when he went back to Portugal. He went from being a writer who couldn't finish anything and worked as a waiter to looking like a successful businessman in tailor-made suits. Maybe that was it.

Or maybe the craziness was always there, but never had the opportunity to explode before. Certainly, relieving him of the need to make a living left him a lot of free time to explore whatever was going on in his head. Until I came along, he'd had to hold a job, which meant keeping his temper reined in. With platinum records worldwide, I had plenty of money to care for both of us. With my money, he could stay home and write his books. He was a brilliant writer, up there with a Styron, or a Tolstoy. I thought I was doing something good, giving him the opportunity to stay home and write.

Major mistake. When men in our culture don't have to earn a living, they start expecting the world to hand them money. In this case, the world was me. He bought an RV as a birthday gift for me one year, with my credit card. He bought jewelry for me, with my credit card.

Some people need to act out the script they were given as children. In Tino's case, the script was that all women are cheats, all women will betray you. He needed me to become a cheat and betray him. I never did, and it helped make him crazy.

I told Dora I didn't want to live alone. I was too scared. She offered me her second bedroom, and I stayed there for the next two years. It was a lifesaver. I'd been living in a war zone for so long, I'd forgotten what it was like to live normally. I was used to keeping my face blank when Tino entered a room, until I could find out what kind of mood he was in. I'd become accustomed to a cross-examination every time I came home, so when Dora walked in from work, I'd report my day. And no matter how much I was hurting, I knew better than to cry, so I held it in. I flinched every time a door slammed. I started every time a car stopped in front of the house.

Those feelings didn't go away quickly. I lived in a state of siege long after the siege was over. I was paralyzed for several months after the gun incident, paralyzed by the death of my dreams and the loss of my future.

Dora patiently listened to everything I had to say. She'd point out discrepancies in my behavior when I was caught between doing what I wanted, and automatically wondering if it would be all right with Tino. She said I'd been brainwashed, and it would take time to recover, but that I would recover, make no mistake. She encouraged me to continue with Stella and the ballet. She even let me play piano for the classes once in a while, which was so demanding that it took me right out of myself and back into music.

I called my mom to say I was getting a divorce. She was sad, but understanding. I was so relieved at her sympathy that I began apologizing for the end of my marriage. *I tried to be normal, Mom. I really did.* Without missing a beat, my mother said, "I know, honey. But it wasn't *your* normal."

I saw Stella as often as possible. I'd gone to her when I first left Tino, a little concerned that she'd try to convince me to go back. She listened closely, then asked what the last straw had been.

He hit me, Stella. He hit me.

She thought for a moment, then leaned in, took my hands in hers, and said quite seriously, "He wasn't Jewish, was he?"

We both roared at that one.

My closeness to her was something I've never felt with anyone, before or since. She understood me, and my work, on a deeper level than I'd have believed possible. I'd send her a new lyric, and she'd dissect it as she would a play, writing down her thoughts and sending them to me on crisp blue stationery.

I worried about her health. At one point, she referred to a "breakdown" she'd had on her return from London five months before. I was sitting in a chair across the table from her, patting her arm. She took my hand in hers, and said, "Janis. You are mother, daughter, sister to me. . . . Will you cure me? Will you? You can, you know."

It frightened me. She was looking at me like I was the Messiah. I would do anything in the world for Stella, but I had no idea what she was talking about. She asked if I'd spend more time with her, lend her my strength. She said she needed my clarity, it was difficult for her to hold on to hers.

A few weeks later, while we were talking before class, she grabbed my hands in hers and passionately said, "You must teach. You must teach. I must hand over this mantle. You can do it, I know you can." I pulled my hands back and told her I couldn't possibly accept. I was a songwriter, not a teacher. And I knew nothing about teaching acting.

Through later conversations, I began to understand that she wasn't talking about acting, or handing over the mantle of her own work. She was talking about handing over the mantle of her artist's soul. Of what she felt about art, what she believed about art and artists. How she articulated those beliefs, and passed them on. Years later, when I began giving master classes, I understood why she'd picked me.

After I left, Tino went on a spending spree, purchasing a $10,000 phone system, clothing, books. I hired an attorney and published a public notice in the newspaper, saying we were separated and I was no longer responsible for his debts. I told my attorney, *I don't want to fight, I don't want some long, drawn-out court battle. I just want him out of my life.*

My lawyer called Tino and told him he could have one of my rental houses, with the mortgage paid off, and a settlement in cash of half a million dollars, in return for a quick divorce.

He turned it down. I was stunned. So was my attorney. Even in a community property state, he was entitled to only half of what I'd earned *after* the marriage, which was nowhere near what I'd amassed before. The offer was generous.

Tino wanted to speak with me in private, without lawyers. I hadn't gone near him alone since the gun incident, but I agreed to meet with him. Not inside, though. Outside, on the front porch, where there'd be other people watching.

We sat outside, in full view of the street, talking. He looked awful.

He asked me to come back. He'd do anything I wanted. We could adopt a child, we could live in New York. Anything, if I'd just come back.

I couldn't believe I was hearing those words! He'd threatened to leave me dozens of times. He didn't desire me. For God's sake, he didn't even *like* me. He'd said it often enough: "I love you, Janis, but I don't like you."

I had no intention of returning, but I was curious enough to ask why he wanted the marriage to continue. I thought I might finally hear an apology, something along the lines of, "I miss you. I was a brute, and I want to make it up to you."

Instead, I heard him say, "Because I don't want to grow old alone."

I mentally slapped myself for thinking anything had changed, then asked him why he'd rejected my offer.

"It's not enough."

All right. How about if I give you a house, mortgage paid, agree to pay all costs for the next five years, and throw in $750,000?

No. He wanted more.

What do you want?! I finally said. *Everything?* I laughed after I said it, sure he'd see the absurdity of his position.

"Yes. I want everything."

You can't have everything! I told him. *Besides, I earned it all—none of it's rightfully yours. All you've done is spend it. Why on earth would you think you're entitled to everything I have?*

"Janis, you're in your thirties. You can make it all back. I'm in my fifties. This is my last chance."

The absurdity of it stunned me. I excused myself and went into the house to get a drink of water and spend a moment alone. While I stood at the refrigerator, Tino came in and began moving toward me. Without thinking, I grabbed a bottle of beer, broke it at the base, and pointed the sharp end toward him.

Do not . . . I repeat, do not *come near me. If you come near me, one of us is going to die. And if it's me, I'll do my best to take you along. No one is ever, ever going to hit me again.*

I left through the back door, watching him carefully. We spent the next few years in court, Tino doing everything in his power to slow down the divorce proceedings. He told the judge I was a lesbian; the judge asked what that had to do with anything. He said I was profligate; Irene Gilbert testified that he'd been paying tuition for several pretty actresses in an attempt to seduce them, which was news to me.

At one point, it actually became funny, as Tino's accent thickened and he told the judge he was just a "poor Portuguese immigrant" who'd been taken advantage of by his sharp-talking New York wife. He said he barely spoke English, and hadn't understood many of the proceedings.

I whispered to my attorney, who stood up and asked Tino where he'd gone to school. "UCLA," Tino replied. And how far had his studies taken him? "One or two semesters before a doctorate." And what had he studied? "English literature."

Even the judge smiled.

The divorce was granted February 25, 1988. In his decision, the judge determined that Tino had already spent his share of the marital estate. Besides, the IRS had moved in by then, and taken everything that wasn't nailed down. There was nothing left for me to live on, let alone support Tino.

He was out of my life now, but he still lived in my head. For more than a decade, through therapy, through other relationships, I caught myself doing things the way Tino liked them done. Or not doing things because they'd displease him.

I stayed scared of him all that time. Even after he lost his health and wound up in a wheelchair, I'd dream of him coming after me. I didn't relax until the day he died, when I finally understood that he could never hurt me again.

FOURTEEN

When Angels Cry

When angels cry, can I stand by?
When stones weep, can my heart sleep?
Wish I'd never heard
the power in a four letter word

The next few years went by pretty uneventfully, as I tried to get separated from Tino and have a life of my own again. They were quiet years, punctuated by the rise of AIDS, and the beginnings of my involvement with that movement.

Back in 1981, Bruce Mailman had called all the investors in the Baths, saying a strange disease was felling gay men on the West Coast. Most of them seemed to be promiscuous, and many frequented the bathhouses. Bruce's lover, a doctor, was following the Centers for Disease Control reports diligently. There had been twenty-six cases of a rare cancer called Kaposi's sarcoma among gay men in the past two and a half years, and eight of them had died.

A 33 percent death rate was terrifying to contemplate. I spoke with Bruce privately, asking what they thought was causing it. There were a lot of theories—mold getting in the lungs, from the dampness caused by the pools. Or amyl nitrate, "poppers," very popular in the dance clubs.

Perhaps it was sexually transmitted, though no one had ever heard of an STD that caused cancer. No matter. We would do what we could, step by step.

Bruce asked us to donate our earnings for a while, so he could begin an education program, and the Baths embarked on a model plan. In addition to passing out free condoms, we had weekly updates by physicians and scientists. There were safe-sex pamphlets everywhere, and we asked clients to sign a pledge that they would practice it.

The programs continued until the New York Board of Health shut all the bathhouses down in December 1985. By then, we all knew the grim statistics: 1981 saw 234 deaths from AIDS. In 1982 it quadrupled; 1983 saw it triple to 2,304, ten times what it was two years previous. By 1984 there were 4,251 deaths, almost double the previous year. It was horrifying. If deaths continued at this rate, pretty soon there'd be no more gay men.

I did a lot of AIDS benefits, often being the first performer because it still bore the stigma of a "gay disease." The first benefit in New York, the first fund-raiser in Nashville, the first pediatric benefit in the country. It seemed like for a while all I did were benefits, as the disease became a scourge.

When the Board of Health shut us down, we decided to fight. If every bathhouse in the country had used our methodology, the spread of AIDS would have been tremendously lessened. Our program of free condoms and education had prevented many men from getting the disease. Even *The New York Times* agreed, editorializing that we should be kept open to disseminate information. But it was not to be, and now, all these years later, Bruce himself is dead of AIDS, and the St. Marks Baths is no more.

MY GRANDPARENTS' sixtieth anniversary was that December, so I went to New York to drive Mom up to Boston for the event. She was degenerating swiftly, lurching drunkenly when she tried to move without a walker. I felt like someone had stolen her quick body and replaced it with a lemon. We'd managed to keep her multiple sclerosis a secret from my grandparents, not wanting to worry them, but it was impossible now. Mom could barely feed herself anymore; the tremors of intention in her arms would cause them to flail without warning.

We tried to make the best of it. We had sushi one night, and after a sudden tremor, I realized my face was plastered with salmon roe. My mother began to giggle, and I joined in, glad that even in these worst of circumstances we could still amuse each other.

Another night, I heard a loud sneeze from the bathroom, then a thud. Sure she'd fallen and been hurt, I raced in, only to find Mom accordioned in the small tub. Both her legs were dangling over the edge, and she was laughing her head off. It was funny, but the next morning we applied to Medicaid for more assistance.

I began encouraging Mom to apply for grants, to reeducate herself technologically. I knew she found living off the government humiliating, that she longed to feel useful. Years before, I'd bought her an IBM Selectric typewriter because it was easier on her failing hands than a manual machine. Now I talked about buying her a computer. I tried to explain that with the new technology, it was possible that even with the MS, she'd be able to work at a job again. It was frustrating, because I couldn't make her understand how fast the technology was changing.

I'd always been captivated by the idea of computers, going back to when my father gave me an Isaac Asimov story about Robbie the Robot. In fact, Peter and I had worked on a huge computer project at Columbia University back when I was seventeen, when they were still using punch cards. I'd bought my own IBM 5160 in 1982. It worked with floppy disks; you could actually save a whole letter for later editing! The machine was enormous, with a black-and-white monitor and its own desk. I'd had to learn DOS Basic, and binary systems, but that fit right in with the newer technology in my own field.

In fact, I flew back to Los Angeles just in time to attend a party at Chick's studio, where he and George Massenburg had just finished installing the first automated mixing board I'd ever seen.

This world is changing faster than any of us could have imagined, I wrote in my journal. *And some things can't change fast enough to suit me!*

I was still supporting Tino; he was still contesting the divorce. Occasionally, he'd call in a rage, threatening to call *The National Enquirer* and tell them I was gay. He was staying inside the house for weeks at a time, wearing nothing but his pajamas. He finally left, to visit his ailing father in Portugal, and I decided to go by and pick up a few of my things.

It felt strange, walking up the steps to the front door. I'd always parked in the back and gone in through the kitchen entrance. For a moment, I felt like an interloper, until I reminded myself that I owned the house.

I tried my key in the door; it worked fine, but when I punched the code to stop the alarm, I discovered Tino had changed it. It was silly to think that would keep me out, since I paid the bills. I just waited for the alarm company to arrive, explained that I'd been out of town, and had them reset it to the old code. Then I took a deep breath, turned the doorknob, and entered the home I'd loved so much.

I entered complete chaos. There were piles everywhere, unread newspapers and letters, untouched magazines, junk mail. Mail from attorneys, the IRS, all sealed and waiting to be read. Six months' worth.

The piles were about knee-high, with just enough room between them to cut a path. They filled the hallway, the living room, the breakfast nook. They filled the entire house. I was up to my waist in piles, as far as the eye could see.

That's when I began to shake.

I went up to Tino's dressing room and looked around. All through our marriage, he'd kept it locked. There was nothing mysterious about it now, just an old armoire, some weight-lifting equipment, and a cedar closet. I opened the closet and stared in amazement. Piled floor to ceiling were shoes and shirts, dozens and dozens. All the same. Blue work shirts, still in their packaging. Brown shoes, still in their boxes.

I thought at first that Tino was hoarding clothes against the day our divorce became final, and he'd have to support himself. Then I thought again. He couldn't have bought them since I'd left; I'd cut off access to my credit cards and bank accounts. He couldn't have bought them with his own money; the Portuguese escudo kept getting devalued, until his income from Madeira rents was just enough to keep him in food. That meant he'd bought them while we were still together.

He'd never believed we'd stay married. He'd always hedged his bets.

I found an old journal tucked away at the back of a drawer. In it, I read that he'd had an affair. The whole time I was in South Africa, he'd had another woman in my bed. In our bedroom. In our home. The affair had continued for months. I couldn't tell if that was the only one.

I closed the door, walked down the steps, took a deep breath, and called my doctor to arrange for an AIDS test.

TIME WENT BY, and life settled into a routine. I practiced, took ballet, read a lot. After all the drama with Tino, I needed some quiet, even if I got it by putting my hands over my ears. I enjoyed leading a calm, uneventful life.

Darn, I forgot: It wasn't so uneventful after all. I was sleeping with my therapist.

At Dora's urging, I'd begun to see a therapist during the last year of my marriage. It was fine with me; I knew I was confused, and miserable. My experience with Gerry had led me to believe all therapists were like him, so I walked into "Cassie's" office with great expectations.

I downplayed Tino's cruelty, ashamed to admit that I stayed through it. I did say he was abusive, verbally, and that he'd hit me once. I told her I was thinking of moving out, but she disagreed, saying I was "too parentified" to live on my own. She suggested instead that I start spending some time away from the house. That seemed like a good idea, so I booked myself into a cottage at a hotel called El Encanto, up near Santa Barbara.

I spent a gorgeous weekend alone, reading and resting. There was no phone in the room, so Tino couldn't reach me to yell at me. Nights, I'd lie on my back in the grass, and watch the shooting stars. One night, I counted seven, and it seemed like a good omen for the future.

Cassie and I became friends outside the office. It felt safe, like Gerry. I'd often go to dinner with her and "Manny," her husband, who affectionately referred to himself as my brother. In retrospect, she enjoyed showing "Janis Ian" off to her friends and family, but at the time, I was so grateful for any kindness that I swept right past it.

As Tino's depression lengthened, Cassie suggested I give him the house. That way, she reasoned, he'd feel like he had property of his own. I might also think about tearing up my prenuptial agreement; she was sure that was eating at him, too. Her suggestions seemed a little over the top to me, but I figured she had my best interests at heart. Still, I wasn't about to give any houses away, but I did disavow the prenuptial. It made no difference.

Cassie and Manny invited me to spend some time with them at their "Vermont" retreat. Cassie had once told me that the only kind of relationships she found exciting were the forbidden ones. Now she confided that she was having an affair with someone they both knew, who lived near their vacation home. She asked if I'd cover for her with Manny while we were up there, so she could see her lover undisturbed.

I said I'd have to think about it for a while. I liked Manny very much; I didn't want to hurt him. Cassie said she understood completely.

At my next session, she was giggly, almost flirtatious. The session after that, she told me she'd always wondered what it would be like to sleep with a woman. Before I knew it, she was sitting on the couch, her arms around me. Next she was kissing me, saying she wanted me.

What about the person in Vermont? I asked. *And what about Manny?*

"I want them, too. There's nothing really wrong with it, so long as they don't find out about each other. I'd like to try it with you, too—I'd like to see what it's like."

Oh. Another explorer. Back to Beth and Tino. Except this time, no one else was invited to the party.

At the last minute, Manny couldn't come, so Cassie and I went up to Vermont without him, arriving just in time for a blizzard. It was a nice place to be stranded, a cozy little house surrounded by woods and fields. The sky was dense with snow, swirling around the trees and covering the thick brush surrounding us. We showered, got into bed, and made love. Or something like it.

Sex with Cassie was one of the most unpleasant experiences of my life, and certainly the least pleasant in my entire life as a sexual being. I'd always known there were all kinds of sex—laughing sex, serious sex, got-to-have-you-right-now-or-I'll-explode sex. Sex for the fun of it, sex for the heart of it. Every lover I'd ever had was right there with me, sharing the pleasure.

Every lover except Cassie. She wasn't there. She was somewhere else, watching herself be satisfied. It was the oddest feeling, knowing she was connected only to herself. As I touched her, I looked at her face. She had a small, secretive smile on her lips. She was a million miles away.

I realized in that moment that Cassie didn't want a lover—she just wanted to be serviced. She wasn't sleeping with me, she was watching herself be slept with. Sex for Cassie was just narcissism, with a healthy dose of mental masturbation thrown in.

For me, it was the last step into complete self-loathing. My ego shattered, torn apart by the guilt I felt toward Manny and the anger I felt, but couldn't show, toward Cassie. I'd gone to her for help, and instead she'd seduced me. I'd gone to her after six years of abuse, hoping to find a safe place, and instead she'd placed me in more danger. Now I was stuck in a remote part of rural Vermont, with no one to talk to about any of it.

Afterward, Cassie expressed astonishment that she'd come, saying, "I must trust you very much." I guess she expected me to be flattered, but I took the words in with a cynical shrug of the heart. Neither of us trusted anyone, truth be told. I showered, then put my head on the pillow to sleep.

In the small space between waking and dreaming, I found myself looking down from a great height into a huge, barn-like building. There were Hasidic Jews of all ages milling about, wearing beards and long black coats. Some were in the stalls, praying and davening. Some were pacing up and down the corridors, arguing with each other and God. In the center was an open area I thought was for stabling horses. I had the strong sense that four or five animals were usually kept there before being moved on.

At the head of the room, there was a pedestal table, with books and papers scattered on it. There was an enormous, ancient book in the center, its covers frayed from much use. I watched as several old men pored over it, talking excitedly and making marks in the margins.

The room became a backdrop for someone's head hovering above, ringed in light. I lifted my eyes to the open barn doors. I saw lush green fields beckoning beyond. As I tried to see what lay past them, the entire scene exploded in a light that seemed to go on forever. I fell asleep wondering why I'd been dreaming about Orthodox Jews and light.

The next morning, Cassie gone to meet her lover, I called my mother. "Where are you?!" she cried. "We've been trying to reach you all night!"

I'm in Vermont. We had a blizzard, the phones were down. Why, what's up?

"Your Bubby Fink died."

My father's mother. My grandmother, who'd always dreamed about people just before they died. Who firmly believed in dybbuks, golems, and the power of her rabbi to hold up his staff and force a pack of wolves to draw away from their cart. Apparently, the apple hadn't fallen far from the tree.

Cassie saw her lover; I got the flu. She told me I was just upset because she'd seen her other lover; it was all in my head. I had some small satisfaction a few days later, when we were in New York with her daughter and son-in-law. They both had the flu.

When I got home, I took up a new hobby—drinking. Not during the day. During the day I got my work done, took classes, watched over my business. But at night, I'd drink enough to fall into oblivion. It was easier than dealing with everything. If I didn't drink, I'd start going through my journals, trying to figure out where I'd gone wrong. If I didn't drink, I'd start thinking about Cassie.

She was still enthralled with me. I'd begun a special project for an Australian company, and she visited the studio often. The album, *Uncle Wonderful*, was full of disjointed songs set to a thumping beat, and eventually spawned a minor dance hit with "Heart Skip Too Many Beats." She found excuses for us to spend time together, with and without Manny. Since I had nothing better to do, I went along for the ride. Cassie would say she loved me, and I'd laugh. I was done with believing anything anyone said to me. If someone asked what I wanted, I'd freeze, knowing it was a trap. They'd only exploit what I said to make fun of me, or to use it against me later. Look how Cassie and Tino had used me.

IN NEW YORK that May, I spent an evening with Stella. There were two Pirandello plays she wanted me to see, and afterward we went to the Russian Tea Room for dinner. Stella said she was proud of me, but she was also worried. She told me all of *Uncle Wonderful* shrieked "Someone *hold me!*" She said it was autobiography, a complete revelation of self. I told her my writing was crap, and she told me to stop worrying, to trust my talent.

I talked about Cassie and my confusion. Stella smiled, saying, "Ah, sex . . . at your age, the fires still burn. People have been trying to figure out sex for hundreds of years; they never have. It remains a necessity."

I was relieved to hear my friend calmly assessing my life, without judgment. As we walked outside, she turned, took my head in her hands, and kissed my forehead. Then she said, "So . . . you have all these talents, and they elevate you, and they destroy and confuse you. Feed your soul, Janis. Feed your heart." Then she walked into the night.

I began searching for music that would satisfy my hunger. I went to see Oscar Peterson at the Blue Note, and it was like hearing a miracle. I went to see Yves Montand, Tina Turner, Natalie Cole, and started hanging around the jazz clubs again. I was trying to come back to myself, and it began to work.

I cut off contact with Cassie. When she tried to see me, I said no. She said she needed to talk to me. I replied, *Cassie, I don't want to talk to* myself *right now, let alone to you.* She sent letters: "I'm heartsore about the cessation of emotional contact." She called again, warning me that if I told anyone what had happened, she could lose her license. *I'm not telling anyone, Cassie. I'm not even telling myself.*

I searched for musicians I knew who lived in the area. I spent some time with Nina Simone, until she began reminding me of Tino. I'd met Nina decades before, when "Society's Child" first came out. My mom was an enormous fan, so I took her to see Nina at Carnegie Hall. The only seats available were onstage, and I remember the relentless power she exuded as she came close to us, microphone at her lips, singing and shouting and whispering her heart in our ears.

Years later, we'd gone to see Nina at the Village Gate. She was having a rough night; she'd start a song, stop, move on to something else. The entire show was disjointed, and she ended after only twenty minutes. Someone leaned over and asked why I kept going to see her perform, when more and more of the shows were like this. I whispered back, "Because in twenty minutes of Nina, even at her worst, I learn more than twenty hours of anyone else."

Mom and I went backstage to visit. Nina was mourning her own mother, saying she missed her dreadfully. *Well, you can have mine for a while,* I said and we made plans for brunch the next morning at Mom's apartment. Nina arrived with James Baldwin in tow, and we spent four or five hours fixing the world, while she and James drank themselves into a stupor. Long after he'd left, Nina was still going. She finally passed out on the couch, and we carried her down to a taxi, giving the driver half of a hundred-dollar bill and promising the rest when he came back after depositing her safely at home.

Nina always had a streak of craziness, but anyone could see it was getting worse. One day in L.A., we went shopping for shoes. She found a pair of sandals she liked and brought them home, wearing them all afternoon. Then she decided she wanted to return them.

You can't, Nina, I said. *They've been worn outside.*

"Never mind what I can or cannot do, Janis. Drive me to the store."

I drove her to the store, where she regally presented the sandals to a puzzled clerk, who refused to take them back. She argued for a while, then swept imperiously out the door and back into my car. "Take me home, Janis, I have things to do."

When we got there, Nina told me to stay in the car. She walked into the house, coming back with the sandals still in hand. She told me to take her back to the store, and I did, following her curiously as she strode toward the counter. Once there, she called for the clerk who'd refused her. When he sauntered over, she pulled a gun out of her pocket, pointed it at him, laid the sandals beside the cash register, and said,

"*Now* will you take them back?" He quickly opened the cash drawer and gave her a full refund, carefully placing the money in her hand, then holding the door open as she strolled out of the store.

The last time I saw Nina, she was playing a small jazz club in L.A. Things were even worse than before. She saw me in the crowd and began to sing "Stars," but she only got through half a verse. After the set, she came over and whispered, "Let's go get a drink." I said I thought she'd stopped drinking, and she replied, "I only drink in my car, now." The trunk was full of small airline liquor bottles, empty and full. She searched around for a minute, then quickly downed a few.

After the second set, I was backstage talking with Nina and the club personnel when she got a wild look in her eyes. "Where's my money, Janis?!" she demanded, shaking a fist at me. I took a step back and responded that I didn't know what she was talking about. "Where's my money?! Why do you think I recorded your damned song, anyway?"

Nina, your record company pays you for recordings. I don't, I said.

"That's why I recorded it in the first place! Where's . . . my . . . money, Janis?!" She moved toward me, and I stepped back a pace, arguing, *Nina, you didn't write the song. I did. You don't get publishing. You can check with Paul Adler from ASCAP if you don't believe me.*

She grabbed the pay phone and dialed Paul's number in New York. It was three in the morning there, and she woke him out of a sound sleep. Apparently, she didn't like his answers. After she hung up, she ripped the entire phone out of the wall. Not just the handset, mind you—the entire pay phone.

It was pretty impressive.

Years later, staying in a Paris hotel, I got a call from one of her flunkies. "Miss Simone would like you to call her," he said. I replied that Nina still had five fingers and was perfectly capable of dialing a phone herself, then went back to sleep.

. . .

BY THE END OF 1985, I was restless to be working. I had no desire to go back on the road, or make records, but I did want to write. And writing without a publishing deal was writing in a vacuum. If I didn't record or perform, no one but me would ever hear the songs. I needed a publisher.

I called Ina, and she set up meetings with Lance Freed of Almo, and Leeds Levy of MCA. I met with Lance first. I was very excited; at the time, his publishing company was the best in the country for a serious songwriter. His staff didn't just pitch the songs; they *believed* in them. If they thought a song was great, they'd stick with it for years, trying to get someone to record it. I thought the meeting went well, but when Ina called, she said Lance had turned me down. So I went with MCA.

Later, I found out that when Dave Anderle, one of the most respected A&R people in my business, asked Lance why he'd passed. Lance responded, "She scares me." Dave smiled and said, "But, Lance . . . those are the ones you sign!"

MCA came up with a plan. Leeds and Rick Shoemaker, my point man there, said, "Janis, you write great, deep songs, but they're not very commercial. We want to send you to Nashville. We think if you can team up with someone who has a real talent for marketable songwriting, the combination could be killer. What do you think?"

I thought it was a great idea. I knew that, as a songwriter, I needed an education. All my life, I'd written blind. If something worked, great. If it didn't work, I threw it out and started over again. I had all the talent in the world, but very little craft. Nashville was steeped in craft. Maybe I'd finally start writing songs that pleased me again. I was more excited than I'd been in years.

I spent a week assembling some bits and pieces I'd started, then got a haircut. Buzzed and dyed deep purple on one side, curly and black on the other. And on March 11, 1986, I flew off to Nashville to make my fortune.

FIFTEEN

My Tennessee Hills

I'll go home, I'll go home
where the wild shadows roam
and the dawn over mountaintops spills
Where the deer pause in flight
on the edge of the night
I'll go home to my Tennessee hills

I set foot on the tarmac, and the oddest thought popped into my head: *I'm home. I'm finally home.* I wondered where it had come from. I knew nothing about the town, and next to nothing about country music.

The Nashville MCA office had asked around to see if anyone was interested in writing with me. It was hit or miss; the town was tired of songwriters coming in from L.A. to make a quick buck, thinking country was easy to write. They looked at me with a jaundiced eye. I was Northern. I'd had hit pop records. I'd probably turn out to be a know-it-all little snit, so why bother trying to write with me?

The first morning, I was dropped at MCA's writers' house with no fanfare. Writers' houses are a peculiarly Nashville institution, much like the old Brill Building. Owned by the publishing company, each has a bunch of rooms songwriters can use. Some of them rotate, some of them belong to a particular writer. Lots of them have keyboards, and even guitars, along with couches, chairs, and coffee tables. It's a lot easier than going to a new place each day, and for writers with children or roommates, it's a lifesaver.

You get used to a space. I can write anywhere, but I vastly prefer my own little writing room. The couch is low enough that my feet don't dangle. The coffee table's just the right height to lean over a guitar and jot down lyrics. I look out onto trees and grass. The plaster walls are circa 1901, so they're thick, giving the room a great echo. It's small, intimate, and safe.

I was sitting on a couch, waiting for something to happen, when an old-time writer named Frank Dykus ambled in. He looked me up and down, sat, then said, "Huh. You're that Janis Ian girl, right?"

Yep, I replied.

"Huh. Guess you've come from L.A. to show us how to do it."

Nope, I answered, enjoying myself immensely. I grinned at him.

"Ya got purple hair on one side. You know that?" Frank grinned back. I was glad I hadn't taken the color out; it was a good conversation starter.

Must be the water. I laughed.

"You're short," Frank said. "Real short."

Yeah, I know. I'm hoping Nashville will stretch me.

"What do you know about country music?"

I thought a minute, then answered honestly. *Not much. I know Hank Williams, and Jimmy Reeves, 'cause I grew up on folk music. That's about it. I'm here to learn.*

"To learn . . . huh. That's a first." Frank rose and said, "See ya," then left.

Later, I found out his wife was a big fan of mine. When she asked him what I was like, he said, "Looks like a rat terrier with a perm . . . but she'll do."

Word spreads quickly in Nashville. Within days, his comment was all over town, and writers were asking to work with me.

I had all my preconceptions shattered in those two weeks. One day, I was writing with Russell Smith, and we went out to lunch. Now, when I think *redneck*, I think Russell. It's no slur; he'd be the first to agree. I had a mess of fixed ideas about the South, and rednecks. So when Russell spied a member of the Ku Klux Klan standing on a street corner asking for donations, I got nervous.

I grew more nervous when Russell swerved and headed toward him. Then I froze. What was I going to do? Obviously, Russell was going to make a donation. Should I say something? If I said something, I might ruin myself in Nashville. If I didn't say something, I'd ruin myself in my own eyes. I sat there, wanting to jump out of the car.

Russell pulled up and rolled down his window. The Klansman strolled toward us, holding a grocery bag. He smiled and lifted the sack to the window. Russell calmly took the car ashtray, overflowing with stale cigarette butts, and dumped it in the bag. The Klansman was flabbergasted. "We don't want your kind here," said Russell. "Go on home, now."

I have rarely been so astonished. From that moment on, I resolved to lose any notions I had about Nashville, the South, and most of all, rednecks.

There was a Nashville Songwriters Association show on my last weekend in town, and I'd been asked to perform. The audience would be writers and industry people, which worried me. I hadn't set foot on a stage in years, and I had no idea what kind of reaction I'd get. I had fifteen minutes, so I decided to go for broke. It worked for me in Philly, it might work here. So I opened with an a cappella version of "Jesse," moved on to something funny, then closed with "At Seventeen."

It went down really well. I got a standing ovation, and more fun still, got to sit around in the group dressing room and meet other songwriters after the show. One struck me in particular. Her name was Kye Fleming, and she had beautiful eyes. Pat Halper, from MCA, filled me in on Kye's career stats as we drove back to the hotel. She was extremely successful, named BMI Writer of the Year four times, once trumping the Beatles. She'd written most of Barbara Mandrell's hits, and a slew of others. She'd been partnered with Dennis Morgan for years, but they'd burned out, and she was now with Almo, looking for a new writing partner.

Kye had asked me what I'd seen of the town. *Nothing,* I told her.

"Nothing? No one's taken you around, or had you over to dinner?"

No, I said. She clucked her tongue and invited me to her home the next day, promising we'd take in some local acts and have a good meal.

True to her word, Kye picked me up that Sunday morning and took me for a quick tour of Nashville. We wound up sitting by the Harpeth River, talking about our lives. At some point, I said, "I have a friend who always tells me to stop rushing the river." Kye laughed and said it would make a good song title.

We climbed in her truck and went back to her place, where there was a wonderful baby grand piano. I sat down and began playing, my friend's words still echoing in my head. Kye sat next to me and began singing, "Don't rush the river," and we had the beginnings of a song.

It was the easiest song either of us had ever written, and we both wanted to try for more. Unfortunately, Kye was fully booked for the rest of my time in Nashville, but we made plans to get together for dinner a few times, and go to the Bluebird Café.

Now, the Bluebird is an institution, a venerable coffeehouse specializing in singer-songwriters. Back then, the club had been open only a few years. Kye took me to see a group of songwriters playing "in-the-round," something new for me. As we entered, I saw four men form a square, then pull out guitars. Schuyler, Knobloch, Overstreet, and Schlitz proceeded to play some of the best songs I'd ever heard. On top of that, they were terrific guitarists.

It was horribly depressing.

Energized by the show, Kye and I went back to my hotel room, where I showed her an unfinished lyric called "Every Love." It began with:

Every love is different, every love's the same
Every love has sorrow, every love has pain
I knew love at thirty, and I knew love at nine
but the love I know right now
is the sweetest love I'll ever find

I confessed that I'd been stuck for weeks, trying to come up with a second verse. "Oh, that's easy!" said Kye, picking up the pen. She wrote:

Every town's familiar. Every town is strange.
When you're feeling lonely, every town's the same.
I have dreamed of Paris, and I have dreamed of Rome
but the dream we're in right now
is the sweetest dream I've ever known

We stared at each other, beaming with glee. This was incredible! How could something that was always so hard suddenly be effortless?

We wrote as much as possible over the next few nights, after our other appointments were over. We wrote, and wrote, and when we didn't feel like writing anymore, we talked about everything under the sun. I went back to L.A. with thirteen new songs I liked, four of them with Kye.

We played them for our publishers. They were thrilled. Almo suggested flying her out, so we could write uninterrupted for two weeks. We spoke every day on the phone, passing ideas back and forth, spilling our secret hearts.

Writing, at its best, is a naked profession. When you cowrite, the best way to do it is to be completely open, and let your creativity flourish. I don't mean you have to spill the dark secrets of your life every time. But writing, like the human heart, is mysterious. If you can open the door a little, it's surprising what comes through.

We fell in love, of course. It was inevitable. When we were writing, we breathed together, as one soul. That sounds corny, but it's true. Some of the best writing I've done in my life was with Kye. Our songs were seamless, unlike our lives.

She flew out to Los Angeles in mid-April. The second day she was there, I took her for lunch at my friend Mary's restaurant. Mary served great food, in a nice atmosphere, but she was struggling, barely able to keep the business open. She'd been really unhappy of late, and I was hoping to cheer her up.

Instead, I made it worse. While Kye and I were babbling about our new songs and how happy we were together, Mary announced that she was thinking of suicide. We were dismayed. *Why on earth would you do that?!* I demanded.

"It's all right for you two," she shot back. "You've made a real difference to a lot of people. Your work will live after you. But me? No kids, no lover, no nothing? In a couple of years, no one would miss me. It'd be like I never existed."

We went back to Kye's hotel, thoroughly depressed. Kye paced up and down in the small room while I picked up a guitar and idly played the opening chords to "Jesse." I looked up and said, *You know, I've always hoped to write another "Jesse," or at least a ballad as good.*

"What we should write about is Mary," Kye responded. "And how she feels."

I played a few more chords, but Kye continued to pace. She wheeled to face me, tears in her eyes. "You know, some people's lives, they just . . . they just run down like a clock. It's awful!"

Awful? It wasn't awful! It was a great line. I changed my second chord to a minor, added two more, then sang at her:

Some people's lives
run down like clocks

and she shot back:

One day they stop
That's all they've got

I sang:

Some lives wear out

and Kye sang back:

like old tennis shoes
no one can use

so I finished with:

It's sad, but it's true

We were off and running.

I'd never had an experience like that with a song. I'd had songs that obsessed me, songs that played in my head all day and night. I'd written songs I just *had* to finish. But I'd never spent three days living, breathing, and giving birth to a song like "Some People's Lives." It was incredible.

We wrote in the shower. We wrote in the bed. We had dinner at Lance's, and wrote in the car parked outside his house. We wrote until we were dizzy with it.

When we reached the last chorus, we got stuck. There was, as Kye said, no "wrap." We spent a full day on the last two lines, but nothing worked. So we went to Mary's for dinner, hoping it would inspire us. While we lingered over coffee, Kye suddenly looked at me and grinned.

"I've got it!" she said. "How stupid am I? It's been sitting right in front of our noses. The last chorus should be:

"Doesn't anybody tell them?
Doesn't anybody see?
Doesn't anybody love them
like you love me?
'Cause that's all they need."

I agreed that it was fantastic, but it didn't scan. She'd added an extra line at the end, and it wouldn't fit the music. "Then change the melody," Kye insisted. I spent half an hour playing with it in my head, writing down ideas for chord changes on one of Mary's precious cloth napkins. And finally, I grinned at Kye the same way she'd grinned at me, and said, "How stupid am *I*?! It's right in front of my nose!"

We went back to the hotel and I played her what I'd done. I'd transposed the next-to-last line up a whole step, so we could resolve back to the original key after the extra line. It worked like a charm.

An hour later, we went back to the restaurant and I played "Some People's Lives" for Mary. She began to weep. *See what a difference you've made?* I said triumphantly. *See?!*

The next morning, we took the song to our publishers. Brenda Andrews, our main confidante at Almo, almost fainted when she heard it. She swore it was going to be covered by someone huge; she'd work it until it went platinum. Lance smiled and said, "Now, *that's* a copyright. That song'll make money for decades. We'll find a good home for it, no matter how long it takes."

And it took a long time. I went over to Mel Tormé's place and played it for him; he agreed that it was a great song, but he wasn't recording. Kye called Jennifer Warnes and we played it for her, but she was between deals. Anita Baker loved it, but it wasn't right for her next album. Streisand loved it; it wasn't right for her album. It was four long years before a major artist finally recorded it. By that time, Kye and I were just a memory, but the song endured, and finally, Bette Midler released a double platinum album titled *Some People's Lives.* Lance and Brenda had been true to their word; they'd worked it all that time.

I'd been living at the Chateau Marmont, an L.A. institution, but now I rented a house. Tino still wouldn't vacate our Hancock Park home; it would be another year, and the IRS, that finally got him out. I found a sweet two-bedroom in the heart of West Hollywood, and we moved in. We were stupidly happy together, but there were major problems.

Kye was a Pentecostal Christian. Her world condemned us. When Kye's mother came to visit that July, her first words after asking if we were gay were, "I'm going to have a heart attack," followed by, "I'd rather you'd died at birth than done this to me."

In her heart, Kye condemned us as well. I've never understood how people who are gay could believe they're going to hell for it, but in her bad moments, Kye was sure of it. As time wore on, that belief made it harder and harder for her to be with me, in any sense of the word.

I give her mother big points, though. When she got back home to Fort Smith, she went down on her knees and prayed. She prayed openly, asking God to lead her, rather than asking Him to change Kye. And at the end of three days, she told me, God said, "This is not your business; this is between Kye and me." I never heard a criticism from her again, and she told me I was always welcome in her home. Not many people are that brave.

Despite that life was pretty idyllic over the next few months. We wrote all day, every day, in every possible key and every conceivable form. Kye wasn't just a great lyricist. She had a terrific gift for a commercial melody, and when I threw a line out at her, she'd often sing it back to me much improved. We began creating an eclectic catalog of songs that ranged from solid jazz to almost classical. It was a constant surprise to Kye that we could throw away the formulas and just write for the love of it, letting the music take us in any direction. And our instincts proved right over time, as that catalog was covered by people as diverse as Diane Schuur and Kathy Mattea.

The songs were so good that I decided to book a short tour and try them out onstage. About a week before I left, Kye took me to our favorite restaurant for lunch. I was feeling great until I stepped out of the car, and the world tilted. It was like being dosed again; suddenly, everything turned on its side. I broke out in a cold sweat and sat down on the pavement. Kye helped me into the restaurant, where a drink of cool water seemed to settle things.

Because I felt fine soon after, I put it down to stress and excitement. I was thrilled about the last few dates of the tour. I'd be finishing off the run with a show at the Kennedy Center, then the Philadelphia Folk Festival. The first week went smoothly. I liked being a performer again, and it showed. I was using everything I'd learned from Stella, trying to be "in the moment" every moment onstage. I'd repeat what she'd taught me like a mantra before I went on: "Entrance. Focus. Energy. Exit."

Things started to fall apart during the second week of the tour. Suddenly, I couldn't focus. My bass player, Chad Watson, took me aside one night in Florida and asked if I was okay. *I'm fine,* I said. But by the middle of the next night, I was breaking out in sweat every few minutes. Forgetting the words to songs I'd sung a thousand times. Not feeling well at all.

The third day, there was a dull pain in my lower abdomen. *I've got a urinary tract infection,* I thought. I bought some cranberry juice and began drinking it by the gallon. Stan Schnier, my road manager, was with us. He'd probably have some penicillin if the juice didn't work.

We had the next day off, and Stan and I went to the movies. When we walked outside, I got faint. I asked if he had any penicillin with him and explained that I had a UTI. He told me he wasn't going to give me any antibiotics until I'd seen a doctor.

I don't need a doctor! I'm on the road, for Pete's sake. What do I need to be poked and prodded by some stranger for?! I was adamant. My last experience with a road doctor had been in Amsterdam. I had a minor infection, and the hotel recommended a nearby physician. After sitting in his waiting room for hours, I'd finally gotten into the office, where he wrote me a prescription for penicillin without looking up, and told me to remember to wash after sex. I snorted, realizing I was in the red-light district and he thought I was just another hooker complaining about an STD.

I went back to bed and lay there with my knees drawn up, clutching my abdomen. The people next door were making love, and their headboard was banging violently against the wall behind my head. She was calling out, "Tito! Oh, Tito!" For one hallucinatory moment, I wondered if Tino was stalking me. I took two Tylenol and tried to rest, but the pain was getting worse.

Stan called and invited me to a seafood restaurant. I declined. Minutes later, he was at my door. He grabbed my arm and pulled me toward the car, saying, "That's it. When you turn down lobster, your favorite food in the world, something's really wrong. We're going to the hospital."

I owe him my life. I argued all the way there. *I have gigs, Stan. I've got Philly Folk Fest next weekend. I don't have time for this.* He wouldn't listen. The pain stopped right after I walked into the hospital, and I argued some more. *It's just a UTI, Stan. I feel fine.*

Yeah. I felt fine because the abscess my body had built around my ruptured intestine, trying to protect me from its septic contents, had burst. Now, it was flooding my bloodstream with poison. When they asked me to hold my breath for an X-ray, I saw stars and fainted dead away.

Stan, cool and collected, called a cousin of his who sat on the board of Mount Sinai Hospital. His cousin called "the A-team," a group of highly regarded surgeons, and they had me transported to their facility at midnight. They wanted to talk with my next of kin. Stan said they were unavailable. He lied through his teeth and told them he had full power of attorney. The doctors told him no one knew what exactly was wrong, but by now, it didn't matter. If they didn't go in and find out, I wouldn't be alive by morning.

I was blissfully unaware. I was starting to fade. My white count was triple. I had blood poisoning. The lead doctor, Peter Segal, leaned over the gurney to insert an intravenous line and said, "You have about forty-five minutes." *Oh, good,* I said. *I should call my folks and Stella to tell them not to worry. Otherwise, they'll hear it on the news.*

He smiled. "No, Janis. You don't have forty-five minutes until surgery. You have forty-five minutes, and then you'll be dead."

That's the last thing I remember before I came to the next evening in ICU. I woke up because I heard chanting. When I listened harder, it was the Jewish prayer for the dead. Groggily, I opened my eyes and peered through the open door. There were Orthodox Jews walking down the hallway, blowing the shofar and singing the Kol Nidre.

My great-grandparents were right! I thought. *Shit shit shit. I should have kept kosher. Now they're taking people up to heaven, and I'm not going to get in. I'll have to do this all over again. Shit.* I fell back asleep with a groan.

The next morning, I found out it was Yom Kippur, our highest holy day, and the day we mourn our dead. A local synagogue was holding services at the hospital for those who couldn't leave.

My surgeon, Harry Sendzischew, kept me in the hospital for ten days, then he and Stan put me in a nearby residential hotel for two weeks. Kye flew in and stayed with me. Mom called and wrote, heartbroken that the MS wouldn't let her travel. Stella also called, offering to come down and stay until I recovered. Even Tino called, after hearing about it on a newscast, and offered to come help me.

Yeah, right.

The effects of the septicemia took months to get over. I'd lost more than twenty-five pounds, a quarter of my body weight. I was anemic, with a temporary colostomy. I'd need follow-up surgery to close it, but I'd have to get healthy first.

I hadn't been really ill since my bout with pneumonia. One afternoon, I decided to take a look at my scars. I stood nude in front of a full-length mirror, staring at my shrunken body. I looked a hundred years old. The scars were huge; there wasn't time to make them pretty, Harry said, they'd had to hack their way in as quickly as possible.

I'd always hated having large breasts, had longed to magically wake up a 32B. Now the illness had accomplished that for me. I looked down at them and muttered, "You poor things." I looked at my face in the glass and said, "You poor thing." Then I collapsed on the bed and wept a river.

I did everything Harry asked, taking pills for anemia and forcing food down my throat so I could gain some weight. I was on my own; Stan had to go back to his children, and Kye had a BMI function she couldn't miss. She worried all the time about Nashville discovering our relationship; she said people already thought it strange that she'd flown to Florida because her writing partner was sick.

We decided I'd convalesce at her Nashville place. When I walked into the kitchen, every conceivable type of candy and cookie was there, waiting for me. "I know you don't like sweets, but you've got to put twenty pounds back on," Kye said, holding out a chocolate bar.

Then she informed me that her parents were coming to visit. *Oh, no . . .* I groaned. *Can't I just go to a hotel?* Her folks were the last thing I needed, but she was getting an award, and they wanted to be there. I wanted to be alone with Kye, held by her, told everything would be all right. With her parents around, she'd sit on the opposite side of the room, and we'd sleep in separate beds.

We all went to the movies later that week, and as we were walking, I began to feel faint. I put my hand on Kye's shoulder to steady myself and she jerked away. "Stop it! My parents will see!" I burst into tears.

I put the weight back on, and just before Thanksgiving, Harry operated again. Prior to the surgery, I spoke with the gynecologist who'd been part of my original team. He said when he'd checked my womb then, it was filled with fibroid tumors. He recommended a hysterectomy.

I told him about trying to get pregnant, and asked if it would ever be possible. He looked at me with sympathy. "Even if you'd been able to get pregnant, you'd never have been able to carry to term. Your uterus wouldn't have held on to a child. I'm sorry."

It wasn't my fault after all. Since I'd left Tino, whatever thoughts I'd had of becoming a single parent had been put off for the distant future. Now, that option was closed forever. It was actually a relief, knowing I'd never have to think about it again.

This time, I recuperated at my rented house in L.A. A few weeks after I arrived, I got a call from a business associate, saying my check had bounced. *I'll get it straightened out,* I promised, and called Sam. A mistake—he said. A mistake. He'd fix it right away.

A month later, going over my statement, I found a $10,000 error. And $5,000 that should have been deposited, but wasn't. Then all my checks began bouncing. I called Sam again. It was a bank mistake—he'd take care of it right away.

I phoned Ina. *Something's not right. I think he's stealing.* She said that was ridiculous. He'd been with me for decades. There'd been plenty of opportunities to steal before, and he hadn't taken them, had he?

I wasn't so sure. I called Stan to ask what he thought.

"Janis, you worry too much. Mistakes happen. Come on, relax. The worst is over. You got through two surgeries, you're writing again. You're in love, you've got a roof over your head—what more could you want?"

Then the roof fell in.

SIXTEEN

Stolen Fire

When the new wears off, the weak ones fade
Some whore moves in for the kill
I could hear her thunder in the love we made
I can hear it still

The IRS liened my bank accounts, taking everything. It came out of nowhere. I called Ina in a panic, and she recommended I hire a tax specialist named Michael Zimmerman. When he heard why I was calling, he told me to go to a pay phone and call back collect.

"Are you sure you don't owe them any money?" he asked.

Absolutely sure. Do you have any idea how much I pay in taxes every year? I've seen the statements.

"Are you sure the statements are correct?" Zimmerman wanted to know. "Have you cross-checked them against the checks and bank statements? Done an audit?" No, I hadn't. He sighed and said he'd call Sam. In the meanwhile, I wasn't to discuss this with anyone.

What's the worst that can happen? I wanted to know. Well, they could put a lock on my door and deny me access until they'd inventoried everything in the house. If I'd been served notices and ignored them, they could put me in jail. *But I didn't get any notices!* I protested. Well, maybe I did, maybe I didn't. He'd know more after speaking with Sam.

I called Tino to warn him there was no cash, and he accused me of lying about the liens. Then he announced he was suing me for support.

It took three days for Sam to return Zimmerman's calls, but what he said was a relief. No, there weren't any notices. The whole thing was a silly misunderstanding over some old tax shelters. Michael was welcome to come and go through his files.

Michael went the next morning. Sam handed him the keys, then left without a word. Rummaging through the files, Michael found seven IRS notices of deficiency, dating back to 1981. I hadn't known about any of them. By the time we added interest and penalties, I owed more than I was worth.

He called the IRS agent in charge of my case, a Mr. Granite. (Really. Do you think I could make that up?) Granite wasn't very helpful. As far as he was concerned, I'd been avoiding them for seven years. Michael tried to explain. Granite wasn't interested.

Michael called me. Perhaps, if he and I spoke to the agent together, I might be able to convince Granite I hadn't known what was going on. Hopefully, we could work out a payment plan that would allow me money to live on while things got sorted out.

We set up a conference call. When Granite picked up the phone, I introduced myself, then told him I'd never gotten the notices. They'd all gone to Sam, who'd kept it from me.

"Tell it to the judge," he sneered. "I know all about you fucking performers."

I held the phone away from my ear, staring at it in shock. This was his first sentence to me?

The conversation went downhill from there. I asked about a payment plan. "Nope. We're gonna take every dime you've got, every cent you earn, until you've paid what you owe."

I argued, saying they had to leave me money to live on. "Yep. You get seventy-five dollars a week."

But what about my mother? I cried. She was completely disabled. I'd been sending her $500 a month for years now, to cover everything Medicaid wouldn't pay for.

"She gets fifty dollars a week," he told me. And with that, he hung up.

We needed the rest of my paperwork. I called and called. Michael called and called. Sam wouldn't respond. I finally flew to New York and told Ina I was going to fire him and get my records. *I really think I should go up there with a U.S. Marshal and a court order,* I told her. *I don't trust him to turn everything over.*

She demurred. Sam had been a friend of ours for decades. At worst, he was incompetent, a poor record keeper. There'd be no problem.

I walked into Sam's office alone. He looked up, unsurprised. I told him he was fired, and I wanted all my records. He stood up and shouted "That's fine! That's just fine! Because I know all about you fucking artists. You waste money, you get in trouble, then you blame somebody else. Well, you know what? Fuck you!" Then he threw one of my checkbooks at me and stormed out.

I grabbed as many records as I could carry and brought them back to L.A. Then I started trying to get the rest of my paperwork. Sam had everything I'd accumulated over the past twenty years—contracts, tax records, correspondence. After months, and the threat of a lawsuit, I finally got twelve boxes. The note from Sam said that his staff had "lost the rest in spring cleaning."

The IRS liened my royalties, then demanded any property I owned be sold. With that, Tino finally moved out, taking my rare book collection with him. Once he was gone, I held a huge garage sale, getting rid of everything possible and pocketing the cash to keep myself going. I sold guitars, stage clothes, furniture, rugs, anything I could get my hands on.

Kye had decided to buy a condo in Santa Monica, and I spent part of the sale money going in on it with her. I brought very little with me; some recording equipment and books, a couple of instruments, my car, and my Bösendorfer. The IRS couldn't force me to sell it, because I needed it for my work.

I'd always spent two to three hours a day playing, but now I spent all my spare time at the keyboard. I played like a drowning man who'd just been handed a rowboat. If I could have, I'd have crawled inside the Bösendorfer and slept there. It was the only place I felt safe.

I started selling my houses, and running out of money. The sales would help satisfy the IRS, but I owed taxes on any profit I earned. For better or worse, I was a good businesswoman, so most of the sale money was pure profit. Since the IRS took every dime, there was no money left to pay the new taxes, and I was in even more trouble.

I protested to Michael. What was I supposed to live on? More important, what was Mom supposed to live on? We'd finally gotten her moved into handicapped housing, and she had an aide, but she was terrified about money. That $500 a month paid for more than food and diapers; it gave her some peace of mind.

Zimmerman couldn't believe I had no cash socked away. Surely I had a stash somewhere?

Michael, why would I hide money? I always paid my taxes, as far as I knew. Can't you talk to Mr. Granite, ask him to ease up a little, just for my mom?

No, Mr. Granite wasn't going to ease up. In fact, he seemed to be enjoying himself. And I couldn't even challenge the amount he said I owed. The rule then was that you had to pay the entire amount they'd assessed, before you could challenge it. I was stuck.

I spent hours each day going through what remained of my financial records. It seemed like an impossible task; items had been systematically removed. There'd be a year's worth of check stubs, but no checks. Or there'd be checks, but no stubs.

Still, I started finding discrepancies. There were two sets of books on the same Chemical New York account, with the same check numbers. Sam had used one to ostensibly pay my bills, never sending the checks out. He used the other for his own bills, with the same check numbers. I'd find two same-numbered checks to American Express, for the same amount—only one went to pay off his account, while mine never went anywhere.

There was a million-dollar life insurance policy on me, with Sam one of the beneficiaries—my signature had been forged. There was authorization for the IRS to audit as far back as they liked; Sam had signed, saying he had power of attorney. There was a photocopied POA form, signed by me at the bottom, with most of the provisions I'd put in limiting it whited out. The original had disappeared.

And finally, there was a series of checks made out to cash and signed by Sam, for tens of thousands of dollars. They were all endorsed and cashed by him.

I borrowed money from Kye and flew back to New York to show Ina and Stan my proof. While I was there, I checked on my mother and freaked. I'd explained what was going on to her as best I could, promising I'd be able to send some money soon. Now I discovered she'd been trying not to eat, to save money. She was down to sixty-nine pounds.

I sold my Bösendorfer.

I used all the money for my mother. I didn't think I'd be needing it; my third year at MCA Publishing was approaching, and they were supposed to pay me a hundred grand. Ina said she'd work out a way for me to have access to that money while the IRS was being settled.

A few days before my term ended, Rick Shoemaker called and made me an offer. They would pay me half the amount the contract called for. In return, they wanted a fourth year tacked on, with no advance for the extra time. Take it or leave it.

I was furious, and told him so.

"Well, you can't really afford to be picky about it right now, can you?" he said.

I could not believe it. They knew about my IRS problems, and instead of helping me, they were using my poor circumstances to hold me up. It was blackmail, pure and simple. They wanted to cut my fee in half, and get ownership of twice as many songs on top of it.

I took a deep breath, then said, *You're absolutely right, Rick. I can't afford to be picky right now.* I paused, then followed up with, *But I'd rather sleep in my car than give in to blackmail, Rick, so go screw yourself.*

In January 1988, I sold the last house I owned. The IRS had pocketed more than $850,000 by now, but Granite wouldn't let up. He seemed to have it in for me personally. He didn't like people like me, "spoiled singers who think they don't have to pay taxes." The liens stood, with more added to cover the money I owed for the sale of the houses.

I compiled a dossier of all the illegalities Sam had perpetrated and sent it to John Clark, a noted litigator, to ask whether he would help me sue Sam. I reasoned that since he held himself out as a CPA, he'd have malpractice insurance. Maybe it would even pay the rest of the IRS bill.

After reviewing everything, John called with good news. "Janis, my firm never takes these cases on contingency, but we're willing to do that with yours. The evidence is so very clear, and you've been so damaged, we think you have an outstanding case."

I was ecstatic. I'd have the full weight and resources of Abeles, Clark, and Osterberg behind me. I trusted the firm; decades before, Bob Osterberg had successfully defended me when *The New York Times* and I were codefendants in a multimillion-dollar libel suit about Phoebe Snow. A reporter had interviewed me for an article about her, and I'd defended Phoebe's professional reputation. One of her former managers felt I'd libeled him personally, and even though we'd never met and I didn't even know his name, he'd sued—but he'd lost.

I was in an upbeat mood the day Clark met with Sam, until John called to say I should drop the case. "First of all, Janis, he's not a CPA. He's not licensed as one, whatever he told you. He's just a bookkeeper. Second, he has no insurance. Last and most important, he's become very good friends with your IRS adjuster. They're buddies. Sam told me that if you sue, he's going to tell Granite you've got money hidden all over the world, and watch you spend the rest of your life disproving it. Drop the case, Janis, at least until you're done with the IRS."

That was that. I had no money, and no prospects. If I got a new publishing deal, the IRS would pocket 100 percent of my advance. If I tried to tour, they'd show up at the door and take the box office receipts, leaving me no way to pay the band or crew. I had no one to turn to but Kye, who was there every step of the way. As the list of people I could trust grew shorter, I placed my faith in her. When I had no faith in myself anymore, she kept faith for me. Whatever problems we had together, they paled next to my trust in her.

I sold instruments, one by one, and lived off the money for as long as I could. I sold the jewelry I'd held back, doing the same. It was tight, but I was managing. Ina and Michael carried me, as did my divorce attorney.

Kye and I had been together now for two years, spending most of that time in Los Angeles. She didn't like going back to Nashville. We'd each kept our own residence, so she could keep up the fiction that we just stayed with each other when we were writing. Still, she worried that someone "back home" might put two and two together and wonder if we might be something more than friends.

It was exactly the opposite for me. I wanted to spend as much time in Nashville as possible. I loved knowing there was a community of songwriters. I'd never had that before; the closest I'd come was the Village, back when I was a kid. Knowing there was a place where people understood, and not being able to spend time there, drove me nuts.

I also loved working with other songwriters, but Kye wanted to be the only person I wrote with. Writing and living with her, day in and day out, was beginning to feel like living with Beth. Kye had no life of her own, and it concerned me.

She began talking about wanting a baby. At first, she spoke of wanting to adopt a retarded child, or a deformed child, one no one else would want. I was appalled; our life as writers didn't really lend itself to full-time caretaking. *Do you think gay people don't have the right to a healthy baby, Kye?* I asked. Yes, she thought that. I finally talked her out of it, and we went to meet with an attorney who specialized in gay adoption. She suggested that since the process could take so long, we also pick a sperm donor. Kye was more than willing to carry the baby.

It was time for me to think about recording again. Kye was good friends with a Nashville duo, "Nancy Dawn Montgomery" and "Dell Ward." The two were making a name for themselves locally as "Montgomery Ward," attracting the attention of people like Sting's manager. I was friendly with them, and admired their work. Ina wanted me to record three or four songs she could pitch for a record deal, and I asked them to produce. We arranged to start recording in early fall. There was next to no money, but I'd interested a couple of small investors who were willing to front some costs. Nancy Dawn flew out to spend a week with us and pick the songs. Kye cried when Nancy left, saying she missed the South.

We planned to start working with a fertility clinic when we returned from Nashville, so Kye and I went ahead and picked a sperm donor just before our departure. We hit Nashville in a good mood, ready to write and do some recording. A few nights after our arrival, I got a call from Maureen Weiss—Gerry had suffered a fatal heart attack. The funeral was Sunday; could I come?

It was a Friday night. I called American Airlines and begged for a cheap rate, telling them my father had died. Then I asked Kye to lend me plane fare. I took the first flight out, staying with Maureen and Randy, hardly able to believe what had happened. Gerry was only fifty-nine, but he'd suffered two previous attacks. More than half his heart was gone from the first incident, and he'd been on the Pritikin diet for decades. The last time I'd seen him, he'd finished off dinner with a pint of ice cream. When I scolded him, he said, "I'm sick of living like an invalid. I'd rather go sooner than live like this."

I wasn't sure how to behave, or whose car I should ride in. I'd stayed close to Gerry, but it had been years since I'd spent time with Maureen or Randy. When it came time to leave for the funeral home, I stood there uncertainly until Maureen grabbed me and told me to get in the limo with them. *But . . . but . . . I'm not family. What about Gerry's mother?* Maureen snorted and told me I was, indeed, family, and to get in the limo.

I was glad to be at Randy's side, because if I was a wreck, he was even more so. Maureen had an open casket, against Jewish tradition, because so many of Gerry's old clients were flying in to see him one last time. When we reached the funeral home, I put my arm around Randy's shoulders and we walked to the coffin.

I looked down at the man who'd given me back my heart. I was glad to see he still had his glasses on. There was no fake smile planted on his face. He looked like a sleeping Gerry. I began to cry, and Randy comforted me.

The graveside service was short and sweet, and somehow incomplete. After they lowered the casket, people began to leave, including Randy and me. When we got to the car, I realized what was missing. I grabbed Randy's hand and pulled him back to the open grave, took a handful of dirt, and threw it in. I motioned for him to do the same. Then we both lost it, and fell into each other's arms, sobbing our hearts out.

I returned to Nashville and thought about starting therapy again. I looked back on the past few years and realized an awful lot of bad things had happened to me in that period. Though I'd managed to push Cassie to the back of my mind, Tino was still very much alive in there. And I wanted to talk to someone about Gerry, someone who'd understand how deeply I mourned my loss. I also wanted to figure out why Kye was still unable to let go of the cop inside her, who judged her every time we made love, and found her wanting.

A lot of people I knew recommended one therapist in particular. I made an appointment with Leigh just before Kye was due to leave on a riding trip with Nancy Dawn. They were both horse fanatics, and I thought it would be good for Kye to spend some time with someone other than me. Frankly, I needed the break.

It was a short drive from Nancy Dawn's to Leigh's office. I walked into the waiting room one morning and sat there, nervously twitching my leg. When the door opened, I faced a friendly-looking woman, about twenty years older than myself, who gave me a welcoming smile.

She asked me to take a short test, and when I finished, she motioned me into her office, then went out to grade it. She came back, shaking her head. When I asked what the test had shown, she said, "I rarely see this . . . but you don't trust anybody, including yourself. Somehow, someone or some ones have totally destroyed any sense of safety or hope in you."

Shades of Gerry. Damn. We talked for an hour, and I decided to continue seeing her. As I was leaving, I turned and said, *You have no idea who I am, do you?*

No, she didn't. She'd never heard of me.

That's a relief, I said.

I saw Leigh again while Kye and Nancy Dawn were away. I talked about how supportive Kye was and the child we were going to raise. At some point, Leigh said, "It sounds like you've put all your eggs in one basket." I laughed and said, *I guess I have, but that's fine with me. I trust Kye absolutely; she'd never let me down!*

I was house-sitting for Nancy Dawn that week, enjoying being out in the country with nothing but empty fields and silence around me.

They were due back Saturday morning, but they never showed. By nightfall, I was really worried, and when Kye finally called, I let her have it. *I was just about ready to call the police! What do you mean, not even calling to tell me you'd be a full day late?*

Kye seemed surprised that I was upset. She said they'd run into a storm and taken shelter; there hadn't been a phone, they were out in the middle of nowhere. They'd be home in a few hours.

They didn't get back until late the next night. I was excited to see her, but Kye seemed disconnected, reluctant to spend any time with me. After a short conversation, she told me to go ahead to bed, she was getting in the hot tub. From the upstairs bedroom, I could hear the sound of her laughter as she and Nancy Dawn splashed each other with the warm water.

The next morning, Kye said, "Janis, I need some space." I didn't understand. "I need some space. We're together all the time. This trip made me realize that I need some time on my own." I asked if she was leaving me. Absolutely not, she said. She just needed space.

The next few months were a nightmare. I'd go to the studio, and Kye would be there, along with Nancy Dawn and Dell. She was polite, but distant. The three of them held long, whispered conversations while I tried to work. Nancy Dawn was perpetually late, and I'd have to wait for her while the clock ticked away. Kye fell asleep while I was doing vocals. The work slowed to a turtle's pace, straining my tiny budget.

I couldn't understand what was happening. Both women denied they were having an affair, but it certainly felt like one.

I asked Kye if she'd meet with me and a mutual friend experienced in mediation, and she agreed. During the meeting, she vehemently denied there was anyone else in her life. She just needed space. She explained to us both that she and I had been growing apart for years. She couldn't understand why I'd be so bothered by her taking some time off to find herself. It didn't matter if we spent six days or six months apart; she'd been intending to do that for a long time, anyway.

That was news to me. I looked at our friend in confusion and said, *This is really out of the blue. I didn't see it coming, not an inch of it!*

Our friend leaned toward Kye and said, "You keep saying you weren't planning a future with Janis—but you've been talking about a baby. What about the baby?"

Kye looked blank, then said, "Oh. That."

It was devastating. Leigh had been right; I'd put all my faith in Kye. With her gone, it felt like I had nothing left.

I'd wake up in the middle of the night, heart pounding, begging God to turn back the clock. I was sure that if I could just do it over, we'd still be together. We had some songs that needed finishing; Kye bailed, over and over again, saying she had to do this or that. Then I'd hear from a friend that they'd seen the two at the movies that day. I couldn't understand why they kept lying. If they weren't having a physical affair, they were certainly having an emotional one. If it was over, it was over—why put me through this pain?

Then I realized the why of it. Nancy Dawn wanted to keep producing my project. It was Barry all over again. I canceled the rest of the session time and fired everyone. Nancy Dawn started telling people I was having a breakdown!

Don Schlitz was my saving grace through that period. He defended me to everyone, telling them it was nonsense, that they should be proud to have me around. He'd come by to hug me, and fill me in on the local news. He and Thom Schuyler began urging me to move to Nashville permanently. "We can use people like you, Janis," they said.

I wouldn't even consider it. My home was in Los Angeles. I'd lived there since 1981, longer than I'd ever lived in any one place. After seven years in the same city, I didn't want to uproot myself. And maybe Kye would come back.

Or maybe not. Weeks turned into months. I was still being gaslighted, they were still denying the affair, Kye was still saying she just needed space, and I was getting sick of it all. Leigh urged me to begin making a life for myself, to accept the loss and move on, saying, "Remember the story of the straw that broke the camel's back? Even your back's not broad enough to take all this weight." That last straw was only a heartbeat away.

I'd put whatever cash I had into the Santa Monica condo when Kye bought it, making her promise to hold on to it at least five years. I wanted to make sure that when I gave up my cheap digs in L.A., I'd have somewhere to live for a while. It didn't mean that much to Kye, who owned several other properties, but it meant a lot to me. It meant stability.

Our mutual business manager, Al Hagaman, called me one December afternoon to say Kye was selling all her properties. He hadn't been consulted, and the tax consequences were going to be enormous. Could I try to make sure she didn't sell the condo, her main investment?

I laughed and told him I was sure she had no intention of selling it. Kye had told me that, just a week earlier. He could rest easy.

I hung up and sat down to work on a song. The phone rang again. It was our realtor in Los Angeles, saying she was ready to show the house and needed to know where the spare keys were. I called Al to let him know, and asked him to try to get an honest answer out of Kye. When he called back, he apologized and told me Kye was giving me two weeks to get my stuff out.

I can't possibly make that time frame! I argued. *I don't have any money to get back there, and she knows it!* Al said he'd arrange for Kye to buy my airline ticket. I told him it could be one-way; I'd find a new place to live in L.A.

I told Don I was going back to Los Angeles. "Why?" he asked.

Because my stuff's there, I answered.

He looked at me and laughed. "That's a stupid reason to live somewhere."

I realized he was right. I was staying in Los Angeles because that's where the memories were. I didn't need to be reminded of my life with

Kye or Tino every time I turned around. I called Al back and said, *Make that a round-trip. I'm moving here permanently.*

It was one of the best decisions of my life. I moved to Nashville a few years before it became trendy; people from New York and L.A. still considered it a hick town, filled with ignorant hillbillies. In fact, Ina suggested I lie and tell people I still had a place in Los Angeles, and was only living part-time in Nashville to do some cowriting.

I've never felt that way. Nashville gave me a home when the rest of the world had turned its back. People like Don and Chet Atkins welcomed me, inviting me into their world and becoming lifelong friends. To this day, I feel fortunate that circumstances led me to make that choice.

When Kye found out, she was absolutely furious. She said I had no right to live in her town, no right at all! *What, are you saying the town's not big enough for both of us, Kye?* Yes, she said, the town's not big enough for both of us. I actually started laughing, the line was so trite.

I flew to Los Angeles a few days later, got to the condo, and found my things had already been packed. I was livid. Kye and Nancy Dawn had gone through my clothing, my instruments, even my journals. They'd packed all of it themselves. I felt like I'd been raped.

And things were missing. The two songwriting notebooks I'd been using were gone. My baby blanket, the only tangible thing I had left from my childhood, wasn't there. Kye had wanted a cookie jar Bruce Mailman had given me, the only thing I had left of him. I'd said no; now it was gone, too. And my Grammy Award was nowhere to be seen.

Months later, I was sitting in Hagaman's waiting room when an associate walked in, carrying a large box. He dumped it on the couch next to me. There were my missing things. *Where'd you find all this?* I asked. "Oh, Kye packed it with her stuff by accident. She just now got around to opening the box."

It was a hard time, with a lot of hard lessons, both for myself and for Kye, I'm sure. She's still the best writer I've ever worked with, and so many years have passed now that whatever pain we caused each other is just dust on the wind. When I run into her now, it's like seeing an old and distant friend, someone you loved very much in your youth. That, in its own way, is a lovely counterbalance.

But good Lord, I sure couldn't see that then! I moved to Nashville with four pieces of furniture, my guitars, and the rest of my song notebooks. It was all I had in the world. I didn't even have winter clothes; I hadn't needed them for years. It was January, and my borrowed convertible had no working heat. I earned some cash playing in-the-round, then went to a used-clothing warehouse, where for forty dollars I bought a secondhand coat, boots, warm socks, heavy jeans, pajamas, and some sweaters and flannel shirts. I felt wealthy beyond words.

I proudly brought my loot home, laid it on the couch, then looked around the seedy room. I was living in a complex, surrounded by a parking lot. I'd been trying to put aside enough money for a rent deposit on something decent. I had $640 saved up; I counted it carefully, added the change from my shopping expedition, left it on the coffee table, then went to bed.

I always laid out pants and a shirt before going to sleep, a habit from my L.A. earthquake precautions. When I woke the next morning, I noticed a dollar bill sticking out of the back pants pocket. I couldn't understand—the dollar should have been added to my little pile of savings.

I went downstairs, got a cup of coffee, and noticed the back door was ajar. Impossible. It had a dead bolt; I always checked it at night. I spun around. My guitar was still on the couch, but the coffee table was empty. The money was gone.

I called the police, who dusted for fingerprints and found nothing. I kept asking how someone could have entered, and they insisted I'd left a door or window open. The detective helped me install locks on all the windows, cautioned me about making sure the door was closed at night, and left.

I went to see Leigh that afternoon. I was angry at the break-in, furious over the loss of my savings. Since I had no one else to get mad at, I took it out on her. *You've been trying to convince me to stop trying to see around corners, Leigh . . . you keep telling me to stop looking over my shoulder—but every time I relax, something bad happens!* I glared at her as though it were all her fault. *Why should I ever trust anyone again?!*

"You shouldn't," she said.

I stared at her. What the hell?

"I mean it," she told me, leaning forward to emphasize what she was saying. "I mean it, Janis. You shouldn't ever trust anyone so much that you give 'em a blank check. That's what you've been doing, with Tino, with Kye, with Cassie. Even with Sam. And I'm telling you, until you learn to trust yourself . . . you have got to believe you're safe *with yourself.* That's the main thing. Until then, you won't really trust anyone else, anyhow."

Leigh leaned back in her chair, and I leaned forward in mine. *Okay, I get it. Or at least, I think I get it . . . or maybe "getting it" is knowing that I don't really get it, but I'm willing to learn . . . or . . . oh, hell, Leigh. I have no idea what I'm talking about! Do you?!*

Leigh smiled. "Maybe you're finally growing up, Janis."

For the past few sessions, we'd been talking about Cassie, and my relationship with her (if you can call it that). Leigh had finally worked me around to the idea that what Cassie had done, she'd done *to* me. I wasn't responsible for the affair; Cassie was. Each time Leigh pointed that out, I'd protest, saying, "Leigh, I was in my thirties—an adult. Of course I was responsible." Leigh would sigh and start over, but I remained unconvinced. All my life I'd been told I was responsible for everything in my life (and sometimes in everyone else's life, too). It was hard to think I'd been played for a sucker.

My friend Laurie really turned the tide on that one. A counselor herself, she'd said, "Janis, as a therapist, my job is to help you break down your walls, then rebuild them. While you're rebuilding, you need to be in a safe place. Part of *my* job is to keep walls up around you, while yours are down. Cassie did just the opposite. Your walls were down, and she invaded."

Leigh had been trying, subtly, to convince me to file charges. It was hard; I really didn't want to deal with it. But Leigh was concerned that Cassie's amorality would impinge on current clients. How would I feel, knowing that what had happened to me had happened to someone else, and I might have been able to prevent it? Cassie had totally destroyed whatever ego I'd had left after Tino finished with me. She'd ruined my trust in the world, and in myself. Was I willing to let someone else go through the same thing?

But Leigh, I protested, *she told me I was the only client she'd ever slept with.*

Leigh regarded me patiently, then said, "How do you know, Janis? How do you know?"

I sat there, astonished at the thought. I really *didn't* know, did I? Cassie lied so much, she might have lied about that as well. Why not?

The next afternoon, I dialed the number for the California Board of Behavioral Sciences, but I hung up as soon as they came on the line. Conflicting feelings came rushing into my heart, and for a moment, I was paralyzed by them. Cassie loved me—she'd said so. *How could she love me and do what she did?* She might lose her license; how could I live with that? *And if she doesn't, how will I live with that?* I was special to her. I was the only one. *I wasn't special, I was just famous. A tool. A convenience.*

I picked up the phone again. The board therapist I spoke with told me 80 percent of all therapists who did this once did it again. But if I filed charges, I wouldn't be able to sue Cassie in civil court, or collect money for my subsequent therapy, which I deserved. The therapist suggested I call Cassie and try to get her to at least pay for a portion of my current therapy before I filed.

I thought it was a good idea. I hadn't been able to pay Leigh for months, but she insisted I come in. I kept careful track of what I owed her, fully intending to pay it all back one day, as I'd done with Gerry. It would only be fair if Cassie, who'd taken so much from me, gave a little bit back.

Leigh agreed, and that evening, heart in hand, I phoned Cassie's house. Manny answered, and we spent a few minutes chatting while Cassie made her way to the phone. I explained to her that I was in therapy, dealing with what had happened between us. I wanted her to fly in and meet with Leigh and me, try to resolve some of the issues that remained. I wanted some acknowledgment that she was sorry. I wanted her to pay for the therapy.

In my secret heart, I wanted to prove Leigh and the board therapist wrong. I wanted to hear that Cassie loved me, wanted to protect me, would help me in any way she could.

Cassie said she hadn't been feeling well. She didn't want to fly any-where. The question of money wasn't addressed. There was no apology. There was just more of Cassie telling me what she'd been doing and how she was feeling. The longer she talked, the clearer it became that she didn't give a hoot about me. She cared only about herself.

I hung up the phone and the next morning I called the board, saying I was ready to file charges. A district attorney came on the line and ex-plained that they wouldn't file unless they had an airtight case. Once they'd assembled the evidence, they'd confront Cassie. She'd be shown the charges, then offered two choices: she could resign for health rea-sons, in which event she'd have to shut down immediately, or she could refuse.

If she refused, the district attorney's office would explain the next step. The government of California would go to court, loudly and pub-licly, seeking any and all publicity for the case—and there'd be plenty, given that I was a public figure.

I started to get nervous. The whole thing embarrassed me. I thought it made me look like an idiot, getting taken in that way. I wasn't sure I could handle a public demonstration of my stupidity.

He said the way I felt was normal, but to look at it this way—if it came down to a trial, I'd have the weight of the state behind me. All of California's legal resources would be used on my behalf. If I really had a case, and the board therapist thought I did, justice would triumph. Cassie wouldn't be able to do this to anyone else.

I sent in the paperwork a few days later. The board determined there was more than enough evidence to proceed. Ultimately, Cassie was charged with thirteen violations on behalf of two ex-clients, and her license to practice in California was revoked. She denied the sexual charges to the end.

I SAW LEIGH that afternoon. I was feeling really good about myself, feeling like I'd cleared out a lot in the previous months. I'd been saving as much as possible, and felt flush enough to pay a hundred dollars on my account with her. I actually joked about being a survivor, saying, "I've managed to keep my sanity, while all around me were losing theirs!" I went back home in a self-congratulatory mood, worked on a new song, and went to bed early so I didn't have to waste any heat.

I woke the next morning and reached across the bed for my jeans. Out of the corner of my eye, I saw a dollar bill sticking out of the back pocket. *Oh, God, no, not again!* I threw my clothes on and ran downstairs barefoot. The back door was ajar, and my savings from the past months, carefully hidden in a drawer, were gone.

I called the police. The same detective came, accompanied by a young policeman. After reviewing what had happened the last time, and noting that there were still no signs of forced entry, the policeman asked delicately if I'd ever been in a mental institution.

Institution? *No, no, I'm not crazy!* I protested.

Well, it certainly was strange that this had happened again, he said, closing his notebook. Perhaps I should see a therapist?

I was so rattled that after they left, I called Leigh, asking if she thought I was nuts. Was it possible that after all this pressure, I'd just lost my mind? Could I have caved, and not even know it?

Leigh reassured me. I wasn't having a psychotic break, she said. Just a streak of bad luck.

It was about to get worse.

SEVENTEEN

Days Like These

It's years like these that make a young man old
Bend his back against the promises that life should hold
They can make him wise, they can drive him to his knees
Nothing comes for free, in days like these

After the second robbery, I went through my little apartment with a fine-tooth comb. Then, feeling like a complete paranoid, I decided to check the bedroom closet for a hidden door. I felt pretty foolish, taking a stepladder inside and pressing my hands on the ceiling to see if it gave way, but lo and behold, there it was. The seams were so tight, you couldn't even see them from the ground, but there was a trapdoor just big enough to poke a body through. I cautiously opened it and stuck my head up. Sure enough, there were fresh footprints. I thought of getting a bear trap and letting whoever'd been breaking in suffer, but settled for nailing it shut.

I got through the winter, somehow, though it was rough. On really cold nights, I'd sleep in my clothes for warmth. By spring, Mr. Granite had collected over a million dollars, but he still treated me like a criminal, much to my attorney Michael's dismay. Then one afternoon, Mike called to say Granite was going on vacation. In his absence, we could try going over his head to speak with a supervisor. While it was risky, it might be worth a shot.

Zimmerman spoke with Granite's superior, complaining bitterly that even though there was no evidence I was hiding funds—in fact, I'd done my best to assist them in uncovering assets Sam had set aside—I was still being treated like a criminal. No consideration was given to my other obligations, or the fact that any remaining debt had resulted directly from the sale of assets to satisfy the original liens. Granite was still unwilling to discuss abating any penalties, even though he had proof none of this was my doing. The clock was running full tilt on my new debt. I was living hand to mouth, unable to support myself because Granite grabbed every dime I earned, allowing me only the minimum the law required.

The IRS had proof that the powers-of-attorney had been tampered with. They had proof of Sam's forgeries, which had created the debt in the first place. Against my specific instructions, Sam had purchased seven questionable tax shelters by forging my signature. Other people who owed much more, and were less cooperative, were allowed to work out payment plans. Why was I being penalized this way?

The supervisor said he didn't understand why Granite was behaving like this, but he couldn't undercut an agent. He could, however, strike a deal; I'd be allowed to start a bank account, provided the balance never went over $1,500.

It doesn't seem like much of a concession, but I was thrilled. My credit was shot; Granite refused to notify the credit companies that my debt was going down, so all my report showed was that I still owed something like $1.3 million, plus the taxes on the sale of my properties. It looked like I hadn't paid anything at all. For over a year, I'd been living on cash, paying what bills I could with cashier's checks (which I hated mailing) or driving down to the utility buildings with cash (which cost gas). Now, I could have a bank account again. I felt like a person.

I'd put together a small band, and we'd done a few shows under the radar. I had all of $1,200 saved toward my current rent, and a new apartment. I proudly entered a local bank and opened an account, then went to the Bluebird Café and splurged on a burger and beer.

The club had a strict policy about comps, understandable in a town full of songwriters. No one got to sit at a table without paying admission. You could avoid buying a ticket by sitting at the bar and spending the two-drink minimum, but that was more than I could afford anymore. I'd avoided going to the Bluebird at all that past winter, but Melissa Etheridge was playing, and I really wanted to see her.

I'd run into Melissa at Almo, while I was still in L.A. When we were introduced, she'd literally dropped to her knees, saying she worshipped my work. I was embarrassed, thanked her quickly, then moved on. But my friend Craig Krampf had produced her first album and given me a copy. There was some great stuff on it, and I was curious about her live performance. So I waited in line with the rest of the audience, then made for a seat at the bar.

The Bluebird's owner, Amy Kurland, stopped me and gestured to a two-top, saying if I didn't mind sharing, I was welcome there. I hung my head and mumbled that I didn't have the cover charge. She walked me to the table, sat me down, and said, "Order one drink and we're square." Until I was on my financial feet again, that offer stood, and I'm forever grateful for it.

I fell asleep content that night, with Melissa's songs still ringing in my ears. The next morning, Al called. Bad news. Granite had returned from vacation and liened my new bank account, taking every cent. I had no money for rent, let alone a new place to live.

But I have a signed agreement with the IRS not to touch that account! I yelled. He knew, he knew. But there it was.

I have never been so depressed in my life. I hung up the phone and leaned against the wall, trying not to cry. I'd been a fool to think I could turn things around. I couldn't. I'd stay where I was, watching drunks careen through the parking lot all night long. I'd fall asleep to the sound of lovers arguing in their cars while the radio blared. I'd stay in this cheap furnished room, with the couch full of holes, and the carpet that would never look clean again, until the day I died.

I sank to the floor and sat there for a long time, staring at nothing. Everything was gone. I'd never own a piano again. And where was I going to get rent money? I'd have to sell my remaining instruments, if anyone would buy them. What a loser I was. My mother's health continued to deteriorate, and I couldn't even afford to visit her. My father was working three jobs; he had nothing to spare. My brother and his wife were raising three sons; their cupboard was bare.

Life was over. Why bother going on?

I pulled out a guitar and picked out a dirge. The strings were skanky, corroded from age and use, but there was no money for a new set. They felt gritty against my fingertips, and I wiped them down with my shirt-sleeve as I thought about everything I'd lost.

My home was gone. My life with Kye was over. I'd never again feel the comfort of my mother's arms around me. What did I have left?

Somehow, as I was adding up the list of things that were gone, the dirge turned into a simple melody. I kept thinking, *Days like these. It's days like these that make you want to pack it in.* Before I knew it, I had a first verse:

> *On days like these, when the rain won't fall*
> *and the sky is so dry that even birds can't call*
> *I can feel your tears disappearing in the air*
> *Carried on the breeze, in days like these*

My life had become a desert. The landscape was so bone-dry that tears evaporated before they had a chance to hit my cheeks. There was no point in crying anymore. Easier to give up.

Still, there was always a choice. That's what Gerry used to say, that I always had a choice. I was only thirty-seven. My circumstances sucked, but maybe I was still young enough to rise above them. Somehow. At the least, I could try to figure out a way. I'd never be able to do that, if I gave up now.

You can't reap what you don't sow
and you can't plant in hollow ground
So let us fill this empty earth with hope,
until the rains come down

By the time I hit the third verse, I'd remembered something they hadn't taken from me. Something they could never take from me. My talent.

In lives like these, where every moment counts
I add up all the things that I can live without
When the one thing left is the blessing of my dreams,
I can make my peace with days like these

In later years, people would ask how I got through that period of my life. I'd shrug and say, "What else could I do?" In truth, that song was the turning point. When I finished it, I knew that until the day I died, my dreams, and my talent, would always be with me. No one could take them away. It was up to me to make the most of them, in whatever time remained.

I picked myself up and went back to work, studying other writers as much as possible. The Bluebird is where I got my education, completing my plan of years before. With Amy's blessing, I went there as often as possible, sometimes five and six nights a week. After writing all day, I'd hit the early show so I could study up-and-coming songwriters like Beth Nielsen Chapman and Gary Burr. I'd stay for the late show, so I could study the A-team writers. Even when I skipped dinner to save the cost, I went home feeling like my belly was full.

One night, I went to the Bluebird and watched a young man from the hill country, Lance Cowan, sing a song about the Holocaust. I was chagrined. Here I was, a Jew, and though I'd always wanted to write about the death camps, I'd been scared I didn't have the chops for such a huge subject. Now some kid with no personal investment had gone and written a good song about them. It made me feel small. It made me feel like a coward.

I grabbed my napkin and jotted down two lines:

Her new name was tattooed to her wrist
It was longer than the old one

For the next two weeks, it was "Some People's Lives" all over again. I worked on it in the car. I worked on it during other writing appointments. I worked on it late at night, when I could barely keep my eyes open. I tried half a dozen different choruses before finally deciding the song didn't want a chorus. I got stuck on the ending and sat there, stymied, for a month. I finally took a friend, Rabbi Beth Davidson, to lunch to discuss it. The song needed some resolution. Did she have any ideas?

Rabbi Davidson shook her head. "Janis, there isn't any resolution for a concentration camp survivor. . . . It doesn't go away. It gets better, but it never goes away."

That gave me the key I needed, for an ending that never really ended:

Surgeons took the scar,
but they could not take it far
It was written on her heart
Written on her empty heart
Tattooed

When I was finally finished, I took my new song to the Bluebird and played it for a bunch of other songwriters. Their mouths dropped open. No one had ever heard anything like it. With lines like,

> *Gold from a grandmother's tooth*
> *Mountains of jewelry and toys*
> *piled in the corners, mailed across the borders*
> *Presents for the girls and boys*

It was at once an indictment of the Nazis, and a heartfelt account of one woman's destruction at their hands:

> *Centuries live in her eyes*
> *Destiny laughs, over jack-booted thighs*
> *"Work makes us free," says the sign*
> *Nothing leaves here alive*

One of the writers said, "That's the most powerful thing I've ever heard." Another told me, "You make me ashamed to be human." And another said, "Janis, no one's ever going to sing that but you. You need to start thinking about making another record."

A record? What a laugh.

Years later, "Tattoo" was chosen by the Dutch government to represent their country during the Europe-wide festivities that marked the fiftieth anniversary of the end of World War II, and Queen Beatrix herself thanked me for it. But I didn't know that would happen back then, and the chance of my having another recording career was lower than my getting struck by lightning.

Michael kept hammering away at the IRS, saying I was no good to them dead of starvation. They finally allowed me to tour for a month and keep the proceeds. It cheered me immensely. I played Los Angeles, and took a night off to see Ella Fitzgerald performing with Joe Pass at a small club in Santa Monica. It was a real thrill to see them working as a duo, only yards away from my seat.

I went backstage after, praying Ella would remember me from the Grammys years before, and she didn't let me down. She broke into a huge grin and threw her arms around me, hugging me and then holding me at arm's length, taking me in. She shook her finger in my face, scolding me with mock severity. "Girl, where's my record? What's taking you so long? I need some new music from you!" I couldn't believe it, that Ella Fitzgerald was waiting for my next record. It gave me hope.

I talked to Chet Atkins about making a new record, asking what he thought about the state of the music industry. Chet had been great to me from the time I'd moved to town; I found out years later that he actually called a number of people he thought might have problems with my being gay, and told them, "She's mine. Don't mess with her, 'cause she's mine. She belongs here. Leave it be." He'd introduced me to Waylon Jennings, played my songs for Mark Knopfler, and in general made me more than welcome. I knew he thought I should record again, and I knew he'd give me a straight answer.

"Chet, what are my chances?" I asked. "Seriously."

Chet shook his head. "Shoot, Janis . . . Waylon can't get a record deal. Waylon! Willie can't get a deal. Willie Nelson, one of the great writers of our time!" Chet grimaced, waving at the gold records lining his office walls. "Heck, I don't even know if I could get a deal right now. . . ." He looked at me sadly, then patted my hand, and said seriously, "But you've got to try, Janis. You've got to try. The songs are too good to waste."

Allan Pepper, owner of the Bottom Line, asked if I'd come to New York to do an in-the-round at the club. Since there'd be four of us splitting the take, there wouldn't be much in the way of earnings, but he wanted me on the bill. When I sheepishly told him that I didn't have the money for airfare, let alone hotels, Allan offered to pay my expenses

out of his own pocket. As humiliating as I found it to accept, I grabbed
at the chance, because it meant I could see my mother and meet with
Ina. I wanted to talk to her about selling my songs.

I'd begun to feel slightly schizophrenic when I'd have to deal with
people from what I'd begun to consider my "past life experience." People
in Nashville knew me as a pretty regular person, who'd moved there to
better herself as a writer. They understood that I was broke, and it was
okay. Nobody expected me to keep up with the Joneses—why should I?
From their point of view, what I was doing right now didn't matter
nearly as much as what I'd already done. I'd written "Jesse." I'd written
"At Seventeen." To the Nashville songwriting community, I'd always be
a great writer, even if I never had another hit.

In New York and L.A., everyone assumed I wanted to make a come-
back, was in search of a major label deal and a big hit record. They
couldn't understand how trivial that seemed, when I was worried about
whether I could afford to buy winter socks. They still thought of me as
famous, and assumed I wanted to become more famous.

Let me tell you how I felt about fame at that point in my life. Fame
was something you wanted before you grew up and out of it. Fame was
something people worked all their lives to attain, then whined about
ever after. From the bottom of an empty bank account, fame looked like
a pretty silly goal, believe you me.

I'd allowed myself to drift into obscurity, and I never regretted it.
Not once. Not for an hour, a minute, a second. Not when I couldn't pay
my electric bill. Not when I couldn't fly up to see my mother. I never regretted it, because when I had it in spades, it was killing me.

Imagine what it's like at the height of success. Not the cool parts,
not the parts I've already talked about. The underbelly, the part no one
outside of the business thinks about. The part that starts to eat you
alive, rips you away from the daily life that made you a writer in the first
place.

Imagine living like this. You can't drive yourself, because of the liability—twice, people in other vehicles recognized you and deliberately tried to cause an accident so they could collect a settlement from your insurance company. You take limousines instead, and only with drivers you know, because you worry about being kidnapped and held for ransom (and you never quite trust that your record company would pay it . . .). You keep the windows up all the time, grateful that they're dark; you learned that lesson the hard way, when you left them down and two people immediately tried to jump in the back to get close to you.

You've finally got enough money to take your family to nice restaurants, but they won't go out with you anymore because it always becomes a mob scene. You can't go shopping without attracting a crowd; they grab at you and your clothes until security comes and hauls you away in tears. And you keep thinking to yourself, *This is what I wanted. This is what I worked for.* But eventually, you realize that it really *is* an either/or scenario. You can be really, really famous—and spend the rest of your life trying to stay on top, never having a life of your own. Or you can stop, and wait for things to return to normal.

I stopped, and I've never regretted it.

Don't mistake me—I'm not whining. I loved the ride. After all, when would somebody like me, coming from my background, get a chance to travel the world? To go places most tourists are never allowed? To dine with queens and princes, to ride in a limousine when it wasn't graduation day or a marriage? It's a fantastic, unbelievably exhilarating ride.

But like all rides, you have to get off eventually.

Living in Nashville, spending my time as a writer rather than a performer, I began finding it hard to believe I was ever that famous. That I'd set records in Japan that have yet to be broken. That I'd broken records in Europe, in Australia. That I had toured America with a crew of fourteen, two semis, and two buses of my own. Time dimmed those memories, and daily life at the bottom of the financial pool made them too painful to reconsider.

I flew up to New York early morning and went straight to my mom's apartment, spent a few hours with her, then met Ina at her office. She'd offered to take me to lunch, and we wound up at a very expensive sushi restaurant in Midtown Manhattan. Toward the end of the meal, I began trying to explain what my life was like now. I wanted her to understand that it bore no resemblance to the life I'd lived before. I tried to make her see that I might never have another record deal, might never be "famous" again, and that I didn't really care. All I cared about was getting out from under, and the only way I could see to get my head above water again was to sell my songs, my publishing catalog, to the highest bidder.

"You don't have to sell anything. It'll be fine," she said, motioning for the bill.

I sighed. *Ina, my life is schizophrenic enough without you refusing to see reality. . . . Please, just listen to me. I'm thinking that with the yen so strong against the dollar, maybe we should talk to a couple of Japanese companies. They've always done right by me in the past, and I've still got some friends over there who might—*

Ina cut me off with a curt glare. "You'll sell your publishing over my dead body!" she announced as the check arrived.

I stared at the $200 bill, then at her. She didn't get it. She owned her apartment. She made a good living, and got to keep what she earned. She didn't see that I was budgeted down to my last nickel, dreading the forty-dollar electric bill waiting for me at home. She didn't understand what the last few years had been like. How could she? I was the one living them.

What's the point of owning my publishing if I can't sell it when I'm in dire need, Ina? What's the point?

"You're not in dire need. We'll get the IRS thing straightened out, you'll start recording again, everything will be fine." She slipped the credit card back into her purse.

I almost wept with frustration. *Ina, can't you understand? I don't have a credit card anymore. Heck, I don't even have a purse, because I have noth-ing to carry in one! I can't go on living like this, scared all the time, feeling like a criminal. I need to take care of my mom. I need to take care of myself. If selling my publishing does that, what's wrong with it?*

I never did succeed in making her understand, and I felt like a char-ity case at the Bottom Line that night, as Allan insisted on buying me dinner and giving me cab fare to the airport. It was a discouraged song-writer who arrived back in Nashville, and things didn't get any better when I checked my mail. There was a tribute to Stella Adler in two weeks, and I still hadn't answered Irene's invitation to sing at it. I wanted to, more than anything in the world, but I couldn't see how I could af-ford to get out to L.A. for it.

The next morning, Bruce Mailman called. He was putting on a big AIDS benefit that weekend. Donna Summer was supposed to perform, but she'd canceled at the last minute. Was there any way I could leave for Fire Island that afternoon, spend a night at his house there, and do a show the following night? He'd pay my expenses, feed me, and throw in a round-trip ticket from Nashville to anywhere in the country.

"Of course," I assured him. This was perfect; I'd be able to help Bruce out, *and* make Stella's tribute! My luck finally felt like it was changing.

I went to Fire Island and spent a lovely evening with Bruce and some friends. Having been in landlocked Nashville for so long, it was a real treat to sit on the dunes and watch the Atlantic Ocean roar by. There were no cars on the island; the only sounds were surf and wind. Bruce cooked dinner, we had a couple of drinks, and I went to bed, waking early the next morning to the sound of waves against the beach.

I did the benefit, caught the first morning ferry, and flew to L.A. Dora picked me up at the airport and took me back to her house, chat-ting and laughing all the way. I felt strangely subdued; I'd intended to do some business that afternoon, but by the time I arrived, it felt like I had the flu. I got into bed around dinnertime and slept straight through until noon the next day, then woke with chills and a fever.

I called my local doctor and went in to see him. He confirmed my suspicions; it was the flu. I couldn't afford to be sick; the tribute was Saturday, just days away. He told me to rest as much as possible, drink lots of fluids, and check back if I didn't improve.

Resting was no problem; I couldn't stay awake. I'd lie down for a nap and get up three or four hours later, disoriented and fatigued. I couldn't seem to remember the simplest directions; even though I'd lived in L.A. for years, I kept getting lost. Dora finally ended up driving me to the tribute. I got through Stella's show, somehow, and arranged to spend part of the next day with her.

For an eighty-eight-year-old, she was in rare form. She hugged me, and I thanked her for her many letters, saying they'd kept me going on many a dark night. "Oh, Janis, I'm just an old broad from Odessa!" she laughed, patting my arm. I asked her if she wasn't tired, after the gala tribute. She laughed again, saying, "Janis, at my age I don't get tired anymore. I just get nervous."

Seeing Stella cheered me, and I flew back home in a good frame of mind. I'd finally been able to save enough money to rent half a small house, and I now looked out onto green trees and a little lawn. My home was Zen-like in its simplicity. I'd managed to buy a coffee table and a bed on time. I had the four pieces I'd brought from L.A.—a desk, an oak library file that held my cassettes and guitar equipment, a night table, and a couch.

The house was so empty that when people came to visit, they'd say, "Where's your stuff?" But I had everything I needed. I slept on the bed, ate and wrote on the coffee table, and worked at the desk. I even had a piano again. Brian Williams, a local banker, had just opened the first "Music Row" division in town, and I'd gone to him, asking for a loan. He gave it to me on my word that I'd pay it back, an act of kindness I've never forgotten.

I loved my little place. My apartment in the parking lot had been rented on a month-to-month basis, and I lived ready to be kicked out at any moment. Now I had a year's lease, and it wasn't embarrassing to bring other songwriters there. I can't begin to tell you what a relief it was.

Once I hit Nashville, the flu returned. I couldn't wake up, no matter how long I slept. The glands in my neck swelled until it was painful to swallow or turn my head. I ran fevers that made no sense; they'd spike up to 103 degrees, then drop down to 96 an hour later. It was late summer, and my neighbors were out gardening in shorts and T-shirts, while I was wearing every piece of clothing I owned and still shivering.

I began losing my hair; I'd sit up in the morning and turn around to find small chunks of it lying on the pillow where my head had just been. I was dreaming, too, strange Technicolor dreams that made no sense, and left me dragged out and dog-tired when I woke. I tried to sit at my desk, but it took everything I had just to stay upright. My neck muscles didn't want to work; my head kept dropping to my chest. It would have been scary, but I was too tired to be frightened.

I slept through my next appointment with Leigh, who called, concerned. Her next visit to Nashville, she stopped by my house, and was shocked at how pale and listless I'd become. I complained that I couldn't even find the strength to sit up anymore. *My doctor in L.A. said it's the flu, Leigh, but it's been going on since Fire Island. That's weeks now!* Leigh leaned forward intently and asked if I'd been dreaming much.

Yeah. Funny that you mention it. They're weird dreams. And they're so bright! It's like in The Wizard of Oz, *when they go from black and white to color. Except I'm going from color to ultracolor.* I leaned back on the couch and groaned. Leigh wrote something on a slip of paper and handed it to me, saying it was her physician's number. I should call him, go in, get checked out.

I went to see Dr. Murray Smith, who listened to my complaints, took blood, and gave me a complete physical. A week later, I received a letter with his diagnosis. He believed I had something called chronic fatigue syndrome, or CFS. I'd have to take a bunch of tests to rule out any other possibilities, but all signs pointed to this. The Centers for Disease Control had thirteen criteria for determining if someone had it; I fit twelve. He'd like me to come in three times a week for a while, so he could draw blood and compare the results.

I was outraged. I told him he was dead wrong, it was just the flu. I couldn't have anything chronic—I couldn't afford to treat it. He said that was no problem, since there were no medications available. Well, I couldn't afford to see him that often. Again no problem; since they'd be studying me, there'd be no charge.

Yay.

I went downhill rapidly as the disease took hold. Murray theorized that my body was trying everything possible to fight it off; when one thing didn't work, it moved on to the next. My glands swelled to golf-ball size, then went back down to nothing. My white count doubled; two days later, my red count did the same, while the white returned to normal. I had the highest yeast count on record, then the lowest. I slept eighteen hours a day, and still woke exhausted.

Murray suggested that since traditional medicine had no treatment, I try alternative medicine. I started working with a chiropractor who also dealt in homeopathy and nutrition. I cut out nicotine, caffeine, and sugar, just in case they were making it worse. Nothing seemed to help.

The disease began affecting my ability to think. I tried to go shopping at a local supermarket, and wound up sitting on the curb, weeping into my folded arms. I couldn't remember if I'd walked there, or driven myself. I couldn't even remember how to get home.

I was having trouble remembering names, too. I'd look at someone, knowing I knew them, but the name wouldn't come to the surface. It was humiliating when I'd run into a person I'd known for years, and wasn't able to greet them by name. That problem is with me to this day.

I became aphasic. Language had always delighted me; now it became the enemy. Words I knew, and had always used, couldn't seem to make the journey from my brain to my tongue. I felt like I was speaking a foreign language, but without enough vocabulary. I might want a burger, but I'd be reduced to saying, "That animal that eats grass and we raise it for food, it has four stomachs," because I couldn't find the word "beef."

And I got stupid. I felt like Charly in *Flowers for Algernon,* going from brilliant to well below normal. I couldn't do the *Times* crossword puzzle anymore. I couldn't even make sense of the *TV Guide* crossword. I had trouble following the plot of *Happy Days.* It was dreadful.

It was also humbling. I hadn't realized how arrogant I was about my intelligence. I'd always taken it for granted, and in my heart of hearts, I'd thought that if stupid people just tried a little harder, they could be smart, too. Maybe not supersmart, but smarter than they were. Now, with my brain on half-track, I realized how condescending I'd been.

Murray poked and prodded, the chiropractor tested homeopathic remedies, and I underwent every exam known to man. I developed dark circles under my eyes, looking like I hadn't slept in months. I avoided everyone, because people kept exclaiming over how bad I looked. When I'd tried explaining the CFS to the third person, and heard yet again, "Is it really a disease? I mean, there's no test for it, right? Are you sure you don't just need a good therapist?" I gave up.

In October, I received a notice from the IRS's criminal division, saying they were investigating Bruce Mailman and wanted to interview me. I called Bruce to find out what was going on. Two agents, Frank Primerana and Holly Cusick, had been hounding him for several years, accusing him of everything from money laundering and tax evasion to dealing drugs. Bruce was convinced it was because he was gay.

The agents insisted on meeting me at Al Hagaman's office that October ninth. I was outraged; it was Yom Kippur, the highest holy day on the Jewish calendar. They refused to change the date, warning me they'd issue a federal subpoena if I didn't comply.

The meeting was surreal. They were obviously playing "good cop, bad cop," doing it so badly that it made me giggle at first. Cusick was the bad cop; she opened the meeting by saying she knew about my "relationship" with Bruce, and I was in big trouble. Primerana was the good cop; he laid a hand on her arm as if to calm her down, then told me I wouldn't be in any trouble if I just told the truth.

They asked when I'd seen Bruce doing cocaine. Not *if,* but *when.* I said I'd never seen him do drugs. Cusick insisted I had, saying Bruce was a known drug runner, that he and Billy Nachman had built a multimillion-dollar business out of it. I laughed. The idea was so ridiculous, it beggared belief, and I told them so.

They were adamant. They knew I'd stayed at Bruce's home on Fire Island—how many times? *Once,* I replied. *I was there once, to do an AIDS benefit.*

They shot knowing looks at each other. "And how many kilos of cocaine were stored there?"

It was the third or fourth time they'd asked that. *None,* I shot back. *None. I keep telling you, I never saw Bruce with any drugs.*

They wanted to know how Bruce got the drugs into the country. They thought maybe he had a rowboat.

I snickered. *Let me get this straight. You're telling me Billy Nachman, who is about the size of a string bean, and Bruce, who's not much bigger, get into a dory at night, row out into the Atlantic past the three-mile limit, load it up with bales of cocaine, row back, drag it on shore, then transport it over the dunes to Bruce's house? Get real!*

By now, the interview had gone on for more than an hour. I was doing my best to stay focused, but I was starting to have trouble tracking the questions. I was tired, and said so. Too bad, they answered. They wanted proof that Bruce and Billy were coke dealers, and I was going to give it to them. Otherwise . . .

Otherwise what?! I asked. Primerana leaned toward me and smiled. "You know, we're aware of your . . . other problems with the IRS, Janis."

I glowered at him.

He smiled again. "We have some pull there. . . . We could make your life a lot easier. A lot easier."

Cusick bent forward and grinned nastily, then said, "Or, we could make it a lot harder. A whole lot harder."

That was it. I jumped up from my chair and faced them both, shrugging off Al's restraining hand. I didn't care anymore, and I told them so. *First, let me raise a formal objection. You've forced me to come in here on my highest holy day, a day I normally spend at synagogue. You've spent the morning trying to put words in my mouth, and no matter how many times I correct you, you insist on putting them there. You've done everything but ask me to lie outright. And now, you have the unmitigated gall to threaten me?*

I continued, letting off the steam that had been building up since they'd called Al. *This is bullshit. This is all bullshit.*

I stalked to the door, turned around, and said, *You dare to threaten me with the IRS? You fools . . . what do you think you'll take? You think there's anything left?!*

And with that, I stormed out the door. The last thing I heard was Al saying, "Sorry. She's had a rough week."

Years later, the truth finally came out, but not until it had ruined Bruce financially and emotionally. After being indicted for everything and anything Primerana could come up with, Bruce filed charges against the Assistant District Attorney helping Primerana and Cusick. He charged that prosecutor James McGuire had told him point-blank that he'd been "indicted because he was gay and the government was interested in penetrating the gay community." McGuire was eventually suspended on other charges.

In 1992, Primerana was indicted and charged with obstruction of justice, making false statements, and fabricating a memorandum of a confession by Billy to gain IRS and Department of Justice approval to prosecute him on tax charges.

Although Primerana was eventually acquitted, the Justice Department's own review found that "evidence was apparently falsified." After that, all charges against my friends were dropped. Fat lot of good it did them. By then, Bruce and Billy were both dead of AIDS. What a travesty.

THE CFS CONTINUED to rule my days. I canceled my writing appointments; I kept sleeping through the alarm clock. I tried to stay hopeful, but it was getting hard. No one knew of a treatment. No one knew how long it would last, or if it would ever go away.

I went to the bookstore to see if there was anything in print, and got fantastically lucky. Not days before, a book had come in by Jesse Stoff and Charles Pellegrino. In 1989, it was the only thing in print about my illness, and I took it home and devoured it.

I met with Murray to discuss what I'd learned. Stoff recommended something called ART, or Active Relaxation Therapy. Murray agreed that in the absence of anything else, it sounded like a good idea.

I'd need help. Murray met with some of my friends one night, and explained what he knew of the disease. I was obviously in poor physical shape, but I was also neurologically affected. I couldn't be expected to remember why I'd entered a room, let alone their names. We were going to try something radical, and take all responsibility away from me for a while. Hopefully, that would give my body a chance to concentrate on healing. We couldn't be sure it would work, but it was worth a try. Would they help?

They would. At Barbara Short and Dorothy Gager's suggestion, they formed something called a "telephone tree." Each friend took on some of life's daily chores—shopping, garbage, driving me to the doctor's. When one was done with their task, they'd phone the next in line, who'd begin theirs. I'd go on ART, and literally do nothing for two months.

I took to my bed, or rather, my couch. People came and went at all hours; if I was sleeping, they let me be. When I woke, someone was there with food, or had the shower running. They'd help me into it, then wait and help me get dressed again. My arms felt like lead weights, and I couldn't remember how buttons worked.

I kept getting worse, and I was too tired to care anymore. Headaches, earaches, sore throats—everything hit at once. The glands all over my body swelled, until it was painful to move. I was grateful the house was so bare, because any kind of sensory input was overwhelming. My short-term memory was nonexistent. Friends would remind me to call my mother, then sit there patiently to make sure I didn't put the phone down before the call ended.

I shook with chills much of the time, and took hot lemon baths every night to try to get warm. I'd intended to do some reading, but I couldn't concentrate long enough to get through more than a sentence, so I just lay there in a daze.

I saw Leigh regularly, trying to deal with the idea of being chronically ill. No one knew if CFS could be cured, or even sent into remission. I might never write again. I might never play again. Leigh concentrated on giving me hope.

She asked what good could come of this. How was having CFS helpful to me?

That was easy. It slowed me down. I'd always been a workaholic; if I wasn't working, I was thinking about working. I worked on vacation, if I bothered taking one. I worked during meals. I was always juggling four or five projects at once.

Now, I learned not to work. I started learning to relax, instead. It was a revelation. Even though it was winter, I was beginning to stop and smell the roses.

I was also learning to accept acts of kindness. There was a small article in the paper about my being ill; for weeks, strangers left food on my doorstep. Orson Scott Card, a writer I greatly admired, e-mailed to ask why I hadn't been in touch. I told him I was sick, and needed to be on the couch rather than at my desk. Two days later, a laptop arrived, with Scott's return address on the package.

I'd never been able to ask for help before. Even with Gerry, I hadn't really asked. Now, I was learning what it felt like to receive, openly, with no ability to give back. It made me feel powerless at first, but I came to realize there was just as much power in taking as in giving. I submitted to the ministrations of my friends, followed my holistic regime, and slowly began to get better.

One evening, I got out of a bath and realized the house was warm. It was the first time in months that I'd accurately read the temperature around me. I was delighted. A few mornings later, I woke up feeling hungry, and put away half a plate of food. Best of all, about a week after that, I slept dreamlessly.

Now that I was feeling a little better, Murray said I needed to start building up my system. "Your grandparents were right—I want you to take twenty minutes of sun a day. If it's too cold to sit outside, then sit by the window, but make sure you get it. That'll do more good than anything I can prescribe." So I sat by the living room window every day, staring at the dry November leaves. And I continued to improve.

I'd been ill for ten weeks, though it felt like ten years. Now, still confined to the house, I was starting to get restless. I didn't have the energy to do much, but I did what I could in short bursts, careful to stop before I got tired. I learned to watch for the slight stinging behind my eyes that signaled the CFS's return. When that happened, I dropped whatever I was doing and lay down. As the days wore on, I began to long for new faces.

I complained to Leigh that I'd seen the same fourteen people for months. And while I loved and honored my friends for taking care of me, I really wanted someone to play chess with. Now that my brain was functioning better, I was hungry for some intellectual exercise. Murray couldn't promise the neurological problems would go away. I needed to do what I could to help myself. I thought chess might help me regain some of my ability to think.

Leigh said she had a friend who might do, and gave me the number. I called the next day and left a phone message: *Hi, this is Janis Ian. I hope it's okay that Leigh gave me your number. I've been pretty sick, but I'm getting better, and I'm looking for a chess partner. Here's my number.*

A few days later, Leigh asked if I'd called. Yes, but no one had called back. Leigh humphed and said she'd call to find out what was going on. When I got home, there was a breathless phone message. "Hi! I thought my friends were playing a joke on me, saying it was Janis Ian, but Leigh just called and told me it was really you. So I'm calling back. I'd love to play chess, but I have to go now, my dryer's on fire."

Hmm, I thought. *Hmm.* I called back and politely asked if she'd managed to put the fire out. Yes, she had. Did I want to get together for lunch sometime?

Lunch. What a concept. Eating outside my house. I hadn't done that in months. Yes, absolutely. I was sure Murray would okay my driving two miles during daylight hours, especially if I promised to rest the entire day before. We arranged to meet the following Thursday, and Pat walked into my heart.

EIGHTEEN

Through the Years

It's a miracle of nature
just to be alive tonight,
awake in your arms
The world and its charms
lit up by candlelight

I've always been an idiot about come-ons. Pat says she doesn't worry about me cheating on her when I'm touring; I have to be hit over the head with a baseball bat to realize someone's interested. She's always maintained she knew we were going to spend the rest of our lives together in that first five minutes. I just thought we were having lunch, even though we talked right through to dinnertime.

She brought me a book, *Flattened Fauna*. She'd read somewhere that I'd been married five times, and she figured I'd be a snotty diva. The book was a test; if I laughed, I was probably all right. I laughed.

Ten days later, she invited me and two friends to dinner. I still wasn't allowed to drive at night, so they picked me up en route. I entered the small house and looked around appreciatively; there was a roaring fire, and a beautiful Doberman lay stretched out on the couch. A delicious smell was coming from the kitchen, and there were books everywhere.

I didn't realize the dog was artfully arranged to cover a large hole she'd eaten in the sofa that morning, or that Pat hated being in the kitchen. She says years of cooking for her daughter used up all her patience, and she stays out of there whenever possible. In fact, that may have been the last full meal she ever made me.

Dinner was wonderful. She'd made paella, and we chuckled and chattered through the meal. It was the first time I'd been with a group in months, and I reveled in it. Pat was funny—I laughed longer than I'd laughed in years. She was bright, and competent. At one point, she excused herself and went outside, returning with her car battery in hand. She explained that she had to bring it in whenever the temperature went below freezing.

I'd never met a woman who could remove a battery before. I was impressed.

I admired a sparse line drawing hanging on the wall. The strokes were minimalist, but it caught the mood of the face it portrayed, at once serious and whimsical. Pat took it down and handed it to me, saying, "It's a self-portrait I did when I was thirteen; I want you to have it."

I called her when I got home, saying, *If Nashville had a coffee shop open this late, I'd invite you for a cup to show my thanks.* I heard her say, "I'll be right over," and a few minutes later she arrived with coffeemaker in one hand, coffee in the other. She even brought mugs.

That night, we sat on opposite ends of my couch and talked for hours. Over the next two weeks, life settled into a nice pattern. I'd rest and sleep all day, while Pat went to work. Then she'd come over and spend the evening with me, talking about everything under the sun.

She was fascinating; she'd gotten a full art scholarship to the University of Rome at thirteen, forging the paperwork to add five years to her age. She bought a one-way ticket to Europe at eighteen, arriving in Dr. Scholl's sandals during a blizzard. She bummed around for a few years, working as a chambermaid in Switzerland and living on a kibbutz in Israel, before finally coming back to Nashville to raise her child.

She was a single parent by choice, one of the first I'd met. Now she worked at Vanderbilt University, so she and her child could have health insurance. Her boss had some real problems with gay people, which made things awkward sometimes, but the school was also paying to put her daughter through college. The benefits outweighed the negatives.

We sat on the couch and passed a little teddy bear I had back and forth between us, holding it for comfort as we confessed our secrets. It had been a long time since I'd made a new friend, and I cherished the way our relationship was growing. But really, in all other aspects, I was dim as a used lightbulb. Even after we went for cheap Chinese food, and my fortune cookie said, "You will have a gay old time," I didn't get it.

One night, Pat invited me out to dinner. As we ate, she said something about being on a date. I looked at her in confusion. *It's not a date. You didn't bring a bouquet.* She jumped up from the table and hurried into the parking lot, searching for anything resembling a flower. She returned with a dried leaf, placed it carefully before me, then looked into my eyes.

I felt my heart surge. *Oh. This must be why I've been so giddy lately— I'm in love.* How unexpected. How impossible.

I looked at Pat and carefully explained that I couldn't be in love. Not now. I was still sick. I had no way to earn a living. The IRS hung over my head, and I couldn't be sure of my body from one hour to the next. Besides, I liked living alone.

Done explaining, I looked at her again. How pretty she was! Her red hair flamed in the dim restaurant light. She had ocean eyes, the gray of early morning waves. Damn, this was inconvenient.

She agreed; it was very ill timed. But there it was.

We began living together, though Pat kept her place for six more months, just in case. She supported us financially as I slowly got better. Murray okayed an exercise program that consisted of my walking up the driveway to the mailbox, then back. The first two weeks, I had to lean on Pat for support, resting when I made it halfway. I conquered the mailbox, and moved on to the stop sign at the end of our block. A few weeks later, when I made the hundred-foot round-trip without needing to rest, we splurged, and toasted my victory with a bottle of Perrier.

We were squeezed tighter than a lemon. Pat was already working three jobs: eight hours a day at Vanderbilt, a part-time job as a book-keeper somewhere else, and running the register at a local taco joint on weekends. What little extra she managed to set by went to pay off the credit card debt she'd accumulated as a single parent. Now she was feeding both of us. It drove me crazy to be dependent on someone else that way, but she refused to let me take on any guilt.

Life eased up six months later, when Michael finally managed to get my tax issues reassigned to another agent. Ever helpful, Granite refused to turn them over without a written order from his boss, but eventually, he had to give me up.

Once Agent Keller took over, things began to improve. He agreed that I'd done my best to satisfy the debt, and allowed me to begin re-ceiving a portion of my publishing royalties. It was perfect timing. I was starting to get cuts by other artists again, and Kathy Mattea had just re-corded "Every Love." Although I wouldn't see the money for another year, it would come in eventually. I could promise my attorneys they'd be paid someday.

I'd asked Al to find a buyer for my catalog, and Toshiba EMI Japan agreed to purchase most of the songs I'd written from 1972 to 1981. That gave them ownership of "At Seventeen" and "Love Is Blind," but I held on to "Society's Child," "Stars," and "Jesse." To me, those were the other seminal songs in my life as a writer. I hated to part with nine years' worth of songs, but I was immensely grateful that I had them to sell in the first place.

The negotiations dragged on for several months, and I got nervous. I asked Al if Toshiba would be willing to deposit a third of their offer to show good faith. He doubted it, but I said *If they're serious, they will.*

The money went into an escrow account, and I was allowed to draw on the interest.

When the first month was up, Pat and I headed to an ATM machine and withdrew five dollars apiece. We stared at the balance. Six figures. We each took out another five, dizzy at the thought of twenty unexpected dollars in our pockets. I decided we ought to buy something to celebrate, so we went to a local mall and each bought a pair of socks that didn't come ten to a bag. It had been years since either of us had bought something so frivolous.

To this day, that's the richest I've ever felt. Grammy Awards, platinum records, sold-out shows—they all pale next to those socks.

I'D GIVEN "Days Like These" to every producer and artist I could think of, hoping someone would record it, but no one was interested. Friends like Chet kept encouraging me; he took me to dinner with Mark Knopfler, who said I had to try for a record deal, because "Tattoo" needed to be heard, and I was the one to sing it. But at forty-one, with three careers behind me, I was a has-been again. By pop music standards, I was ancient.

It's a pervasive attitude. Folk and jazz both make room for their elders. They want us as mentors, and examples. Pop has no such sense of history. When I tried to get on Lilith Fair a few years later, one of my former agents, who was in charge of booking it, said decisively, "She's too old, and not hip enough." I was still in my early forties.

Then one day, out of the blue, John Mellencamp called. He'd heard "Days," and wanted to use it in his new film. He asked why I wasn't recording.

No one's interested, I told him.

John snorted. "They're stupid. Come on up—let's see what we can do."

His faith, at a time when no one else in pop music cared, really nourished me. He was incredibly generous. We recorded the song with his band, and he paid for the sessions as well as a video. Then he flew in my own band and cut four sides, again at his expense, so I'd have something to pitch.

John was a real contradiction; a fabulous songwriter who became inarticulate face-to-face. A misogynist who saw past my femaleness to the artist he admired. It's fortunate I'd had good experiences with rednecks, because John was redneck personified. At one point, I played a diminished seventh chord, straight out of the jazz book. John smiled, put a hand on my knee, and said, "No offense, Janis, but those fag chords don't play here in Bloomington." I took no offense; he was right, the chord didn't fit. And despite his use of the word "fag," he treated Pat and our relationship with nothing but respect.

My catalog finally sold, and I paid off the IRS. It took every cent, but I was out from under. Now that royalties were coming in again, I started thinking about buying a house. I wanted something large enough for me to have a home office and a dedicated writing room. Something with thick walls, so I could work when Pat was home, which meant it had to be an older house. Fortunately, no one in Nashville but me wanted to buy an old home back then, and we lucked into a 1901, 4,200-square-foot house that sat on a full acre, right in town. It hadn't been touched in decades, and we got it for the stellar price of $187,500.

Oh, it was fantastic having my own place again! I'd discovered it driving around with my realtor, Berni Nash, who'd said, "What are you really looking for? We've seen fifteen houses, and you didn't like any of them." Glancing down the street, I pointed to the corner and said, *If I still had the money I once had, I'd buy that.* Berni grinned; she knew the house had been on the market for two years with no success. She called the owner, who asked us to come right over. I walked through the door and took a right into the smallest room. *This is a great writing space,* I thought. *Feels like there's always been music in here.*

The night before we took possession, one of the house's former occupants, Anne Goodpasture, called to ask if she could walk through with us. I learned from her that my new writing room had actually been her family's music parlor decades before. She and her sisters held recitals there, playing for their parents and friends. I'd always believed that walls talked; now, they sang.

Sony Benelux approached me that summer, asking if I'd be interested in releasing a Greatest Hits package there, and touring behind it in the fall. We put together the album, and I left for Holland in late September. I wasn't sure about the trip—would anyone remember me, after ten years away? The promoter wasn't sure, either, and offered a very low guarantee. *All right,* I negotiated, *but I want a percentage of the shows.* I couldn't imagine the shows selling out, but we might do a bit better than he thought, and I'd make a little extra money. It was worth the risk.

I did nineteen shows, every single one standing room only. Dublin and London were the same. I was amazed at the reception I got, and came home with more money in my pocket than I'd earned in decades. It was encouraging enough that I began thinking about trying for another record deal.

Unfortunately, the record industry didn't see it that way. No one cared about my overseas success; what had I done in the United States lately? It was a vicious circle; if I didn't have a record out at home, I couldn't tour. If I didn't tour, I couldn't interest a record company. I couldn't figure out how to break the cycle, and I spent hours talking to Pat, trying to find a work-around. Finally, Pat asked how much a record would cost. "I could do a great one for fifty grand," I told her.

"Then let's take out a second mortgage, and finance your record," she said.

We argued about it for a month. I had no wish to jeopardize our home by creating an unsustainable mortgage. On the other hand, without a new record release, I could kiss my career good-bye. There wouldn't be many more chances. I'd already been told by every record company here that I was too old for them to invest in. Who else would do it?

So that April, I went into the studio with Jim Brock, Chad Watson, and Jeff Balding as engineer and coproducer. Jeff was well-known, and well-liked. He managed to talk studio after studio into renting us space for absurdly small amounts of money. Because of the low budget, we recorded when we could, and we didn't finish *Breaking Silence* until August. By then I'd hired a manager, Simon Renshaw, whose enthusiasm was contagious. That December, he proudly announced that Morgan Creek wanted the album. They wouldn't give me an advance, or reimburse the budget, but they'd release it in March of 1993, if I'd tour behind it all year.

My excitement was dampened by Stella's death on December 21. The next day, I received a Chanukah card from her, cheerfully detailing how well she was doing. To this moment, not a day goes by that I don't think of her. With Stella gone, the beacon I used to illuminate the waters went out.

Now that I had a release date, Pat and I began discussing my "coming out." I hadn't given it much thought; it was no secret that Pat and I were a couple, and I saw no reason to emphasize it. Then Urvashi Vaid, at the time head of the National Gay Liberation Task Force, called and asked me to lunch. She urged me to come out as loudly and publicly as possible, coordinated with my record release. She thought the publicity might even help my record.

I wasn't so sure. I wanted the focus to be on the songs, not my sexuality, and I said so. Urvashi began quoting statistics. I was dismayed when she told me that three out of ten teen suicides were because the teenager was worried about being gay. She spoke of Stella as my role model, then reminded me that these youths had no contemporary gay role models. She asked whether I thought it was important, at a time when so many people still said, "I've never met one," to let the public know that the singer of "At Seventeen" was gay.

She convinced me. When *Breaking Silence* came out, I took every opportunity to talk about my relationship with Pat, stressing our monogamy, our commitment, all the things bigots said didn't exist in the gay community.

I decided not to stress it in my shows. While I'd casually mention Pat, or tell a funny story about us, I didn't want anyone in my audience feeling excluded—not because they were gay, and certainly not because they were straight. I didn't appreciate it when people suddenly assumed that "Jesse" was about a woman, and I refused to allow that sort of speculation to get in the way of the songs.

I did press and toured for nine months. It was hard on Pat; until then, if I left, it was only for a few weeks. Now I was in Europe for three months. Money was still tight enough that we couldn't afford to talk on the phone for more than a few minutes a week. I wrote to her every day, but it wasn't the same as being together.

We survived, and I came home encouraged at the success I'd had there, but I was discouraged at the resistance my new work met at home. *Breaking Silence* had sold 35,000 copies there, a hard number to take after selling gold and platinum. Morgan Creek was disappointed, too, and we quietly parted ways. Then the 1993 Grammy nominations were announced, and *Silence* was nominated!

It made my ninth nomination, if I cheated a bit and included a record I'd done for *Sesame Street*. I was ecstatic, and Pat and I flew up to New York that March with high hopes. She clutched my arm as the envelope was opened, and I whispered to her, *Whatever you do, don't cry. No matter who wins, clap like mad and smile, please....* Much as Pat had pinned her hopes on a win, I knew it was a long shot.

I was right. Nanci Griffith took the award, for her album *Other Voices, Other Rooms.* Pat's eyes filled with tears, but I was strangely undisturbed. I liked Nanci's work, and knew she liked mine; in fact, one of my songs was on her album. She'd never won a Grammy before. Her father cried as he watched her take the stage. I felt good about it.

Some part of me accepted that I was moving into a new phase in my life. I had a choice to make: I could stay on the merry-go-round and keep reaching for the brass ring, dislocating my shoulder as it got further and further away. I could try to look younger, prettier, hipper, and see if another major label deal was in the offing.

Or I could accept what Stella used to say: "There are two things you can't play. You can't play sexy, and you can't play young. You either are, or you aren't." I wasn't sexy, and I wasn't young. Maybe that was okay.

The record business hadn't changed much in the decades I'd been a part of it. The major labels still poured millions into young artists, signing them to seven-album deals that virtually guaranteed they'd be there for decades. Anyone with half an eye could see it wasn't working, and something new was definitely in the air. Digital technology was changing everything; people were making albums on a shoestring, often in home studios, and they sounded every bit as good as the more expensive ones funded by the majors.

I'd never have a huge career again, but I could earn a living. That was a lot better than things had been a scant few years before. Maybe it was time to accept that, and do some other things.

Judy Wieder, an editor at *The Advocate*, had been after me for a year to do a monthly column. *I don't write prose*, I explained, and ignored her advances. The next time Pat and I were in L.A., Judy insisted we have lunch together. I made a fundamental error and went to the bathroom; when I returned, she and Pat had struck a deal. Judy explained that I'd be *The Advocate*'s "resident iconoclast"; she felt the gay-oriented magazine was far too serious, and too self-congratulatory. My job would be to poke holes in that.

After some initial terror, I enjoyed myself. It paid well, guaranteeing me a steady income. I had enormous fun with titles like "Lesbian Chic: A Contradiction in Terms," and "Me & My Mammogram," which opened with "I am standing with my tit caught in a wringer, while a mall-haired technician tells me to relax. I am thinking that if men had to put their testicles in a vise as part of a yearly physical, we would have a cure for the common cold by now." I enjoyed being funny, and the experience of having to turn in exactly 1,000 words a month taught me more about deadlines and editing than I'd ever wanted to know.

That same month, Lydia Hutchinson asked if I'd write a monthly column for her new magazine, *Performing Songwriter*. She was starting it on a limited budget, but she was convinced there'd be an audience. She believed my name on the masthead would give the magazine credibility. I agreed, provided I had carte blanche to write whatever I liked. I stayed with her for eight years, covering everything from staying healthy on the road to the death of the old record company paradigm.

I was paying off my attorneys and accountants, though some months I could send them only ten dollars apiece. I hated feeling indebted, and my manager, Simon, knew it, so when he got a call from River North Publishing in Chicago, asking if we'd visit their offices, he jumped at the chance.

It was obvious they wanted to impress; they sent a limo and flew us first-class. We took a tour of their facilities, which included an $11 million state-of-the-art recording studio. I was practically drooling. I couldn't believe my publishing was worth that much to anyone, but I kept my mouth shut.

Over lunch, they made us an offer. I'd have free use of the studio; they'd pick up the cost of musicians and engineers as well. Half a million dollars, not as an advance, but as a signing bonus. A three-year deal, six figures in my pocket every twelve months. All I'd have to do was help their other songwriters learn to be polished professionals. They were a talented group, but they needed a mentor, someone who could tell them when the chorus needed work, or suggest a title change. I'd be able to cowrite with them as much as I liked, and River North would guarantee that everything I wrote would be recorded and released.

Simon and I looked at each other. It sounded too good to be true. There had to be a catch. I thought for a while, then asked, *Doesn't your company specialize in contemporary Christian music?* Yes, they did. *Aren't you worried about having a gay Jewish girl writing songs for you?* No, that was no problem at all.

Simon was grinning. He'd opened his management company with money from a small group of investors; they were starting to pressure him, wanting to know when they'd see a return. This could be the beginning. Between the advances and his share of royalties, the deal could be worth millions to them.

Would you want me to use an alias? I asked. That might actually be fun, and someday, after having dozens of Christian radio hits, I could blow everyone's mind by announcing it.

There was a long silence, then the River North rep said, "Uh . . . that's actually a small problem. You see, we don't want anyone to know our writers need help."

What, you mean I won't get credit, even under an alias? That wasn't good.

No, he told me. No credit at all. We'll work out some way for you to get your royalties, but your name can't appear anywhere. Not even as an alias.

I sat there thinking it over. Half a million dollars. *Phew.* I could pay off the mortgages, and there'd be tons left to put in the bank. I'd enjoy being a song-fixer, and free studio time was icing on the cake.

I was just about to say yes when Simon's fist banged down on the table. We all jumped as he yelled, "No! Absolutely not! Out of the question."

I stared at him in surprise. While I adored Simon, he was nothing if not greedy. Just a few months before, he'd been approached by a William Morris agent who wanted to sign me to write my autobiography. Simon spent days trying to talk me into it, even though I didn't have time and wasn't interested. He and the agent even suggested I use a ghostwriter. When I demurred, the agent argued, "You'd better do it now—lesbians won't be hot forever!"

Simon was more than frustrated when I continued to refuse the offer. Now we finally had a shot at something I could work with, and he was backpedaling. Was he about to do us both out of a huge opportunity? I could barely believe it.

Renshaw turned to the River North people, shaking his finger at them. "Janis's reputation has always been based on integrity. From 'Society's Child' to 'At Seventeen,' she's never wavered. She turned down 'You Light Up My Life,' knowing it would be huge, because she didn't think she could sing it honestly. And now, you have the unmitigated gall to ask her to live a lie?"

Simon rose from the table and offered me his hand. I couldn't move; I was in shock. He pulled at me. "Come on, Janis, we're leaving. Right now." I followed him to the waiting limo, and we drove back to the airport. Without a deal. I was still flabbergasted.

Simon, I can't believe you did that. . . . I just can't believe it. You turned down half a million dollars! You need the money almost as badly as I do. Are you crazy?

He sighed, patted my leg, and said, "Don't worry, darling. Something else will come up."

It surely did. We parted ways amicably a few years later, when his group the Dixie Chicks hit the charts. Today, he's one of the biggest managers in the world, with a roster any record company would envy.

And just think—we both could have crossed over into the contemporary Christian market instead. . . .

NINETEEN

I Hear You Sing Again

In my heart, I hear you sing again
Every note as natural as then
When I sing those songs to family and friends,
in my heart, I hear your voice again

M y mother had been dying by inches for so long that sometimes it felt like the world was comprised of marks on a
yardstick.

Here was the mark where she first felt a tingling and a numbness in
her legs, and here is the diagnosis ten years later. Here is a mark for the
day she refused to hold her first grandchild, lest she drop him. And here
is the mark of our last full conversation together, before she lost the
ability to speak.

I marked her last steps. I marked her final descent into a wheelchair.
And I marked the point where I finally stopped demanding she be herself, and began instead to love the stranger she'd become.

Everyone told me I resembled my father—eyes, nose, and hair—but
as I watched my mother being bathed one day, I realized that regardless
of any cosmetics I'd inherited from him, my naked body was entirely
hers. Flesh of my flesh, bone of my bone, the very shape of my hips

belonged to her genes. Later that day, I napped on her bed, taking comfort in the familiar scent permeating the sheets. The scent of my childhood, safe against her breast.

My mother had been dying for so long that it became easy to forget how much I missed her, how I longed for the comfort of her arms around me. When life is reduced to inches, small things become large.

Here is the mark of the government man's yearly arrival, to verify she hadn't been miraculously cured, wasn't cheating Medicaid and just too lazy to work. Here is the day her weight dropped below seventy pounds, and they wouldn't pay for Ensure because she could still swallow oatmeal.

One visit, my mother told me in a whisper that her aide was drunk all the time. I discounted it. A few weeks later, the aide passed out on the couch, then assaulted the police who came to remove her. Here is the mark of Cain on my forehead, for assuming my mother's handicap had also affected her mind.

And here is the day I realized the disease had, finally, reached her brain. She called to demand that $5,000 in small bills be sent immediately, because the bed was leaking green phosphorescence and had to be replaced. She told me they were rounding up all the handicapped people to put them in camps. She needed blankets, and canned goods, to take with her.

Here is a mark for the moment she herself realized what was happening, telling me, "I know it's just backfire, but I think it's gunshots, and they're coming for me. I get so frightened, Jan. I get so frightened."

I make a mark by each of her prescriptions: Valium, Prozac, everything we tried to keep the door between what-is and what-is-feared shut tight.

My dreams about her became the stuff of nightmares. I envisioned her assaulted as she lay helpless on the bed, strangers playing with her private parts while she, fearing worse punishments to come, dares not tell me.

Here is a mark for the time a former friend said, "I know I should visit, but it upsets me so much to see her like this." Here are my memories of him, sitting at my mother's dinner table every week, eating her food, asking her advice.

I mark the year we didn't speak, too angry at each other to even attempt détente, and I mark the moment when we both decided there was more to us than mismatched opinions.

These are the marks of the things I gave her—backstage late-night jazz clubs, money to go back to school, season tickets for the opera. Sometimes they're overshadowed by the marks of my own regrets—why didn't I take her with me to Japan, why didn't I haul her wheelchair around Macy's one last time, why could I walk when she could not?

I cling to the good I did, and agonize over the rest.

There are good marks on my yardstick, marks that make the world a taller place. Jeff Evans and Jan Sugarman, two fans we'd known since the early 1970s, visited my mom faithfully every week for years. My Uncle Bernie, her older brother, came down from Boston each month, bringing a potato knish and making her smile.

I visited when I could, playing the clown, trying to provoke her laughter. We watched television in silence; I'd learned to make no demands. My mother, who ran funding drives for universities and obtained a master's degree at fifty, was content to live in a state of Zen-like simplicity, where all answers were reduced to *yes* or *no*, and *maybe* was two letters too long for comfort.

Watching the marks on a yardstick build up, you become thankful for what you have. Lula McMillan and Willie Mae Duncan tended my mother for the last decade of her life. They cared for her around the clock, forcing her out of bed when she cried to be left alone, insisting she tell them the day and month to orient herself. They compelled her to interact with a world that had turned its back, massaging arms that barely felt, legs that spasmed and flailed in some rude dance when the drugs weren't enough.

A year before she died, my mother contracted pneumonia. She'd named me her medical executor, trusting me, literally, with her life. I was in Europe when my brother called to ask if he should take her to the hospital. *Yes*, I said, *I don't think she wants to go yet.*

When I got home, we met at her bedside. I looked down at my mother's sleeping form, so much smaller than she'd been, and felt a wave of tenderness sweep over me. Her breathing was labored, but the worst of the pneumonia was over. I began to weep, and Eric squeezed my arm as I drew in a deep breath and told him how lucky we were.

She can speak a little, Eric. She can see. She can hear. . . . I'm so afraid of doing the wrong thing, Eric, I'm so afraid she's suffering.

I turned to my brother in anguish, tears rolling down my cheeks. *Do you think I should smother her, Eric? She trusted me to make sure she wouldn't suffer. Do you think I should smother her? I don't know what to do.*

THE HOSPICE WORKER who'd taught my mother to catheterize herself decades before called on a Thursday night. She'd returned to New York after three years in Africa, and decided to drop in and say hello to my mom. She was blunt. "Pearl's dying. Get up here."

I caught the next flight, meeting up with my brother at Mom's apartment. In a strange confluence of circumstances, both Lula and Willie Mae were off that weekend, and a temporary aide sat in the living room. I was relieved; they were both very close to Mom, and I didn't want them to have to endure this.

I began the bleak business of calling family members, asking if they wanted to see her once more before she died. My uncle called, to ask if we wanted him to fly down. No, we assured him, we're fine.

The hospice worker visited again on her way out of town, and I sat with her and asked if my mother was in pain.

"She's not in pain, Janis. She knows she's dying; they always do. It's the family around them who don't want to hear it."

What can I do to help? I asked. *I don't want her to die early, but I'm sworn not to let her linger.*

"Turn the oxygen up all the way. Give her a good last day. That's all you can do."

There was a bit more we could do, and we did. My mother adored the opera; Eric and I detested it. We brought a VCR into the bedroom that afternoon, and ran tapes of *Aida* for her. As the opera reached its crescendo, my brother and I put our hands over our ears. *You're doing this on purpose!* I accused. *You're doing it to get back at me for that time you forced me to go to the Met, and I fell asleep until Don Giovanni caught fire!* Mom laughed; she remembered it well. I had indeed fallen asleep, waking when the stage lit up as the protagonist was sucked into the fires of hell. At intermission, my mother had announced to the entire lobby that I was a changeling, switched at birth with her "real" child, who would have adored the opera.

I turned up the oxygen that night, and she rallied. The next morning, Mom sat up in bed for the first time in years. She asked for something sweet, and I spooned ice cream into her mouth as my brother poured a shot of Bailey's to chase it. She drank, hiccupped, then giggled.

We had a good day. A very good day. I told her that if I didn't send her to the hospital, she would probably die. She nodded, and managed to say she was glad her children were with her. There was a lot of laughter, a lot of remembering. Eventually, we all fell asleep, me curled up at her feet, Eric nodding from his makeshift bed in the wheelchair.

Sometime just before dawn, I came awake with a start. I stared into the darkness, trying to make out my mother's form against the sheets. She was still breathing—long, slow breaths that struggled from her chest. I reached out and put a hand on her leg, before I remembered that she couldn't feel it.

Something entered the room behind me; I felt my shoulders tighten and instinctively ducked toward my mother's body to protect her. Then I relaxed; it didn't feel threatening. The room seemed to grow blacker, and I felt a dark shadow move over me, hesitate, then move on. When it lingered over my mother, then disappeared, I knew.

I shook my brother's arm. *Wake up, Eric. Wake up. She's gone.*

My brother and I stood by the bedside, looking down at her. I said I needed to call the undertaker, but Eric worried it was too soon. "Jan, are you sure she's dead?"

Yes, I said, *quite sure.*

"But how can you tell?" he asked. "We ought to make sure!"

The tension of the past few days hit me, and I started to laugh. *What do you want me to do, hold a mirror under her mouth like they do in the movies?*

There ought to be a road map for death. There ought to be a field guide for people like us, standing by the bedside, not knowing what to do next. In my grandmother's small village, everyone would have felt my mother's passing. The women of the community would have come to comfort us, helped me to prepare her body. Death is very personal, very profound. In America, death is lonely, and it shouldn't be.

I stroked Mom's cheek; it was already growing cold. *It's time to call, Eric. We have to let her go.* I shivered, and complained, *It's cold in here. Where's the extra blanket?*

My brother put an arm around me and quietly said "Jan, she doesn't feel it."

I want to cover her anyway, Eric. I don't want her getting cold.

When the man from the funeral home came to collect the body, he treated my mother tenderly, lifting her onto the stretcher and gently pulling the sheet over her face. I was suddenly afraid for her. *Please make sure she stays covered!* I begged. *She had a lot of pride. Please make sure she stays covered. . . .* Tears stained my eyes as I begged the man for mercy. In this moment of heartbreak, I was completely dependent upon the kindness of a stranger.

He promised he would treat her with respect, and then she was gone.

. . .

I MAKE TWO last marks in the yardstick. One is when my father dies, three years later, and I find myself an orphan. The other is when I begin to dream of my mother at night.

In the dream, she is walking toward me, through a field of green filled with chaotic wildflowers that embrace and enfold her as she moves. She is rushing to greet me, arms outstretched, legs whole and strong. She feels every motion of the wind against her skin, and as I fall into her arms, I am home, and safe again, at last.

I love that dream.

FOR MONTHS after my mother died, I'd burst into unexpected tears during conversations. I looked at strangers in the grocery store, wondering if they still had a mother. Old bills were forwarded to me, and I'd have to write "Deceased" across the envelope and send them back. I'd run across something of hers in the house and clutch it tight against my chest, flooded with memories.

The item I was proudest of was my mother's master's degree. For that last decade of her life, it hung on the wall next to a picture of Eric and me. Confined to a wheelchair, she could see both her lineage, and her achievement, from anywhere in the room. Sending her to Goddard was the best thing I'd ever done.

With my tenth-grade education, it seemed to be part of my destiny to put other people through college. A few years before, I'd figured out that if I stayed on the road as much as possible, Pat could go back to school and fulfill her dream of becoming an attorney. She'd slogged through the three years at UT Knoxville and graduated with a degree in jurisprudence; now she had her own law firm. I admired her greatly for that, as I admired my mother.

I'd like to do something to honor my mom, I told Pat. *Going back to school at her age, fighting the MS all those years? She was absolutely re-markable!*

"Why don't you endow a scholarship in her name?" Pat suggested.

I laughed. *With what money?*

She paused and considered the problem. "Well . . . you could hold an auction, couldn't you? For that matter, you could do it on the Internet. I bet your fans would love to buy memorabilia, and you could use the money for a scholarship."

I thought about it. This was early 1998; most of the world didn't even know how to use a computer, let alone own one. My website had been up since 1995, but I was one of the few artists I knew who had one. I wasn't aware of any Internet auction sites. When I checked around, there was only one tiny site called auctionweb.com, which dealt in antiques and used computers.

I asked a computer-savvy friend, Michael Camp, for help, and out-lined a plan. I'd go through my house, digging out anything that might be valuable to a fan, then write a brief description of the item. Since I'd be touring on and off all year, I could promote the auction at my shows. There was no money in it for any of us, but there was good karma—if we managed to raise $15,000, that would endow a full scholarship at my mother's alma mater. I doubted we'd reach that, but we could try.

Michael jumped in with enthusiasm, and as I began cataloging, the list grew. And grew. By the time I was done, there were more than three hundred offerings, from old master tapes to personal photos of me with Billy Joel and Bruce Springsteen. First drafts of songs, often written on the back pages of science-fiction paperbacks I'd read on the road. Jewelry I'd worn on album covers, annotated studio charts, and a "living room concert," where I promised to spend an evening with a fan and their friends, singing and telling stories. I even auctioned off the glasses Nina Simone and James Baldwin had used during brunch at my mother's.

I toured the United States from February through September, pro-moting my latest CD, *Hunger*, and pushing the auction at every show.

Enthusiasm among the fans was so high that we revised our plans completely, deciding to begin September 15, 1998, and end a full two months later. Since there was no online infrastructure for credit card payments yet, let alone cash, we'd have to trust the buyers would send checks that wouldn't bounce. I put together photos and descriptions of each item, and Michael wrote hundreds of pages of code to accommodate the landscape of my life as an artist.

In early September, as we finished up on the West Coast, I began getting stomachaches. At first, I put it down to too much spicy food; I loved Thai cooking, and usually ordered "Thai hot." I tried switching to blander foods, but the pain kept getting worse. It was waking me three and four times a night, no matter how many antacids I took.

I had some recording sessions starting on September 11, with a producer named Jim Cregan. I really wanted to work with him, so rather than seeing a doctor right away, I just took more Tylenol and put up with the cramped feeling around my abdomen. Our project, "The Last Great Place," was going to be the featured single for Japan's Expo Day, a huge festival to educate people about ecology. We had to meet the deadline.

But by the second session, I couldn't ignore the pain any longer, so I called the doctor Murray had recommended when he'd retired, and made an appointment for the next week. I had no doubt that this was something simple, to be cured with a quick dose of modern medicine.

We finished the single, and I flew home on the first day of the auction. It opened at noon, and bids started pouring in. Fans were chatting away on the message board, pointing out items to one another, promising that if one won a certain lyric, they'd gladly photocopy it for another in return for a small donation to the college fund. From the first, it felt like a community was forming online—one of the earliest, I'm proud to say.

I saw Sally, my new doctor, that same afternoon. She quickly checked me for ulcers; the test was negative. Sally sat back and said, "Well, Janis, ordinarily I'd say give it a few weeks, but since you're the queen of rare diseases, I'm recommending further testing." She got me an appointment the next morning, and I went in and drank a quart of noxious, heavy liquid in preparation for the test. The minute I got it down, the stomachache disappeared. I called Sally excitedly to tell her I was cured. She told me to finish out the tests, anyway.

By September 22, the date of my next doctor's appointment, Michael and I were beginning to realize we had something special on our hands. We were treating the auction as interactively as possible, posting daily updates for the fans. I kept track of what was going for too little, and what I thought was overpriced, letting them know my own feelings. Since there were so many items, we featured something every day, adding a little more background material each time.

It was pre-eBay (which is what auctionweb.com eventually became), and we had no way to notify people when they were outbid. So we kept the bidding open, allowing everyone to see, item by item, when a higher bid came in. Longtime fan Anna McCabe bid a stunning five thousand dollars for the living room concert, asking if it would be possible since she lived in Ireland. I quickly replied yes, then added a "U.S. Living Room Concert" so the fans at home could have a shot.

With Anna's contribution, we were sure to hit $7,500, the minimum contribution Goddard required at the time. I started to relax, and entered Sally's office in a cheerful frame of mind. She looked up from my chart with a sympathetic smile.

What's up, Sally? Don't tell me it's anything serious! I couldn't imagine it, not when things were going so well.

"Janis, it's one of five things, and three of them are what we call 'bad actors,'" Sally said. She looked at me and frowned. "I'm sorry."

Now, when your car mechanic says, "I'm sorry," you brace yourself for a big credit card charge. When your doctor says it, you shrink back in your seat and prepare for the worst.

Sally said I'd lucked out with the radiologist; he'd spotted a small mass many people would have overlooked. She showed me the test results. I couldn't make head or tails of them.

I wasn't liking this; it was scary. *Sally, give me the worst case, then the best.*

"Your pancreas looks swollen, so pancreatic cancer is a possibility. The other two bad choices aren't much better. But there's also the possibility it's a benign tumor. There's a possibility, Janis."

I sat frozen, trying to digest the news. I'd lost a favorite relative to pancreatic cancer a few years before; she'd lived only a short while after the diagnosis. I tried to take a deep breath, but I couldn't seem to get any air.

Can I use your phone to call Pat? I asked. Yes, of course.

I dialed the number. Pat picked up.

Honey, I'm at Sally's. My test results . . . the tests . . . I began crying then, huge, hiccuping gulps of tears. I couldn't talk through them.

"I'll be right there," Pat said. "Just wait. Don't go anywhere. I'm coming."

After I hung up, I turned to Sally and said, "If . . . if I have something like that, can you still be my doctor? I mean, I know I'll need a specialist, but can you?" Sally hugged me and said of course. I started crying again, and she handed me to her assistant, Terrie, who rocked me in her arms and kept reassuring me that it would be all right.

Pat arrived, and Sally repeated what she'd told me, then arranged for us to consult an oncologist the next day. The specialist would review my results and examine me further, possibly recommend more tests. Pat listened in shock.

I barely took any of it in. I was too busy trying to figure out what to do next. Was my will in order? Would Pat be protected? What about the auction? What about my next record? Jim Cregan had already set three months aside, as had his engineer. Musicians were booked, the release date was scheduled. Show dates were on hold. This couldn't be happening.

Pat and I drove home in our separate cars, each of us praying. I don't know what hers was, but I was busy arguing with God. *This is not fair to Pat. You absolutely cannot do this to her. Pat's spent her entire life struggling, and now, just when it's getting easy, you're going to take it away? It's not fair; you can't do it to her!*

We got home and sat on the screened-in porch I'd built as a surprise for her fiftieth birthday. We looked at each other, but there was nothing to say. We'd have to wait two weeks, until the rest of the tests were done. After that, I'd get a second opinion from Harry Sendzischew, who'd operated on me back in 1986. Until then, there was nothing to do but wait.

The trees were beginning to lose their leaves; fall was in the air. I found myself hungering for the sight of greenery. That entire afternoon, I sat there on the porch, thinking over and over again, *I just want to live to see another spring. I just want to see another spring.*

Weeks passed in limbo. I went through test after test. The results were encouraging; it looked like a benign tumor, but we wouldn't know until they operated. At the end of the two long weeks, we were able to rule out pancreatic cancer.

I called Harry, who reviewed the scans and results. He called back at his most reassuring. "Janis, it wasn't there in 1986, but it's there now. The good news is, it might have been there in 1987. It might be slow growing. And from what I can see, if you had to have a tumor on your liver, it's in the perfect place."

Oh, great. I now had a tumor in the perfect place. Maybe I could get a matched set for Christmas.

"You definitely need surgery," he continued. "I can do it here, in Florida."

Can it wait until December, Harry? I explained about the auction.

Yes, it could wait. He'd reviewed the films with two fellow physicians and two radiologists; all five were in agreement. I sighed with relief and went back to the auction.

We had all we could do to keep up with it. I'd promised every item would come with a Certificate of Authenticity, signed by me, and I spent two days printing them out and putting my signature at the bottom, then attaching them to various items.

I had some tour dates to fulfill, and I didn't dare cancel. The last thing I wanted was to make promoters nervous. Bad enough I'd had intestinal surgery and canceled dates back in 1986; to do it again would leave them thinking I was high risk, and they wouldn't be anxious to book me again. I decided to keep my problem a secret from everyone, as much as possible. The only people who shared it were Pat, Michael, my business manager, the road manager, and my attorney. I swore them all to silence, saying, *It's too easy for rumors to get started. I don't want people thinking I'm dying.*

I had another reason for avoiding publicity, unless it could be on my own terms. The auction was drawing to a dramatic close. My friend Ginger Warder had managed to get a small article into *USA Today*. We were inundated with bids and questions, crashing the server several times. I didn't want people to think I was using an illness to up the price of everything. And I didn't want to scare my fans.

I was scared enough for all of us. I'd tried to make light of it, telling Pat, *You know how I hate the cold. This is a perfect excuse to spend part of the winter in Florida!* But I was terrified. We couldn't be sure I'd live through another surgery. We couldn't even be sure the tumor was benign until it had been removed.

Harry booked my surgery for December 2, 1998, two days before our anniversary. Nine years before, we'd promised each other we would spend our lives together. For Pat, it was the most important day of the year, beating birthdays and Christmas. When she found out, she started crying.

I put my arms around her and smiled. *You always say that no matter how much I tour, you'll be fine with it if we can just spend that one day together. Well, we'll be spending it together this year.* She sniffled, then asked if I thought we could get anything for my tumor by adding it to the auction items.

On November 15, Michael Camp and I sat anxiously in front of a computer screen in his small office. The auction was closing, and fans were going ballistic. Bids were rolling in, thirty and forty a minute. It was incredible. We shut it down at noon, and Michael began adding up the winning bids, while I called the highest bidders myself to tell them they'd won.

"Janis, when you're done, come over here," Michael said, pointing to the screen. I put the phone down and walked over, curious. There was a long line of figures. He scrolled to the bottom. We'd raised more than $66,000.

We looked at each other, stunned. We'd been living and breathing the auction for months. In the past eight weeks, we'd answered at least 6,000 e-mails. Michael alone had put in more than eleven hundred hours since I'd brought him on board. I couldn't begin to estimate how much time I'd spent on it myself. And now, we'd raised enough money for four scholarships!

We posted a newsletter, thanking all the fans and linking to a list of the winners. I added that I was going in for surgery in a few weeks, asking them to keep me in their thoughts. Then I went home and slept for a full day.

In the end, my surgery was successful. When Harry came out of the operating room and told Pat the tumor was definitely benign, and had been removed completely, they both started to cry. I lost two-thirds of my liver, but eventually it all regenerated, better than before. I spent a few months recovering, then got on with my life.

The auction became part of Internet history, and its effect continued to ripple through people's lives. We applied for tax-exempt status as the Pearl Foundation, named after my mother. We use the money we raise to send people back to school, endowing scholarships at various institutions that welcome returning students.

We're a tiny foundation, but we're run right—our yearly operating costs are the price of the foundation's tax return. We raise money where we can—the net profit from my merchandise sales goes there, and we have donation buttons scattered throughout my website. Thanks to living room concerts, a "tip jar" at my shows, and contributions from fans all over the world, we've managed to raise more than $300,000 in scholarship money to date.

Not bad, for the daughter of a waitress and a chicken farmer.

TWENTY

Joy

I wish you roses in the spring
Fledglings on the wing
Fireflies that sing your name
I wish you joy

I n general, I think God knows what he's doing, even though I often disagree.

And as much as I try to control the universe, it rolls over me without a qualm, often leaving pain and confusion in its wake. But the older I get, the more I realize that everything happens for a reason. If Kye hadn't left me, I'd never have moved to Nashville and met Pat. If I hadn't injured my left hand in 1994, forcing me to stop playing piano, I wouldn't have become such a good guitarist. If I'd stayed a big star, I wouldn't have deigned to do an interview with tiny *Vintage Guitar* magazine. Because of that interview, my Martin guitar was returned to me, twenty-six years after it was stolen.

You see what I mean? Things work out, if you let them. It's the in-between that's hard.

For the next few years, life was back to its old routine: write some songs, make a record, tour behind it, then start the whole thing over again. I felt like a broken record, needle scuttling across the same groove until it wore itself out. The half-century mark was just around the corner. I'd be fifty soon—did I really want to spend the rest of my life doing exactly what I'd done since I was fourteen?

Probably not.

I was still writing for *Performing Songwriter*, and Lydia asked me to do an article on downloading music from the Internet. Everyone I knew was against it; people said it was ruining the music industry. I began my research fully expecting to write an anti-downloading piece that echoed what I'd already been told.

Instead, the more I researched, the more I came to the opposite conclusion. Downloading wasn't ruining the industry; we were doing that ourselves. It was obvious that the record company paradigm was no longer working; this new technology offered something the companies should embrace. Instead, they were fighting it tooth and nail.

I did my research meticulously, since I'd be naming names, and backed up everything with source notes. I pointed out the discrepancies in the statistics everyone was tossing around. I homed in on the fact that there were fewer and fewer vehicles for affordable promotion out there, and the Internet was one of them. I argued that we'd made our audience mistrust us, by charging them $15.99 for CDs they knew cost just a few dollars to manufacture. Most of all, I disagreed with encryption, saying it just made buyers angry.

I was convinced that, given the choice between stealing music and affordable downloads, people would be willing to pay. We just had to stop treating them like criminals.

I titled the article "The Internet Debacle," turned it in, and forgot about it. It came out in May 2002, and a few weeks later, my Webmaster called. Was I playing with the hit counter on my site? I logged on; we'd had 50,000 new visitors in the past hour. Someone at

Slashdot.org had posted it, and I was abruptly notorious among the geeks and nerds of the world.

Suddenly, it seemed like everyone was reading my little article. Over the next months, it was featured by the BBC and *USA Today*, translated into nine languages, and reposted on more than a thousand sites. In those first eight weeks, I received more than 2,200 e-mails about it. I answered every single one, beginning dialogues with people like Steve Wozniak and organizations like the Electronic Frontier Foundation. As the fallout from the article continued, I realized I'd exposed my flank in a way I'd never intended.

Many people in my industry were outraged. They accused me of being a traitor. One songwriter wrote that he'd just given away all my recordings. I wrote back to say I'd go him one better, and immediately put ten free downloads up on my own website. Proving my point, merchandise sales immediately shot up by 300 percent.

I wrote a follow-up article, where I suggested a new business model for my industry. I argued for one big site that would offer downloadable music, video clips, links to artists' websites, and any other content we could dream up. If all the record companies got together and made their catalogs available online there, at reasonable prices, consumers would have a real choice. I argued that they would look at us as heroes if we did that.

People thought I was crazy.

A year later, Apple unveiled the iTunes Music Store, and the rest is history. My new record company, Rude Girl Records, was one of the first independent labels to sign up.

Thanks to my research for "The Internet Debacle," I could see that we were losing the trust of the very consumers who kept us in business. Everyone seemed to have forgotten the main thing—we don't really sell records, or the latest technological breakthrough.

We sell dreams.

There isn't a person in America who doesn't have at least one recording that dredges up vivid memories: their first kiss, their first dance. Music is there for them from cradle to grave, rocking their children to sleep, singing them onward when they die. We give voice to the voiceless, give them back a part of themselves they've forgotten. In hardship, we provide a memory of better times gone by—and better times to come.

But no one seemed to be thinking about the noble role we played in human culture. Instead, all we seemed to be providing was number crunching, and plastic performers who couldn't get through a show without using tapes or computers to enhance their voices. I hadn't met a record company employee in years who wanted to talk about music; all they talked about was business. If things kept going this way, pretty soon there'd *be* no business.

I was fed up with the record companies' shortsightedness. Labels that had once been run by music lovers and failed musicians were now in the grip of people who saw music as "a growth industry." Goddard Lieberson, head of CBS, had taught me how to notate triplets over dinner one night. There wasn't anyone like that around anymore. The industry was completely out of touch. Label executives didn't go to record stores. They had no idea consumers were so angry. They'd forgotten that to be allowed into someone's living room, into someone's *life*, was a privilege.

The incredible expansion of the entertainment business had affected me, too, and not for the better. At its best, my business is the business of failure. You fail every single day. I don't know of another business that grinds your nose into the dirt quite so often. You have to be stubborn. You have to have faith in yourself. You have to be egocentric, and stupid about hanging in there. It's impossible.

For five albums now, the record company I'd been with had either folded into a larger corporation and disappeared, or changed staff completely within two weeks of my new release. I didn't have a shot, because with each change, my marketing plans were thrown out the window. My last label, Windham Hill, had kept me on hold for two years while they tried to figure out if they wanted to be based in New York or L.A. They'd replaced almost all the staff two or three times in that period. My last record for them, *god & the fbi*, hadn't even had a marketing manager; in all the flurry, they'd forgotten to appoint one.

At the same time, my personal manager and I had parted ways. I'd always had a manager—I couldn't envision life without one. Then Pat said, "Why? Why do you need a manager? For that matter, do you really want to be with a major label again?"

I spoke with my U.S. booking agent, Tim Drake. He wondered why, too. "Janis, you've been in this business over forty years. You know as much about management as anyone. If you're willing to walk away from the majors, then just do it yourself."

My attorney and business manager said the same, and I realized it was time to reinvent the way I did business. I'd always followed the established pattern; manager, major label, make a record, tour behind it. Now, with the advent of the digital world, I could see that releasing records through independent labels, and managing myself, might just work.

Leaving the majors and controlling my business gave me the luxury of arranging life on the road to include some fun. In the liner notes for *Breaking Silence,* I'd thanked the artists who'd influenced the songs. I'd sent them each an advance copy, along with a handwritten note. Most had written back, and I'd begun a lively e-mail correspondence with several. On tour in Ireland, I arranged a day off to visit with Anne Mc-Caffrey. We'd been writing to each other for years, encouraging each other during our slumps, commiserating when things went wrong, and congratulating when they went right. Even though we'd never met, I felt very close to her.

Anne lived in the countryside just outside Dublin, and we spent a wonderful day together, talking about dragons, writing, and the world of science fiction. I'd always loved the genre. My father had every copy of *The Magazine of Fantasy & Science Fiction* ever released, and I grew up on stories of alien cultures and spacecraft. When I was young, I used to sit by my bedroom window and stare up at the stars, waiting for "my people" to come and take me home. Science-fiction writers had informed my life for as far back as I could remember. The ABCs—Asimov, Bradbury, and Clarke—had taught me as much about human relationships as my own life had. So it was a huge thrill to meet Annie in the flesh.

At some point, she mentioned Worldcon. When I looked puzzled, she got excited. "You must go, m'dear! You must! All the science-fiction writers gather together once a year; the fans put on the convention, and everyone mingles. There are workshops, classes—you'd have a wonderful time!"

Mike Resnick, another writer I corresponded with, seconded her thoughts. Besides, he wanted me to start writing fiction. *Out of the question,* I said. *I don't write fiction.*

"We could meet at Worldcon and talk about it," he persisted.

Pat reminded me that I hadn't had a vacation since my surgery, and urged me to go. I wasn't so sure. It was going to be held in Philadelphia that year, and visiting Philly always reminded me painfully that Gerry was gone. Besides, I didn't like crowds, and I wouldn't know anyone.

Pat kept arguing, and I finally gave in. I left for Worldcon that August with some trepidation, not sure what I would find.

It was magical. For seven days, I walked, talked, and slept writing and science fiction. Not the mass consumption of it, like *Star Trek,* but the literature of it. Mike introduced me to anyone and everyone, and I was immensely gratified to discover that all but one writer knew my work.

It was also overwhelming. I'd brought a book by Connie Willis, hoping to get it autographed. Her story "All My Darling Daughters" had completely changed the way I looked at my writing, and I wanted to thank her in person.

When I was introduced to Connie, I tried to tell her what her work had meant to me, that it had changed my life as an artist. I was so overwhelmed that I burst into tears and fled the room.

Now, people burst into tears around me on a regular basis. They start crying as they tell me what my music's meant to them. Sometimes they even faint. It can be intensely moving, like when a female prisoner of war told me she'd been in isolation for six months, and kept going by singing all my songs to herself. Or when a young man told me with tears in his eyes that they'd buried his mother the day before, and she'd asked to have my albums with her.

Still, I would never have expected it to happen to me, and the experience was profoundly humbling.

By the end of Worldcon, Resnick and I had a project. We would co-edit an anthology of new short stories by my favorite authors, each based on one of my songs. I told Mike none of the writers would have time; he said it couldn't hurt to ask. Then he casually said, "Of course, you'll need to write something for it, too."

I don't write fiction! I said for the umpteenth time.

"Too bad," he said, "because I promised the publisher you would."

I argued that I'd be on the road for months. I insisted I couldn't plot. He just handed me the contract, told me the deadline, and said surely I'd have a day or two off during the tour. I could write it then.

I e-mailed Mercedes Lackey in a panic. *Misty, I'm supposed to write a story. How do I start? Help!*

Misty wrote back with the best advice anyone can give a writer: *Sit butt in chair. Write.*

On my next day off, I sat in my hotel room for an hour, staring at a blank page. Just as I was about to give up, the first line popped into my head. Each time I got stuck, I e-mailed Misty what I'd written. She didn't have many comments to make, but her unwavering belief reassured me enough to keep writing until the end.

When I finished, I sent the manuscript in to Mike. I'd been warned that he was a great editor, but exacting, so I expected pages of criticism. Instead, I received a single-line e-mail: *Thanks. Nice job.*

Before I knew it, other editors were asking for stories, and I was learning to write fiction. I discovered a wonderful thing in the process, something I'd always known in my heart but never put into words before. Writing is writing. If you're a born writer, you're happy when you're writing, whether it's a song, a story, or an autobiography. Words are words, and if you love language, you're happy when you can use it.

I had a good time over the next few years. I'd made the move away from the majors with some apprehension, but self-management seemed to work in my favor. No one cared about my business as much as I did, after all. I worked out a business model where I could make CDs in my own time, funded by affiliates who released them all over the world. It forced me to be in personal contact with the companies, which changed the entire dynamic. Rude Girl's first release, a double live CD titled *Working Without a Net*, was my biggest since 1983.

I toured as much behind my own company's recordings as I had for the majors, but there were huge differences. Because I was the one coordinating routing with my agents, I no longer had to worry about driving six hundred miles in a day, then trying to be bright and fresh for a show that night. Because I could manufacture myself, or buy from an affiliate at close to cost, I could keep prices down and sales up. The profits from merchandise on the road became an important source of income for the Pearl Foundation.

And for the first time in my life, I was receiving a fair share of the profits. I'd recorded "Society's Child" in 1965, but when my statements came in, I still mysteriously owed the record company more than $100,000. Now I was partners with my affiliates, seeing 50 percent of the profit on new work coming back into my bank account. Best of all, I owned the master recordings.

I began spending a lot of time working in Europe. I'd spend my days off with friends there, drinking espresso and talking politics late into the night. They couldn't understand the political frenzy in America over gay marriage—what did it matter to anyone but the couple concerned?

I explained that some people thought it would be the death of traditional heterosexual marriage. "But you and Pat have been together almost two decades," they'd argue. "Surely people don't begrudge you the right to marry. How incredibly provincial!"

I couldn't help but agree. The longer we lived together, the more I resented all the extra steps we had to take, just to ensure our basic rights. If one of us was hospitalized, the other had to bring a sheaf of paperwork just to visit, in case only relatives were allowed. If I died, Pat could only inherit as my friend, paying full taxes on the entire amount. She couldn't get my Social Security payments, either.

In Tennessee, you could be fired for being gay. We had no recourse against discrimination. In some places, it was even encouraged. I knew plenty of people who maintained separate bedrooms, even separate houses, just to make sure their jobs were safe. I knew couples who had to adopt as single parents, and the other parent couldn't even pick their child up from school without dragging along a bundle of legal documents. My straight friends took their rights for granted, while we had to jump through all these hoops. It didn't seem fair.

We were born gay, or at the least, bisexual. It had never been any big deal to me, but I got irritated when people said we were making a "lifestyle choice." It sounded like we were picking out a new sofa.

In most of Europe, my gay friends were being given the right to the same benefits heterosexual married couples had. One morning, I read in the paper that Toronto, Canada, was offering them as well. Worldcon was going to be held in Toronto that year. I thought about it for a few minutes, then went upstairs to speak with Pat.

I know we always said we wouldn't get married until it was legal here, but what would you think about getting married in Canada next month?

"Okay," she said. I felt a little let down at the muted response, until she followed it up with, "And I want our picture in *The New York Times* wedding announcements."

What? Pat didn't take pictures. Even I only had three or four. She hated publicity.

Umm . . . I think they might have run one same-sex photo recently, but it's a really long shot. And do we really want publicity?

Yes, we did. Or at least, she did. I, however, did not want our wedding to turn into a three-ring circus, with hordes of well-intentioned fans and press people competing for space.

We compromised. We'd announce it, but only after the ceremony. And since we didn't want anyone thinking we had anything to hide, we'd also issue a press release afterward.

I looked up the guidelines, had a friend take our photo, and sent it in to the *Times*. They called a few days later. I was the first "star" to take advantage of the change in Canadian law. Would we allow them to send a photographer to the ceremony, and do an interview? They'd just begun using pictures of gay couples; they wanted to make us a feature. It would be the first time they'd done that with a gay couple.

Pat and I discussed it. I really didn't want people thinking I was using our marriage for publicity. I'd seen what it did to other well-known gay couples who used their relationships to get onto the newsstands. Of the three celebrities who'd "come out" at the Triangle Ball in Washington when Bill Clinton was elected, only Pat and I remained standing. Melissa Etheridge's and k. d. lang's relationships had both ended. It wasn't worth the pressure.

Pat was adamant, as well. First of all, this was as much her marriage as mine, and if she wanted our picture in the *Times*, in a feature no less, she should have it. Second, why wasn't I thinking about the good it might do? We were going on two decades together; surely we'd survive a bit of press. I had no record coming out; no one could accuse me of doing it for the publicity. If she was willing to have her honeymoon at a science-fiction convention, I should be willing to do an interview and pose for a photo.

All right. If it was that important to her, we'd do it that way. I asked Mike Resnick if he and his wife, Carol, would be our witnesses. Carol wanted to know what she should wear. Uh-oh. We hadn't thought about that.

"I am *not* wearing a dress, let alone a gown," Pat said, glaring at me before the question was half out of my mouth. That was fine with me; I didn't even own a dress. *We do have to wear something, honey. We ought to get dressed up for this. Let's go shopping.*

"I hate shopping," Pat muttered as we strolled around the mall. "Totally hate it. Maybe we shouldn't get married, after all. We could pull that classic line, excuse ourselves, and say, 'I had absolutely nothing to wear.'"

I was almost ready to agree. We'd been through the dress section, the feminine suit section, even the sports section. Nothing worked.

Walking toward the escalator, I spied a row of Hawaiian shirts. I gestured toward them, and we made for the rack. I called Carol Resnick the next day. *Wear something Hawaiian, girlfriend. That's what we'll have on!*

We were both nervous as we entered Toronto's City Hall, sure we'd trip, giggle, or otherwise disgrace ourselves. The clerk made it easy, laughingly telling us that since they hadn't had time to change the forms yet, one of us would have to be "the groom." Since I was closest to that part of the page, would I mind putting my name there?

No, I wouldn't mind. Maybe it would give me some leverage later. I might even get Pat to hand over the TV remote once in a while.

The ceremony was lovely, though I hardly remember it. We lucked out with our minister, who'd been drafted from a nearby church when the government realized how many gay people wanted to be married, and ran out of judges. Malcolm St. Clair was tall and distinguished, with a beautiful baritone voice and sparkling eyes. We held hands as he recited the blessing we'd chosen:

Now you will feel no rain,
for each of you will be shelter to the other
Now you will feel no cold,
for each of you shall be warmth to the other

When he said, "I now pronounce you married," we hugged each other long and hard, surprised to find our eyes were wet. I'd never expected to be so moved by it. We'd been together for years; this was just a piece of paper. Why did it feel so momentous?

As we stood there in a group, posing on the steps of City Hall, I realized that our wedding was, indeed, momentous. We were legally married. We had the weight of an entire country behind us, according us the same privileges any human being had the right to expect.

On some level, we'd expected to feel like strangers, like freaks. We were prepared for snickers and veiled comments. Yet all that week, people congratulated us on our impending nuptials. The hotel gave us the honeymoon suite. The Starbucks waiter paid for our drinks himself. Every Canadian we met smiled when they heard the news. No one found it weird, or out of place. We were absolutely normal, just another excited couple about to declare their commitment before the world.

It's a powerful thing, knowing the weight of a nation stands behind you.

Plus, as Pat pointed out, being married in Canada virtually guaranteed I'd never leave her. I'd have to take up residence there for a year before I could get a divorce, and I hate cold weather.

We threw a huge party that fall to celebrate, inviting all our friends and relatives. My Aunt Mona, Dad's sister, flew in with my cousin Donna, telling me, "I'm here to represent both your parents." Back when the *Village Voice* article appeared, she was horrified at the thought of my being gay. Now she went from table to table, proudly pointing to Pat and saying, "That's my new niece, there, the redhead. She's a lawyer!"

A few days after the party, I sat alone on our porch, looking out at the late September sky. The promise of winter hung in the air. The trees were just beginning to lose their leaves. I hungered for the spring, five or six long months away, when the yard would explode in green.

Suddenly, I recalled another September day, just five years earlier, when I'd looked out at those same trees and wondered how much time I had left. When my life was measured in minutes, and terror filled my heart.

I'd prayed to see just one more spring that day. Just one more.

I drew in a deep breath, and a rush of joy filled my breast. Every hour I'd had since then was an unexpected gift. How much wonder there was to treasure in this life! Even winter, with its long nights and frigid days, would be welcome now. I would take joy in every gust of wind, every snowflake that might fall. Because I was alive, and that was the greatest gift of all.

"MY AUTOBIOGRAPHY"

I know you and I'll agree
What this world needs is a lot more me
Well, I have got the remedy
Gonna write my autobiography
I've led a fascinating life
Had a husband and a wife
But you will truly be amazed
at just how humble I have stayed

    Enough about me, let's talk about you
    What do you *think of me?*
    You must feel such gratitude
    that you will get to read my autobiography

My life doesn't have a very good plot
Guess I'll have to lie a lot
Should be easy to make things up
There's no one left to call my bluff
A lot of my old friends have passed on
The rest did drugs and their memory's gone
So I'll write my own history
in my autobiography

"MY AUTOBIOGRAPHY"

I'll say I slept with a Kennedy
Don't remember which one
They all looked the same to me
or they did when we got done

Maybe they'll film it for TV
I wonder who they'll cast as me
Should be somebody I look like
Sigourney Weaver'd be all right
Gonna be hard to deal with fame
once the whole world knows my name
but I'll stay humble and grateful to
all the little people like you

A thousand pages more of me
and all I've seen and done
It will be my legacy
and that's just volume one of my autobiography

THANKS

Special thanks for their assistance and generosity to the following: Steve Berkowitz and Vinnie Maressa of Sony/BMG; Nora Guthrie; Etsuko Matsubara, Nancy Weshkoff, and Dag Sandsmark of EMI Music; Harold Woodley and Daniel Wells of Bug Music Publishing; Nancy Ubick of Hal Leonard Publishing; Scott Gunter, Tricia Tierno, and Gary Helsinger of Umusic Group; Arlo Chan of Warner Chappell; Erika Navarette of Alfred Publishing; and last but far from least, Wayne Milligan of GSO Group for his assistance with all the licensing!

INDEX